SARATOGA

Also by George Waller

KIDNAP
The Story of the Lindbergh Case

SARATOGA

Saga of an Impious Era

by
George Waller

Prentice-Hall, Inc., Englewood Cliffs, New Jersey

Library of Congress Catalog Card Number: 66-26229
Printed in the United States of America
T 79114

Prentice-Hall International, Inc., London / Prentice-Hall of Australia, Pty. Ltd.,
Sydney / Prentice-Hall of Canada, Ltd., Toronto / Prentice-Hall of India Private
Ltd., New Delhi / Prentice-Hall of Japan, Inc., Tokyo

For Joan, naturally

Foreword

During the period when this book was taking form, a small, brave body of citizens angrily protested the heedless destruction of public buildings and private mansions which served as monuments to the American past. Across the country, others followed suit with outcries of their own, and the People vs. the Bulldozer grew into a small-scale war.

What the People are fighting for, of course, is not so much perpetuity for assorted piles of bricks-and-mortar, many of which have admittedly outlived their usefulness, as for the tradition they represent. There is an aroused awareness that on every level tradition—the faith, dreams, fashion, manners, morals, habits and so on which join us to the past—is swiftly vanishing from the American scene. We are in danger of losing contact with our social heritage, our personal history.

My purpose in this book is to revive our relationship to an earlier American way of life. My choice of subject was dictated partly by affection (in my teens, the tales I read and heard of Saratoga's legendary summers easily persuaded me that it was a paradise of earthly pleasures and my first order of business should be to get to it as quickly as possible); but in any case Saratoga's unique yet characteristically American history would have induced me to try to recapture its flavor and re-create its fabled personalities and events. As Harper's *Weekly* noted nearly a century ago: "The curious charm of Saratoga life to a student of human nature is the fact that beyond any other American resort it is a social microcosm in which our distinctive national traits are happily portrayed in miniature."

The saga of Saratoga's life and times is the story of an extraordinary era in American culture: impious, opulent, exuberant. Indeed, its peak years, the late 1800's, have in retrospect beguiled so many of us that we have picked *la belle époque* as the period in which we would have chosen to live had a choice been offered.

In the text and pictures which follow I have sought to revive every aspect of Saratoga that made it a fascinating chapter in our social development and a splendid memento of our American past.

Acknowledgments

In my search for prints, photographs and paintings to illustrate the story of Saratoga I was aided and comforted by many persons and places, and to all of them I extend my grateful appreciation. I am particularly indebted to, and particularly thank, the following for their assistance:

Saratoga Springs, N. Y.: Charles H. Hutchins and Bob Mayette, photographers; Elaine E. Mann, National Museum of Racing; Elizabeth Ames, Yaddo; Tsing S. Chu and her associates, Saratoga Springs Public Library; Howard de Freitas, Chamber of Commerce; P. J. Drury, Saratoga Springs Reservation; and Douglas Wheeler, Saratoga Performing Arts Center.

Cooperstown, N. Y.: Frances R. Raynolds, New York State Historical Association.

New York, N. Y.: Elizabeth E. Roth, Nina S. Seco, Janette R. Wedderburn and Jeffrey Dickson, New York Public Library; Beatrice M. Morgan, Frick Art Reference Library; Rosemary Alexander, *Life* Magazine; and George Cole, Gravure Photo Service.

Washington, D. C.: Virginia Daiker, Library of Congress.

Lexington, Ky.: Amelia K. Buckley, Keeneland Library, Keeneland Race Course.

My debt to the artists and engravers who produced the woodcuts and lithographs reproduced in these pages is, of course, beyond measure. Their illustrations of nineteenth-century Saratoga are animated with such perception and skill that we too are there, drawn into the past and plunged into the midst of the fabled personalities and events that made Saratoga a legendary resort.

GEORGE WALLER

Quotations from Copyrighted Sources

The author's gratitude is expressed to the following for permission to quote copyrighted material in *Saratoga:*

Charles Scribner's Sons, New York, N. Y., for extracts from *The American Scene* by Henry James, and from the introduction by W. H. Auden, published in 1946; Harper & Row, New York, N. Y., for extracts from *The Last Resorts* by Cleveland Amory, published by Harper and Brothers in 1948; The Bobbs-Merrill Company, Inc., New York, N. Y., for extracts from *A History of Travel in America* by Seymour Dunbar, published in 1915; Dodd, Mead & Company, New York, N. Y., for extracts from *Sucker's Progress* by Herbert Asbury, published in 1938; The Macmillan Company, New York, N. Y., for extracts from *The American Thoroughbred* by Charles E. Trevathan, published in 1905; Doubleday & Company, Inc., New York, N. Y., for extracts from *Such Was Saratoga* by Hugh Bradley, copyrighted and published by Doubleday & Company, Inc., in 1940; Stanford University Press, Stanford, Calif., for extracts from *A Casual View of America (The Home Letters of Salomon de Rothschild, 1859-1861)* edited by Sigmund Diamond, published in 1961; King Features Syndicate, New York, N. Y., for extracts from the writings of Damon Runyon, particularly *Rope Tricks;* The New Yorker, New York, N. Y., for extracts from *A Saratoga Childhood* by Frank Sullivan, published in 1954; The New York Times, New York, N. Y., for extracts from *Saratoga Discovers a New Gilded Age* by James C. Young, copyrighted and published by The New York Times in 1930, and for extracts from *The Dean of the Horse Trainers* (Max Hirsch), copyrighted and published by The New York Times in 1965; Saturday Evening Post, New York, N. Y., for extracts from an article on Richard Canfield by Alexander

List of Illustrations

PART ONE

Chapter 1

Chapter 2

PART ONE

The Land, The Lake, The Magical Fountains

Chapter One

The visit   Late in August, 1767, a small procession of Iroquois threaded through a forest below the southern foothills of the Adirondacks in the region called Saratoga.* On a litter lightly borne on the shoulders of young braves lay a white man, pale and exhausted.

They came along ancient game trails hardened by the tread of Iroquois hunters who had preceded them over a span of four centuries. The green plateau that stretched ahead of the procession was a favorite hunting ground of the Iroquois, a hide-and-seek land abounding in stately bucks and sleek does, panther, bear, otter, beaver and other succulent game. The Iroquois called it Kayaderossera, "the land of the crooked waters." A swift-running creek they had named Kayaderosseras tumbled from the southern-most Adirondack foothills and flowed in a winding course into a lake, and then streamed on to join the great river named for its English explorer, Henry Hudson.

The path of the hunters led the procession along the western shore of the lake—Caniaderiossera, "the lake of the crooked stream," which would later be called Lake Saratoga—and then along the edge of the winding creek. The litter-bearers were gentle with their burden, for the man lying ill on the couch was the friend, counselor and blood brother of the Iroquois, the white man they esteemed and trusted above all others: Sir William Johnson, Baronet, Superintendent of Indian Affairs in northern America for the British Crown, great white father of the Six Nations Iroquois League.

The young braves escorting the invalid were well acquainted with the history of his devotion to the Iroquois, having heard it often in the winter tales told by their fathers in the longhouses. It had commenced with William Johnson's arrival in the Mohawk Valley in 1738, when he was twenty-three. He had come from his native Ireland to manage his uncle's land and estab-lish a trading post, and soon won the respect of the Mohawk, the most

    * The name Saratoga was derived by colonists in the area from the Iroquois word Sarach-togoe, or a similar Indian name.

powerful of the Six Nations, by trading fairly when it was a common practice among white traders to cheat the Indians.

The wild country and primitive ways of the Mohawk had attracted Johnson from the start. Their habits were better suited to his nature than the formal courtesies and moral restraints of the white communities, and in the forests he felt free to do as he pleased. He mingled with the Indians at every opportunity, surprising and gratifying them by his interest and easy acceptance of them as equals when they were accustomed to being treated by the whites with contempt, fear and greed. He learned to speak their language, shared their food and dressed himself in their clothes. Almost six feet tall with dark brown hair and a strong, vigorous body, he made a fine figure of a Mohawk.

Daubed with paint, Johnson stamped with the braves about their campfires, danced at their festivals and took pride in his prowess in their hunts and games. His rough Irish humor delighted them as he joined with them in devising practical jokes, and his ready Irish tongue slipped effort-lessly into Indian eloquence during the flowery speeches of their powwows.

Eight years after his arrival in the valley of the red men, Johnson and the Iroquois were such good friends that the British commissioned him Colonel of the Six Nations. The Mohawk adopted him, made him a chief and named him Warraghiyagey (He Who Does Much), for in the years of their friendship he had championed their interests in many ways and they looked to him for justice when their treaties were dishonored and for pro-tection against the land-hungry colonists.

In 1755 Colonel Johnson strode before a council of the Six Nations and asked for a greater measure of confidence than he had thus far been given. Braddock's humiliating defeat in the long drawn-out struggle with France for possession of North America had placed the English in a pre-carious position. Rather than deplete their young men by assisting the English, the Iroquois were disposed to stay out of the fight. Johnson flung a painted war belt among the sachems and asked for their boldest warriors to accompany him and a strong force of English militia in a march against the French at Lac du Saint Sacrement. Hendrick, the seventy-year-old chief of the Mohawk, rose to the challenge, and several hundred braves followed him. In the battle Johnson was wounded, Hendrick was killed and the Iroquois casualties were heavy, but the French were routed and America was saved for England, paving the way for the British Lion's ultimate triumph in the New World. In honor of the occasion and England's king, Johnson changed the name of the lake from Lac du Saint Sacrement to Lake George. Two months after the crucial engagement he was made a baronet. He was also appointed His Majesty's Superintendent of Indian Affairs and awarded a hundred thousand acres of Mohawk Valley land.

The war moved north and in the peaceful valley a new and different alliance drew Johnson and the Iroquois still closer together. He took as his mate Molly Brant, sister of Joseph Brant, war chief of the Mohawk and of the entire Iroquois Confederacy. Molly was beautiful, intelligent and charming, but the quality that had set her apart from the powdered and perfumed daughters of wealthy colonials was a spirit as free and undisciplined as the baronet's. Although he was almost twice her age, he had courted her with the ardor of his younger years and she had responded with equal enthusiasm. Such was the fame of their romance that a legend had sprung up in the valley as to how they had met. It had come about at a military field day and festival, when, attracted by the superb horse an English officer was riding, Molly had leaped from the ground to the horse's bare back. Sitting behind the officer with her legs clamped firmly to the horse's loins, her hands at her sides, her black hair tossing while the officer amused the crowd by wheeling, rearing and racing his mount in an attempt to dislodge her, she had stirred the spectators to applause, and when she was ready to dismount, Sir William Johnson came forward to lift her down and ask her name.

He made her the mistress of his baronial mansion, Johnson Hall, in Johnstown, which he founded near the Mohawk River in 1762, and as Lady Johnson she bore him children (he had previously been given two daughters and a son, John, by a buxom young German bond servant whose indenture he had bought soon after his arrival in America, and who had died).* She managed his household and helped him entertain a continual stream of guests, for his success on the frontier had made Johnson one of the most important men in North America, and one of the wealthiest. In 1760, as a token of their affection, the Mohawk had given him more than a hundred thousand acres of land,** and these, together with other vast holdings, had made him one of the largest landowners in the colonial territory. Political and social leaders sought him out at Johnson Hall and found the hospitality so intriguingly different from what they were used to that they frequently returned. Molly was a colorful and imaginative hostess, the baronet's hundreds of tenants and slaves formed an easygoing community on the great estate surrounding the mansion, and the Iroquois camped on his lawns and held festivals and games.

At the crest of his career the impulsive life he had led with the Indians along with the encroachments of middle age produced various aches and pains which sapped Johnson's vitality. Dysentery often placed him in bed for weeks at a time and gout inflamed his legs. To add to his difficulties, the

* It doubtless should be noted that in addition to these more or less legitimate offspring, Johnson fathered over a hundred sons and daughters by Iroquois squaws whose bedding he was invited to share. It was the custom among the tribes to provide a distinguished guest with a pretty companion for the duration of his stay, and as the good friend and adviser of the Iroquois, Johnson availed himself of this custom during his numerous visits to their villages.

** According to a legend, at an earlier stage in the friendship, Hendrick, the Mohawk chief, was visited by a dream in which Johnson gave him a fine coat with silver buttons. Since the Mohawk believed that anything they dreamed was bound to come true, Johnson gave Hendrick the coat. A few days later he told the chief about a dream of his own, in which the Mohawk presented him with a tract of land consisting of many square miles. "The land is yours," Hendrick told Johnson. "But brother, we dream no more."

Hendrick, the Mohawk chief. The thirty-nine X's carved in the tree represented
the number of enemies he had captured or killed in border warfare.

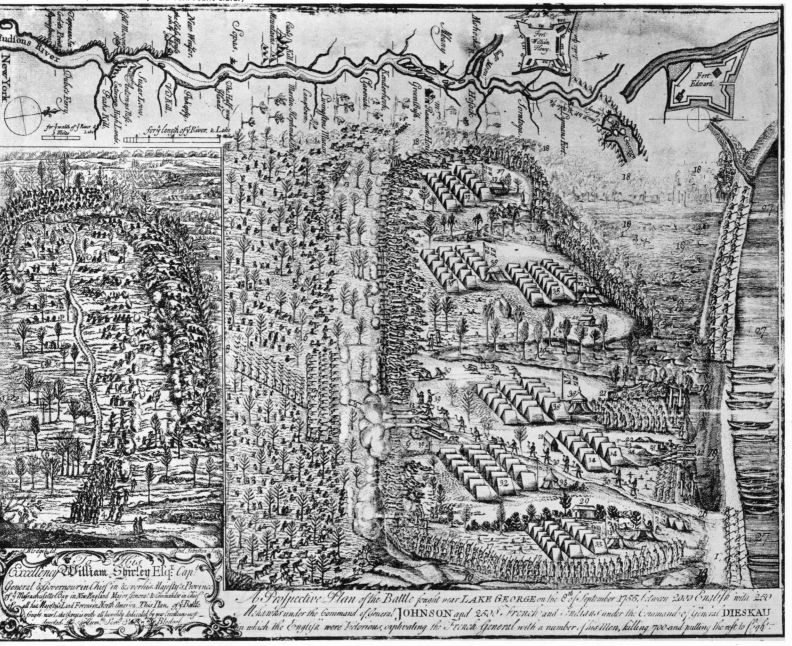

Samuel Blodget's sketch of the battle between the English and the French, both supported by Indians, at Lac du Saint Sacrement (Lake George) in 1755. The battle consisted of two engagements—the first represented in the small panel at left, the second in the larger panel at right.

wound he had received at Lake George—a musket ball had lodged in one of his thighs and had never been extracted—throbbed incessantly during his illnesses and for weeks after he recovered he was unable to ride a horse or engage in active exercise. Skilled in the use of forest medicines, Molly nursed him with herbs, and when his suffering grew particularly acute she sent to Albany or to New York City for a physician.

In the summer of 1767 there was little resemblance between the young trader who had delighted in matching his strength and prowess against the Mohawk and the fifty-two-year-old baronet. A swelling in his legs made it impossible for him to stand or sit. Drugs and herbs were neither cure nor comfort. He kept to his bed, weak with pain.

The Mohawk chiefs met in council. Some thirty miles northeast of Johnstown, in a little valley on the edge of the first southern foothill of the Adirondacks, were the Medicine Springs of the Great Spirit, whose healing waters had repaired and replenished the Iroquois for four hundred years and whose location they had kept secret from the whites. If there was a remedy for Warraghiyagey's illness the sachems were confident that the springs would supply it, and they decided to transport him to the magical waters.

On August 22nd an escort of Iroquois braves set out with the invalid from Johnson Hall. They made their way by boat along the Mohawk River to Schenectady, then over forest trails, with the baronet borne on a litter, to Lake Saratoga and the winding Kayaderosseras. The journey taxed Johnson's depleted resources still further, but he endured it gratefully.

Over the centuries the existence of the springs had become fairly common knowledge. In 1535, while searching for a transcontinental northwest passage to the Orient, the French navigator, Jacques Cartier, had heard of a wondrous, health-giving spring that spouted from a rock in Kayaderossera. Later, other white men had learned of it too, but the Iroquois had been hostile to their attempts to penetrate the prized hunting ground and so far as was known no white person had ever seen the spring. If this were true, Johnson would be the first of his race to visit the watering place, and he was keenly anticipating the experience.

The procession turned north, away from the creek. As a later white visitor would note, "The view before and around him was, in fact, like a wide sea of forest green. To the north and south it lay level and uniform. To the west and northwest, at the distance of a few miles, it was bounded by a low range of wooded hills, while eastward it stretched away for many a league, growing hazy in the distance until it was terminated by a long chain of misty mountains that lifted their blue and billowy tops against the silver brightness of the morning sky."

Johnson stared ahead of his escort, seeking a glimpse of their destination. At first, he had difficulty making it out; in addition to his other infirmities, his sight was failing. Then, as the procession drew close, he saw a curious cone-shaped rock resembling the haycocks thrown up in the fields when the hay was to be carted to the barn, but much larger—five or six feet high and eight to ten feet in diameter at the base, tapering and rounded off at the top. Every so often water pulsed from a nearly perpendicular round hole, some eight inches across, in the top of the rock. It laved the scaly surface, and then sank back to its general level a hand's reach below the mouth of the hole, where it bubbled ceaselessly. All around the rock the ground was tracked with the footprints of animals that had come to drink from the spring.

To make their guest comfortable the Iroquois built a bark hut close to the spring and placed inside it a couch cushioned with forest leaves for him to lie on. He drank and bathed in the salty water, the Iroquois dipping it with dried gourd shells from the hole in the rock. It appeared that the peculiar substance of the rock, which made it seem like some species of giant shell-fish, was due to the chemical properties of the water, which had boiled up from underground over a period of many years and deposited a cone of porous limestone at the point where it burst through the earth's surface. The Iroquois, of course, had a simpler explanation. The healing water, they said, had been created by the Great Spirit in answer to the prayer of a despairing Mohawk chief, whose loved one lay dying from an epidemic that was destroying the tribe.

The treatment continued for four days. Then a runner arrived with letters for the baronet and news which obliged him to hasten home. The chief sachem of the Seneca, one of the Iroquois Six Nations, had died, and the question of his successor would have to be carefully dealt with, for he had been a good friend of the English and troublesome times lay ahead. In addition, a dispute between the Iroquois and colonials over land in the Saratoga region required his attention as Superintendent of Indian Affairs. With his Iroquois entourage, Johnson started back.

The visit to the spring had been brief and he expected few, if any, benefits from it. To his delight, he discovered that the medicinal water had restored a good deal of his strength and that he was able to walk part of the way back to Schenectady. On September 4th he walked into Johnson Hall and was presented with a surprise home-coming gift by his son, John, who had just returned from a visit to London: a pair of new spectacles.

Shortly after his arrival, Johnson took goose quill in hand and wrote to Philip Schuyler, the patrician heir of one of the region's wealthiest and most influential families. Schuyler presided over his mills and acres from his mansion in the village of Saratoga,* where the Kayaderosseras (here called by the colonists Fish Kill) flowed into the Hudson River. "My dear Schuyler," the baronet wrote, "I have just returned from a visit to a most amazing spring, which almost effected my cure, and I have sent for Dr. Stringer, of New York, to come up and analyze it."

* Later, this settlement was named Schuylerville.

In 1856 Jonathan Chapin drew this version of the legendary first meeting of Sir William Johnson and Molly Brant and described Molly in romantic prose: "Formed in Venus' choicest mould, with limbs of a beautiful roundness and symmetry . . . a face of remarkable beauty, just dark enough to show the Indian blood, and yet much lighter than is usually seen among the people of her nation . . . with eyes like the gazelle, shaded by long jet-black lashes, and a splendid head of hair, which floated in the wind behind her—she presented the *tout ensemble* of as fair a creature as ever captivated the eye or won the heart of man."

Johnson in the panoply of his office as Superintendent of Indian Affairs for the British monarchy.

In 1767, ill and in pain, Sir William Johnson was a guest of the Iroquois at their magical healing waters in the Saratoga region later to become famous as High Rock Spring. His visit marked the beginning of the Saratoga Spa.

Thus was launched the spa that would become famous as Saratoga Springs. The news that so distinguished a person as Sir William Johnson had been even partially relieved of his ailments drew other health seekers to the waters, and eventually the resort attracted pleasure seekers as well.

As the future would show, the Mohawk baronet could claim a few additional feathers for his bonnet: he was the first registered guest at the Spa and by choosing August as the time for his visit established a precedent for those who came after him—for August was to become the peak of the social season in Saratoga's celebrated summers.

Chapter Two

Place
of the
swift water

In the beginning were the springs, welling from underground streams formed deep within the earth during the prehistoric glacial era and absorbing the earth's minerals until natural gases thrust the waters upward through the earth's surface and released them in geysers near the southern foothills of the towering mountains which would be called Adirondack.

The animals of the forests came down into the valley of the springs and lapped the saline waters, and pursuing the rich variety of game, more than a century before the time of Columbus, the Iroquois discovered the springs, drank from them, bathed in them and gave them a name.

When the first white men arrived, five Iroquois nations ranged across the region now known as central New York State, their bark-covered longhouses thinly dotting the wilderness from the Genesee River to Lake Champlain. The western part, below Lake Ontario, was the domain of the Seneca, and their neighbors to the east were, successively, Cayuga, Onondaga, Oneida and Mohawk.

The Mohawk possessed a fertile land of forests, plains, valleys and meadows cut by fresh-water streams and lakes, bordered in the east by the great river (the Hudson) they called Oiogue, and in the south by the river Mohawk along whose shore their palisaded villages were poised. In the north the craggy Adirondacks sloped to the Kayaderossera, where there was never a lack of game to be found and where the flesh of the animals and birds was extraordinarily tender and sweet due to, the Mohawk believed, their habits of drinking at the Medicine Springs of the Great Spirit. Four miles from the springs was a sparkling lake, and in the summers the Mohawk hunters left the villages and cast bark shelters on the high bluffs overlooking the lake and fished in its waters.

To this land, extending some forty-three miles north and south and some twenty-eight miles east and west, the Mohawk gave a name spelled by early historians in some twenty different ways, each with a somewhat different meaning. The word Sarachtogoe, "hillside country of a great river," was perhaps most frequently used, but the accepted meaning, "place of the swift water," was derived from Sir William Johnson who attributed it to the pairing of two Iroquois words, saragh, "swift water," and oga, "place of." Whatever Indian name the colonists chose, the English pronunciation almost invariably produced the word Saratoga. And so, after the English came, the land of the Mohawk was called Saratoga.* Eventually, the name was also given to the sparkling lake** and the saline springs.

Late in the sixteenth century the five Iroquois nations formed a confederacy, the Iroquois League. Legend would say that the saintly conciliator, Deganawidah, and his Mohawk disciple, Hiawatha, persuaded the tribes to join together to put an end to their quarrels and live in neighborly harmony based on law and order. However the union originated, it was destined for fame and power. History would show that no other Indian confederacy north of Mexico compared with the League of the Iroquois in political organization, statecraft and prowess in war. The longhouse became the symbol of their solidarity, figuratively spanning the wilderness with a door in the west guarded by the Seneca and a door in the east guarded by the Mohawk, while in the center the Onondaga served as keepers of the fires.

The Mohawk was the most powerful nation in the League and its warriors were the most feared. Many years earlier the Algonquin, who had been driven repeatedly from the Saratoga region by the Mohawk, had called them "man-eaters," an Algonquian epithet that became their tribal name; and in fact man-eaters they were, as their various enemies learned. Late in the summer of 1609, however, the Algonquin and the Huron, another ancient foe of the Mohawk, managed to even a few old scores.

They mustered a war party in Canada, armed with French guns, and accompanied Samuel de Champlain, the founder of Quebec, on an expedition into Iroquois territory. The long journey took them down the St. Lawrence River and the Richelieu to the lake that would bear Champlain's name, and at the Ticonderoga promontory the Frenchman and his Indian

---

* Not until 1791, however, when Saratoga County was established, was Saratoga generally spelled exactly as it was pronounced; prior to that date, in their papers and letters, the colonists spelled the name in a variety of ways: Serachtague, Saraghoga, Saraghtogue, Sarachtoga, Saraghtoga and so on.

** The Mohawk believed that the awesome stillness of Caniaderiossera (Lake Saratoga) was sacred to the Great Spirit, and that if a word was spoken upon its waters the offender's canoe would promptly disappear into the shadowy depths and never again be seen. In the 1850's Nathaniel P. Willis wrote:

> A story is told of an English woman, in the early days of the first settlers, who had occasion to cross this lake with a party of Indians, who before embarking warned her most impressively of the spell. It was a silent, breathless day, and the canoe shot over the smooth surface of the lake like an arrow. About a mile from the shore, near the center of the lake, the woman, willing to convince the savages of the weakness of their superstition, uttered a loud cry. The countenances of the Indians fell instantly to the deepest gloom. After a moment's pause, however, they redoubled their exertions and in frowning silence drove the light bark like an arrow over the waters. They reached the shore in safety and drew up the canoe, and the woman laughed at the chief's credulity. "The Great Spirit is merciful," answered the scornful Mohawk. "He knows that a white woman cannot hold her tongue."

The Iroquois discovered High Rock Spring while hunting game and revered its waters as a creation of the Great Spirit.

A French drawing shows the Iroquois dressed and equipped for battle in 1608.

The victors and the vanquished.

allies were confronted by a war party of Mohawk. The Mohawk attacked eagerly and Champlain, in arrow-proof armor of morion, cuirass and greaves, received them with a shot from his arquebus. The Mohawk paused, awed by their first experience with fire-arms. Again the thunder broke among them; two of their three captains lay dead and the third wounded. The Mohawk turned and ran.

It was a triumph France was to regret for the next one hundred and fifty years, for from that day the Iroquois League nursed a vindictive hatred of the French and stood in the path of their ambitions to expand their empire through the Hudson River Valley. The Dutch, with their own dreams of conquest, equipped the Iroquois with guns, and Iroquois war parties slipped across the Canadian border and employed their new weapons against the French with deadly effect. In the course of one of these missions the Mohawk came upon Father Jogues.

The delicate Jesuit   Directly after he had arrived in the New World at Quebec in 1636, Father Isaac Jogues had been sent to give spiritual guidance to the Huron on the shore of Georgian Bay, the northeast part of Lake Huron. Although he was scholarly, physically slight and constitutionally timid, the young Jesuit priest had overcome all doubts that he was suited to the rigors of the frontier by spending six successful years with the Indians.

In June 1642, he set out with twenty-five Huron in four canoes to receive instructions and obtain supplies at Quebec. It would be a perilous voyage, as he well understood, for bands of Iroquis ranged over the Canadian lake country; however, his superior had had no choice but to send him.

Quebec was reached without a glimpse of the marauders, but on the return trip, early in August, Mohawk braves concealed in a swamp off the St. Lawrence ambushed the voyagers, and the Huron who were not killed or wounded fled. Flung from his canoe into the swamp stalks, Father Jogues lay hidden from the enemy, but among the wounded captives of the Mohawk he saw Huron he had baptized at the Georgian Bay mission. He emerged from his hiding place and allowed himself to be taken prisoner so that he could console them.

In the orgy of torture that followed, the naked young priest fell unconscious, was revived with burning sticks, made to endure new agonies, and fainted once more.

Tiring of the diversion, the Mohawk thrust the captives into canoes and paddled south along the Richelieu and Lake Champlain, then drove the naked men over forest trails through the Kayaderossera to the Mohawk village of Ossernenon* on the Mohawk River, where they were tortured again.

* Later, it was named Auriesville.

When he recovered from his wounds, Father Jogues was adopted as a slave by a Mohawk family. The following March, 1643, in a general exodus from the village, he accompanied his captors on an excursion along the Mohawk River and up the Hudson to a creek, which took them in a winding, westerly course to a lake they called Caniaderiossera. Here they camped and fished for a week during the spring run of herring, catching them in wicker baskets anchored in the openings of stone dams built in the narrow passage where the lake and creek waters intermingled. A few months later the Dutch bought the priest's freedom and took him to New Amsterdam, and Father Jogues mentioned his trip with the Indians in a report he wrote on his imprisonment to his superiors: "The journey was one of four days; the goal, a lake where little fishes are caught, which they [the Mohawk] smoke in order to preserve them, and carry them back to their country—meanwhile living on the entrails alone."

Father Jogues sailed to France and was encouraged to remain there, far removed from war whoop and torture stake, but his experiences with the Mohawk had instilled a desire to return to them as the ambassador of his faith; he went back to Quebec. Anxious to put an end to the border raids of the Iroquois, and agreeable to any enterprise that might improve their attitude toward the French, the Governor of Canada endorsed the young Jesuit's plan and in the spring of 1646 enlisted him as his emissary to submit a peace treaty to the Mohawk. Jean Bourdon, the Governor's surveyor, was instructed to accompany him and map the waterways and land trails they pursued in their travels.

Led by Mohawk guides they journeyed south, and after leaving Lake Champlain came upon a much smaller lake white men had never seen before. The Mohawk called it Andiatarocte, but Father Jogues thought it should have a name suited to its ethereal beauty. Since it was May 30th, the eve of the Feast of Corpus Christi, he christened the waters Lac du Saint Sacrement—Lake of the Holy Communion—and Bourdon inscribed the name on his map. So the waters would be called until William Johnson, a century later, claimed them for Britain and named them Lake George.

Leaving their canoes, the travellers proceeded over an ancient Mohawk war trail through the Kayaderossera to the lake Father Jogues had visited during his captivity. Mohawk fishing parties were camped on the bluffs. A few days later, in canoes borrowed from the fishermen, they came to Ossernenon, and at a council of the Mohawk chiefs Father Jogues presented his gifts and treaty belts. It was agreed that there would be peace between the French and the Five Nations.

Father Jogues returned to Quebec with a light heart. Not only had the Mohawk accepted the proposal of peace, but in his strolls through the village of his imprisonment he had been well received. Surely, it was a favorable time for him to convert these pagans to the precepts of Christ; to go among them not in secular clothes, as the Governor's emissary, but in

Famed for their ferocity in battle, the Iroquois were equally savage in their torture of prisoners of war—prolonging the punishment with devilish imagination and cunning. Fairly typical was this scene, which appeared in the memoirs of a seventeenth-century Dutch observer, David de Vries.

Samuel de Champlain, the chief founder of New France.

In 1609 Champlain invaded Iroquois territory with Indian allies of the French and routed the Mohawk, the boldest warriors of the Five Nations Iroquois, at Ticonderoga. French armor and firearms, which the Mohawk had not encountered before, won a stunning victory. This illustration of the battle is from Champlain's own drawing and is reproduced from a facsimile of the 1613 edition of his *Voyages de la Nouvelle France*.

Father Isaac Jogues came to the New World to give spiritual guidance to the Indians.

Captured by the Mohawk in 1642, the young Jesuit priest was tortured after he was taken prisoner as shown in this drawing reproduced from Bressani's *Missions des Peres de la Compagnie de Jesus dans la Nouvelle France.*

The Iroquois worshipped numerous gods, all of whom they spoke of as the "Great Spirit" and honored with festivals and dances. All that was mysterious in nature— all that inspired them with reverence, awe, terror or gratitude—became deities.

priestly robes, and instruct them, baptize them and establish a church in which they could worship the Saviour.

In September he set out again for the land of the Mohawk, accompanied by Jean de la Lande, a lay assistant, and several Huron. Father Jogues wore his black cassock, with the cowl flung back over his pack and his bearded face exposed to the sun. As they came through the Kayaderossera, he saw that he had been over-hasty in his judgment and that his mission was premature. Mohawk braves streaked with war paint disarmed him and his companions, stripped them naked and drove them to Ossernenon. The village medicine men accused the priest of sorcery, smashed his skull with a tomahawk, cut off his head and mounted it on a stick to expel his evil charms. Jean de la Lande and the Huron were also killed.

Had he lived for another twenty-four years, Father Jogues would have seen his dream fulfilled; in 1670 a good many Mohawk withdrew from the longhouses of the Iroquois League and established a Catholic community. Later, he would be canonized the first saint in North America, an achievement he hadn't at all envisioned.

Historians would credit Father Jogues with accomplishments quite outside his Christian endeavors. So far as was known, as a captive of the Mohawk he was the first white person to set foot on the land that would become Saratoga County, and the first to see Lake Saratoga. Indeed, there was more. He was the first white guest to eat the delicacies of the waters on the lake shore, thus anticipating by two hundred years a social custom that would help make Saratoga Springs a fashionable resort.

The rivals In the years following Father Jogues' death the enmity between the Five Nations and the French flared over wider areas. In 1666 thirteen hundred French and Indians came from Canada through the Kayaderossera over the ancient war trail that took them within a few miles of the saline springs, and struck at the Mohawk villages in reprisal for Mohawk raids along the Canadian border. In 1689 the Five Nations retaliated. Fifteen hundred Iroquois in two hundred and fifty canoes swept from Caniaderiossera (Lake Saratoga) up the Hudson and the almost continuous waterways linking it with Canada, and ravaged the settlements around Montreal. Each punitive expedition led to another until there was general warfare, with the French, Huron and Algonquin on one side and the Iroquois and the English on the other.

The English had replaced the Dutch as rivals of the French for supremacy in North America. Their colonies were strung along the eastern seaboard. Since the Iroquois stood astride the "empire valley" west of the Hudson, the combined land-and-water route over which either of the two colonial powers could attack the other, the English courted the Five Nations and succeeded in enlisting them in their wars against the French.

During the first of these, King William's War, six hundred French regulars, Indians and voyageurs travelled on snowshoes from Montreal to strike at Schenectady on the Mohawk River, and possibly at Albany. Crossing ice-coated Caniaderiossera, they surprised and burned several Mohawk villages, and took so many prisoners that they were forced to turn back short of either goal. Six miles from the springs they were attacked by pursuing Iroquois and English, then fled in a snowstorm, sending word to their attackers that they would kill every prisoner if the pursuit was resumed.

Queen Anne's War brought British troops and colonials into the Saratoga region in ever increasing numbers. They assembled at the village of Saratoga (later Schuylerville), where the winding creek of the Kayaderossera joined the Hudson River, built a fort and set about building a road along the river's eastern shore. It was expected that the army would march over this road and, with other English forces, attack Montreal, while at the same time the British fleet attacked Quebec. The campaign floundered when several ships were sunk after entering the St. Lawrence, and the invasion was abandoned.

The hostilities lapsed. The Five Nations became the Six Nations as the Tuscarora, an Iroquoian tribe driven from North Carolina, was adopted by the Iroquois League and given a place in the council of the confederacy. From Ontario to Tennessee, and from New England to Lake Michigan, the Iroquois were masters of the land.

In 1745 King George's War revived the rivalry between England and France. At the outset the village of Saratoga was put to the torch by five hundred French and Indians, and as the war progressed other raiding parties penetrated the region. Ten years later the colonial struggle moved into its fourth and final phase, the French and Indian War. It seemed to promise victory for the French. General Edward Braddock's attempt to capture Fort Duquesne was a costly fiasco and there were other British failures. But William Johnson triumphed at Lac du Saint Sacrement, and England's prospects grew brighter.

Giving extra muscle to his military arm in North America, the British monarch gambled on a powerful blow that would once and for all win the continent for the Crown. General James Wolfe laid siege to Quebec and in a climactic battle on the Plains of Abraham defeated the French commanded by Montcalm. The next year Montreal also fell to the British, and the long, bloody quarrel was over. The Treaty of Paris in 1763 removed Canada from the control of France and gave it to England, together with that part of Louisiana situated east of the Mississippi River, except the Island of Orleans.

The early history of the Hudson River Valley was stained with the blood of red men and white. Here, in an interlude of peace, traditional enemies guardedly exchange gifts.

The usual exchange between Indians and colonists involved lances and arrows, swords and bullets.

With the surrender of Canada the seemingly interminable border wars expired in a final rattle of musketry and flare of drums, but not even the most optimistic residents of the empire valley predicted a lengthy peace. Long-smoldering resentments between the thirteen colonies and England, kept in check during their fight with the French, flamed into open hostility after the struggle was won and the mother country took disciplinary measures against its unruly children.

The harassment of French and Indian raiding parties, together with a sixty-year dispute between the Iroquois and a company of white land-holders over ownership of the Kayaderossera, had deterred settlers from moving into the Saratoga region. With another war in prospect they continued to hang back, for despite its fertile attractions the strategic position of the region made it a natural battleground, as its history amply proved.

The village of Saratoga could ignore the approaching danger. Although it had been a military target since it was founded by the Schuylers in the seventeenth century, it had plodded ahead with Dutch patience and persistence and prospered regardless of the fortunes of war. But the strong bonds of common origin and purpose that had held the villagers of Saratoga together and served as a shield against attack were generally missing among the families who wished to settle in the Saratoga region. Some were English, some Irish, some Scotch and Scotch-Irish; some were German, Dutch, Swedish, Huguenots and French Catholics, who had come from Canada; and almost all were individualistic. In addition, they were sharply divided in their attitudes toward England and independence. As time went on and tempers grew short in the river valley, setting neighbor against neighbor and frequently father against son, the Saratoga forests, plains and meadows were left virtually unsettled. In 1764 a few families cleared land, built cabins and planted crops at the juncture of Caniaderiossera lake and the creek the Iroquis called Kayaderosseras, but few others chose to follow their example.

In the summer of 1774 the Crown and the colonies appeared permanently estranged, and events hastened toward a showdown. His Majesty's Superintendent of Indian Affairs, Sir William Johnson, pleaded the King's cause before the councils of the Six Nations, and in July, after a protracted and wearisome powwow with the sachems in the arbor behind Johnson Hall, he stumbled upstairs to his bed and died.

The Crown appointed his son-in-law, Colonel Guy Johnson, to succeed him, and with the aid of the Brants—Joseph, the brilliant Mohawk chief called by his people Thayendanegea, and Molly, Sir William's widow—the new superintendent persuaded the Mohawk, Onondaga, Cayuga and Seneca to ally themselves with the British. The Oneida and Tuscarora decided to cast their fortunes with the Americans. After two centuries of unity the Iroquois League was divided.

The following April there was an exchange of shots between colonials and British soldiers, and the rebellion was on. Hastily mustering its energies to deal with the hostilities ahead, the First Continental Congress selected one of its members, Philip Schuyler, to command the patriots in the northern theater of war, and made him a major general.

To some colonials it seemed a curious choice. Schuyler's military background was slight: he had served as a captain in the French and Indian War. While at forty-three he presented an attractive and commanding figure, and was quick and energetic in his actions, he appeared better equipped for the elegant life he generally led than for the battlefield. With his lovely wife, the former Kitty Van Rensselaer, whom he had chosen from a Dutch family as aristocratic as his own, he alternated between his fashionable town house in Albany and his country seat in the village of Saratoga, where numerous servants, an ample stable and a generously provisioned cellar pleasantly accommodated the Schuylers and their guests. Greatly in his favor as a leader in the fight for independence, however, was Philip Schuyler's devotion to the patriot cause, a subject on which he had long been so outspoken that he had alienated a good many of his patrician friends.

Schuyler's opponent in the northern arena was a *bon vivant* whose company he could enjoy in noncombative circumstances, and eventually did. Major General John Burgoyne was at once a soldier, King's friend, member of Parliament, popular dramatist and oft-quoted wit, prince of fashion and pet of British society, sportsman and gamester. In his younger days he had eloped with the eleventh Earl of Derby's daughter, Lady Charlotte Stanley; now, at fifty-three, he was a widower and a man of *affaires* as well as affairs. His troops were as fond of him as were the aristocrats with whom he intimately associated, and called him Gentleman Johnny—a reflection not only of their affection but their confidence in him as a commander well educated in the arts of war.

Burgoyne had proposed a plan for aborting the rebellion that seemed to the British ministry simplicity itself. Divide and conquer; cut through the empire valley and split the colonies in half, then deal with the parts. An army under Burgoyne's command would descend from Canada; another, marshalled by Sir William Howe, would advance from New York City; a third, led by General Barry St. Leger, would drive east along the Mohawk River—the three forces coming together at Albany. With the Crown in possession of the Hudson River region, the rebels would be divided and doubtless disorganized, and their resistance should be seriously weakened.

Burgoyne sailed to Quebec to put the plan in motion and in June, 1777, set out for Albany over the traditional water route to the empire valley. Although his army was considerably smaller than he had anticipated, he could find no fault with its quality. The main force was a proud and

Rivals for supremacy in North America, the English and the French maneuvered to control the great river that flowed through the heart of the "empire valley." This early view of the Hudson was painted and engraved from a sketch of the river at Tappan Zee.

A Mohawk chief in 1710. His face and chest are tattooed and his belt is embroidered with dyed deer's hair. His totem, the Bear, is shown at the right.

Misisagas
Terouto

LAKE ONTAR

LaGara
Fort taken from the
French in July 1759.
Great Falls
Ft Sclosser

Part
of Lake
Erie

Ft
Erie

*The Country West and North
of the Boundary Line having
never been surveyed or
even thoughtly Explored
is chiefly laid down from
my Journals and the
Sketches of intelligent
Indians and other Persons*

Rehasons harbour
Small Village
Canawagus
Chenufsiö

Falls Karandaqual
Very high
Asentus harbour is
capable of receiving
Vessels of Burden

Indian path to the lake
Canadaragev

Anarara

S E N E C A S

There are more
lakes herrab
outs but they
cannot be
laid down
with certainty

Ganushaga
Onondarka
Karaghiyadirha
Gistaquat
Kanestio
Sinsink

Tioniongarunte
THE   SIX

Allegany Mountain

Ohio or Allegany River *as it is Called above Ft Pitt.*

Canaway

Branch of Susquehannah
Great
Part
Chingleclamoock
Bald Eagle Cr
Kittanning
West

A map of the territory occupied
by the Six Nations Iroquois,
copied from the original manuscript map in the State Library
in Albany, N.Y.

*By the Country of the six Nations proper is meant that part within which they principally reside
the rest which is of Vast extent being chiefly occupied by their dependants. The Mohocks are
as they reside within the limits of N. York at Fort Hunter & Conajohare part of the Oneida
lies also within that Province the Tuscaroras who form the sixth Nation are omitted being
southern People that live on lands allotted them between Oneida & Onondaga*

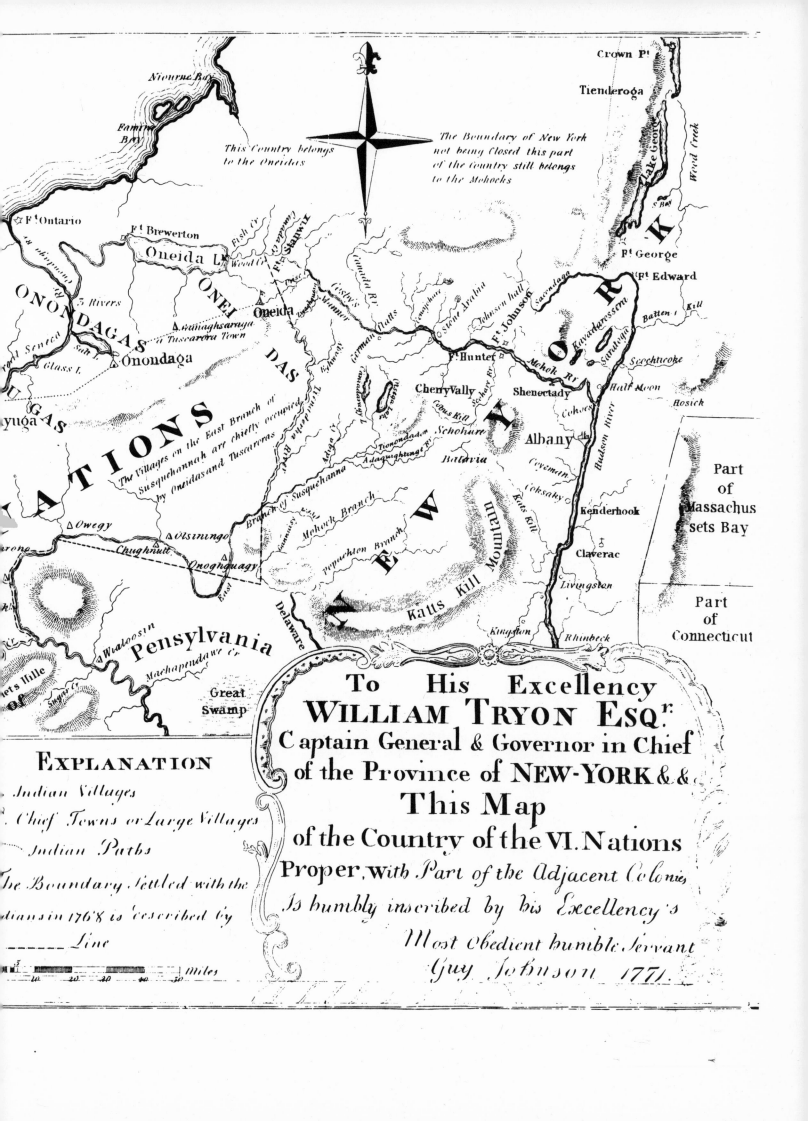

disciplined assembly of almost seven thousand British and German infantry-men, veterans of the assault on Quebec and Montreal. They would be sup-ported by British and Hesse Hanau artillerymen in charge of forty-two field guns. In addition there were two hundred and fifty Tories and Canadians and four hundred Indians. The troops rode on bateaux escorted by ships of the Royal Navy, and the Indians, in twenty canoes each with twenty braves, fanned out ahead of the fleet and served as its eyes and ears.

At the southern tip of Lake Champlain, Ticonderoga, which Ethan Allen and his Green Mountain Boys had seized two years earlier, was re-captured without a fight. A neglected hilltop enabled Burgoyne to place his guns so they would enfilade the cherished fortress and Arthur St. Clair, the Continental commander, abandoned the barricades without firing a shot. The shocking news rippled throughout the colonies and angry crit-icism rebounded against both St. Clair and his commander-in-chief, Philip Schuyler. While he was not responsible for St. Clair's precipitate flight, Schuyler's accusers said, in supervising the defense position he had been astonishingly lax.

Burgoyne came on, the bateaux carrying his heavy guns and stores over Lake George, while his army marched through the forests. When the boats reached the southern extremity of the lake, they and the equipment and supplies would also be brought along forest trails, joining the troops at Fort Edward on the east shore of the Hudson. A decayed relic of the French and Indian War, Fort Edward was a discouraging place to make a stand and Burgoyne doubted that the colonials would use it.

Schuyler had already ruled out the fort as a means of defense. Com-pared to the invaders his army was puny, less than a third the size of Burgoyne's command and many times more inferior in fighting skill, arms and supplies. In open combat the colonials would have little chance. But in the forests, through which the British forces were making their way, Schuyler saw an opportunity to harass Burgoyne and perhaps even turn him back. The tangled woods and tricky streams and the innumerable bogs, swamps and ravines which lay in Burgoyne's path were natural allies of the patriots, and they could be made more formidable by giving nature a hand. Schuyler put his troops to work with axes, shovels and explosives.

As the Crown forces advanced, short-tempered from their exertions in the prickly forest heat, they found newly created obstacles placed in their way: freshly-dug ditches, blown-up bridges, and thousands of trees felled across the narrow road. Twenty days were spent marching twenty miles. Still, they came on, and Schuyler was compelled to fall back.

Hopes had been entertained that the sturdy resistance to Burgoyne would encourage the New England settlements to reinforce the colonials opposing him, but Schuyler's part in the loss of Ticonderoga, and his role a dozen years earlier in settling a bitter boundary dispute between New York and Vermont in favor of New York, had made him anathema to New

An Iroquois brave at the time of the War of the Revolution, from a painting by
J. Grasset de St. Sauveur.

Philip Schuyler, an aristocrat from the Saratoga region, was chosen by the First Continental Congress to command the patriots in the northern theater of war.

Major General John Burgoyne, shown here in a painting by Sir Joshua Reynolds, was Schuyler's opponent. His army, a mixture of British and German troops supported by Tories and Indians, invaded the Hudson River Valley from Canada.

The atrocities committed by the Indians during the advance aroused the countryside
against the British.

When Jane McCrea was murdered by two of Burgoyne's braves a wave of ang...
swept a great many new recruits into the colonial camp to strike back at him.

Englanders. The hoped for support failed to appear, and left to fight alone Schuyler's meager defenders began to desert him in droves.

Seeking a strong position where he might halt the enemy, Schuyler retreated along the Hudson to the mouth of the Mohawk River, a few miles north of Albany, and while his dwindling army was thus engaged an incident occurred that aroused the entire countryside against Burgoyne. Before the British expedition had departed from Canada, Gentleman Johnny had admonished his Indian allies to avoid unnecessary bloodshed, promising bounty for prisoners but punishment for scalps. As Edmund Burke had dryly remarked to the House of Commons, the model major general might just as well have lectured and then uncaged a zoo full of lions. In battle the Indians had followed their usual customs, and as the atrocities mounted the colonists had nursed a growing hatred of Burgoyne. On July 27th a particularly callous deed touched off a cry for vengeance. Lovely, twenty-three-year-old Jane McCrea, who lived a short distance above the village of Saratoga, had gone to abandoned Fort Edward with the hope of joining her fiance, David Jones, a captain in Burgoyne's company of Tories. Two days before the British column arrived at the fort, Indian scouts came upon the girl and promised to escort her to her betrothed. Along the way two of the braves quarrelled over Jane McCrea, and one settled the dispute by clubbing her with his tomahawk and taking her scalp. At the British camp, where the prize was displayed, David Jones recognized the long, lustrous hair, "darker than a raven's wing," of the girl he was engaged to marry, and Burgoyne, appalled by the deed, proposed to execute the assassin. Warned that all of the Indians would desert him if he did, he pardoned the murderer instead.

Congress skillfully publicized the story of Jane McCrea, and to help avenge the crime and protect their villages from similar atrocities groups of New England militia marched to join the army aligned against Burgoyne. Its ranks swelled until it was larger than the enemy. Philip Schuyler, unfortunately, was no longer in a position to appreciate the sight; shortly after the murder he had been removed from his command and replaced by Major General Horatio Gates.

With the painful ordeal of the forests behind him and the Hudson gleaming before him, beckoning him toward Albany, where he would be joined by Howe and St. Leger, Burgoyne's spirits revived. He camped on the east shore of the river, some four miles above the village of Saratoga, and waited for the heavy guns and supplies and bateaux to be brought to him from Lake George. Officers and men settled down to a period of rest and recreation. A great many ladies had accompanied the army from Canada and helped to enliven the stay. Some were ladies of social position, but none was so elegant as Baroness Frederika von Riedesel, whose husband commanded the Hessians and who had refused to let a mere matter of war separate him from her and their three little girls. In her high-wheeled carriage she was a familiar and popular sight from one end of the column to the other; the Germans called her Fritschen, the British Lady Fritz. Burgoyne welcomed her presence; although her carriage was a nuisance, requiring as much attention as any of his military transport, she was gay and charming and a graceful hostess. Too, she was agreeable to his mistress, a lady of greatly inferior station, being but the wife of a commissary in his command, but who amused him and shared his fondness for champagne.

As the days went by, Burgoyne became less immersed in the comforts of his camp than in anxieties as to his present circumstances and future course. Early in August he received word that he could expect no help at Albany from Sir William Howe, as instead of advancing up the Hudson the general had sailed south toward Chesapeake Bay. In mid-August a foray for food and horses into Vermont by nine hundred Germans, Tories and Indians ended in a battle with John Stark's militia and the loss of almost the entire foraging party and a great amount of equipment. In the final week of the month news came that Barry St. Leger had met such stiff resistance at Fort Stanwix in his march through the Mohawk Valley that he had turned back toward Canada. Briefly weighing the significance of these events, more than three-quarters of Burgoyne's Indians deserted him, and he saw that his position was hazardous. Until he received reinforcements and provisions from the north, he was more or less immobilized. Worse, much worse, the three tigers of his invasion plan that had promised to devour the Hudson River Valley were now reduced to one—at present, a rather toothless one. He would have to advance against Albany alone. The alternative, retreat to Ticonderoga, held no attractions, and Burgoyne dismissed it. His only course, he decided, was to press on, engage the rebels and try to disperse them, and hope that Howe would turn about and keep his appointment at Albany. If Howe continued to travel south, he would have no choice but to hole up in the city and wait for help.

Journey's end   In mid-September, having received additional troops and provisions from Canada as well as his artillery and supplies from Lake George, Burgoyne led his army across the river over a bridge of bateaux and poised it for battle. Gates had moved the Americans from the position Schuyler had chosen to a point some nine miles south of the village of Saratoga and fourteen miles east of the saline springs. At this point the Hudson ran through a narrow defile dominated on the west bank by steep bluffs called Bemis Heights, and the colonials had entrenched themselves on the slopes. It was a redoubtable stronghold, fairly bristling with fortifications, and Gates was confident that it would block Gentleman Johnny's march to Albany indefinitely.

His estimate of the situation proved to be somewhat cocksure. On September 19th Burgoyne sent his artillery to occupy still higher ground

As the invaders came on, Philip Schuyler's wife, Kitty, set fire to the cornfields around their country mansion in the village of Saratoga (now Schuylerville).

Baroness Frederika von Riedesel accompanied her husband, the commander of the Hessian troops, as the British forces marched toward Albany.

Under Major General Horatio Gates, who had replaced Schuyler as the colonial leader, the Americans entrenched themselves on Bemis Heights.

On September 19, 1777, the two armies met in the first battle of Saratoga, an engagement which went badly for Burgoyne, and on October 7th a second battle was fought,
in which Benedict Arnold led the patriots to a stunning triumph. Here he is wounded
as the colonials storm a Hessian redoubt.

British General Simon Fraser also behaved with conspicuous bravery. When it seemed
that he would rally the British forces, Timothy Murphy, one of Daniel Morgan's riflemen, climbed a tree, took aim with his double-barrelled rifle and mortally wounded
Fraser. This engraving depicts Fraser's funeral after the battle.

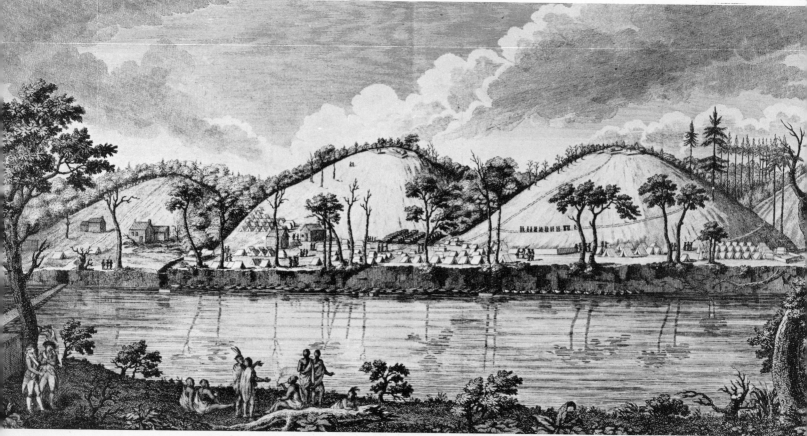

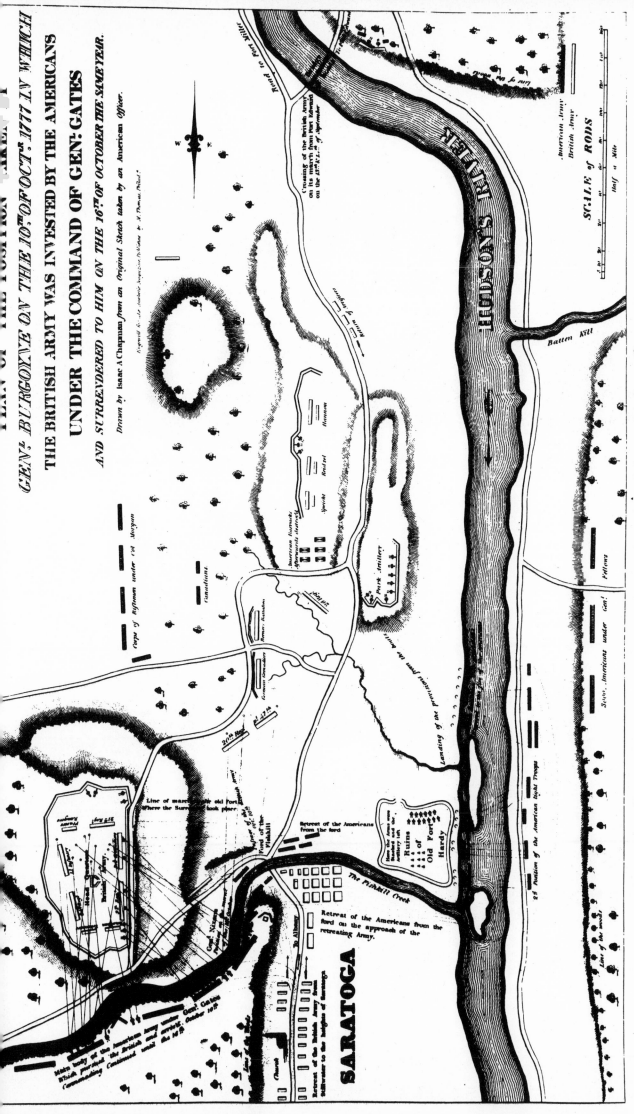

PLAN OF THE POSITION TAKEN BY

GEN: BURGOYNE ON THE 10TH OF OCTR: 1777 IN WHICH
THE BRITISH ARMY WAS INVESTED BY THE AMERICANS
UNDER THE COMMAND OF GEN: GATES
AND SURRENDERED TO HIM ON THE 16TH OF OCTOBER THE SAME YEAR.

Drawn by Isaac A Chapman from an Original Sketch taken by an American Officer.

SARATOGA

HUDSON'S RIVER

SCALE of RODS

This diagram, drawn by Isaac A. Chapman from a sketch by an American officer, traces the advance of Burgoyne's army across the Hudson (far right) and its march through the river valley toward Albany; and then traces the British retreat, following the army's defeat in the second engagement, to the village of Saratoga and the heights of Fish Kill (upper left). Also shown are the positions taken by the opposing forces prior to Burgoyne's capitulation and the place of his surrender.

Two views of the surrender at Saratoga, America's first great triumph of the revolution. In John Trumbull's painting of the ceremony, Burgoyne proffers his sword to Gates as Daniel Morgan, in white deerskin, and other American officers look on (Philip Schuyler was also present, third from left). Subsequently the British army stacked its arms—an event recorded with feeling for the drama of the occasion by the French artist, Fauvel.

from which he could bring his cannon to bear on the carefully prepared defenses, and alert to the danger Major General Benedict Arnold, commanding the left wing of the American troops, begged to be allowed to attack the British before their guns were in position. Gates, who disliked Arnold, sent Colonel Daniel Morgan and his riflemen to oppose the move, but when they ran into difficulty Arnold rushed into the fight, and the battle was joined at Freeman's Farm.

It went badly for Burgoyne. Arnold was everywhere, quick to perceive the British weaknesses and audacious in turning them to his advantage. Convinced that with a little more strength he could end the campaign then and there, he asked for reinforcements. Gates, although several thousand colonials rested on their arms on the heights, rejected the request, and as darkness came Arnold fell back. There was neither victor nor vanquished; both sides had suffered; but the Americans, outnumbering the British, could absorb their losses, while the six hundred officers and men the day had cost Burgoyne were irreplaceable.

For two and a half weeks the armies faced each other with little more than a mile between them and only fitful sniper fire to mark their enmity. To some observers there appeared to be more hostility in the American camp. Gates, exhibiting a flair for petty revenge, had not mentioned Arnold's name in his report on the battle to Congress, and a few days later had removed him from his command. Only the pleas of fellow officers had kept Arnold from leaving the camp.

On October 7th a second battle swirled around Freeman's Farm. It began with a British attempt to by-pass the American position, and once again Gates sent Morgan's riflemen to abort the threat. The sights and sounds of the engagement were too much for Arnold to resist. Ignoring his lack of insignia, he plunged again into the fray, an awesome figure raging with astounding ardor and unbelievable luck into volley after volley of musket balls and grapeshot, brandishing his sword and calling on the half-trained and untrained colonials to follow him, which they did, until his horse was shot down and Arnold himself fell with a bullet that fractured his thigh.

This time there was no need to assess the outcome; Arnold had scored a stunning triumph.

Burgoyne withdrew his battered forces toward the village of Saratoga, where a rise of ground north of Fish Kill Creek was favorable to a defensive stand. He placed his cannon there and established his headquarters in Philip Schuyler's vacant mansion near the Hudson. In every way the great house proved to be an excellent choice. When work was done supper parties, provisioned with hams, beef and other delicacies brought up from the vaulted cellar, relieved the taste of defeat. The Indians brought trout from nearby Lake Saratoga. Champagne flowed at the tilt of an empty glass, and when heads grew heavy, arms locked around waists and officers and ladies mounted the stairs to the many guest rooms and the servants' rooms under the roof. Regretfully, it was pointed out that the house would be an obstacle in the path of British artillery fire from the slope, and so it was burned together with Schuyler's storehouses and mills.

Gates, cautiously pursuing his foe, finally attacked and inflicted new casualties, and Burgoyne decided that further bloodshed would be useless. In the afternoon of October 16th, debonair in gleaming scarlet, gold and white, he rode to the American camp where Gates, the stoop-shouldered, English-born servant's son, awaited him wearing spectacles and a plain blue frock. To some who were present he resembled less a victorious general than a midwife, and since he was delivering Burgoyne of more than five and a half thousand men in a way he was. The next morning the British army marched to the appointed place in the meadows by the river, stacked its arms and set out for Boston and prison. Gentleman Johnny was permitted to continue to Albany, the destination that until then had eluded him; there he was entertained by his deposed opponent, Philip Schuyler, and in the following year he was allowed to return to England.

The news of his surrender at Saratoga raced through the colonies and overseas. It was the burgeoning nation's first great triumph of the war and came when most needed, lifting the morale and stiffening the resolve of Americans everywhere after a disheartening series of defeats. France, which had officially declined to recognize the colonies' independence while secretly supplying the patriots with more matériel, promptly threw caution to the winds and virtually declared itself America's ally.

The war moved away from Saratoga. Soon the land of the Mohawk would belong to the empire builders and their medicine springs would become the site of the New World's most popular spa.

Chapter Three

The
health
seekers
Six years after the first patriotic shots were fired a new flag, starred and striped, flew over the Crown colonies, and the way was clear to unfurl it over the unsettled regions westward as far as the Mississippi River. The prospect was attractive, promising not only land but adventure, and victorious colonials piled their families and belongings in wagons and drove to claim the spoils.

Others preferred prizes closer at hand. The New England militiamen who had rallied to Saratoga and fought Burgoyne had been introduced to an eye-filling region clothed in autumn colors. Some had cleansed and healed their wounds at the saline springs; many had studied the uninhabited plains and valleys and pondered the advantages of the thick forests and fresh-water streams, and when the Saratoga campaign was won had left for home determined to return and settle on the land. Those who did return found the land ready to receive them; for the first time since it had been possessed by the Mohawk, Saratoga was completely free to grant its favors to the colonists.

During their long tenure the Mohawk had warded off all concerted attempts to colonize the region except one, and they had successfully contested the exception until shortly before the war. In 1704 thirteen colonials had applied for a deed to a "tract of vacant and unappropriated land called by the Indian name of Kayaderossera," which they said they had purchased from the Mohawk. Four years later they received from Queen Anne a grant of all the land extending some seven hundred thousand acres north from the juncture of the Hudson and Mohawk rivers—a bountiful domain that embraced the lovely lake and the health-giving springs as well as the Indians' treasured hunting ground. The Mohawk disdained the grant, insisting that they had sold for a trifling sum a bit of land barely large enough to accommodate a farm, and since the colonials made no attempt to survey or settle the tract the matter rested there for more than fifty years. Then, in 1764, a few families had settled beside the lake, and the Mohawk appealed to Sir William Johnson to uphold their ownership of the Kayaderossera. In no mood to antagonize an ally who had helped the Crown wrest the continental north from the French, and whose assistance would likely be needed to keep it from falling into the hands of the Americans, His Majesty's Superintendent of Indian Affairs moved to have the claim of the thirteen colonials vacated by Act of Parliament. The Colonial Assembly interceded, and in 1768 a compromise was reached: the Mohawk were allowed to keep a great portion of the Kayaderossera and were awarded five thousand dollars for the land taken from them. This land was divided among the surviving members of the thirteen claimants, their heirs or assignees, and to the estate of Rip Van Dam went the deed that included the springs. Some time later a wealthy merchant, Isaac Low, purchased most of the Van Dam acres and opened them for settlement, and in 1771 Dirck Schouten came from Waterford and built and installed himself in a cabin near the springs—the first resident of the watering place. Depressed by the remoteness of the spot he had chosen, he departed after two years, and the few settlers who took over his cabin abandoned it after similarly brief stays.

Finally, the war had penetrated Saratoga, and the landowners in the region who remained loyal to the Crown were promptly divested of their holdings after the Crown's surrender. The properties owned by Isaac Low and other Tories, and the bosomy acres Sir William Johnson had bequeathed to his heirs, were confiscated by the Continental Congress; so too was the land held by the Mohawk who, having chosen the losing side, had sought refuge with the British in Ontario.

Saratoga's most prosperous private property, the Schuyler estate, was left in the possession of its patrician owner. Philip Schuyler had been subjected to a court-martial in which he had been accused of negligence in defending Ticonderoga and incompetence or cowardice in retreating with his army down the river valley and allowing the enemy to advance unopposed, but he had been acquitted of all charges, his valor as well as his patriotism vindicated. His mansion, mills and storehouses, burned by the British, had been rebuilt directly after Burgoyne's surrender, and resuming his seat in Congress he had regained the renown his brief military career had cost him. Now he was content to play the role of country gentleman and preside over the thriving enterprises he had inherited from his industrious predecessors.*

In 1783 the great estate overlooking the Hudson was on its way to becoming a summer resort for New York socialites attracted by its elegant

* Philip Pieterson Schuyler had come to America from Amsterdam in 1650, and soon after his sons had achieved their maturity the family had purchased land where the Hudson River was joined by Fish Kill, the creek the Iroquois called Kayaderosseras. There they had established a settlement, the village of Saratoga (now Schuylerville), put up mills and prospered in trade with merchants from Europe and India. In 1745 the village had been destroyed by an attack force of French and Indians, its mills and houses burned, thirty of its members killed, including Captain John Philip Schuyler, and a hundred captured. Despite the tragedy and the loss, the settlement and its enterprises had been restored; and after Burgoyne's act of military necessity, the Schuyler properties were replaced again.

Chalybeate Spring in 1787. The first picture ever printed of the Saratoga springs, it originally appeared in *Columbian* Magazine.

George Washington was so impressed with the benefits of High Rock Spring that he considered building a summer home close by.

Other visitors also praised the waters, but were vexed by the crude accommodations at the springs. One of the most outspoken critics was Elkanah Watson, shown here in a portrait by Samuel F. B. Morse.

mansion and sprightly entertainments, its spacious grounds and the scenic view it afforded of the battlefields where history had been made. To comfort guests who rose from his richly laden table with a twinge of dyspepsia, or complained of constraining aches and pains, Schuyler had cut a bridle path through the difficult country between the village and the "most amazing spring" Sir William Johnson had called to his attention. Later visitors had named it High Rock Spring, and while the growing swarm of health seekers had discovered six more springs within a half mile of its waters High Rock was the favorite. Schuyler's path made it easier for everyone to sample the curative brew, but the journey was arduous even so; wolves and cougars prowled through the forest and in several places the path was no more than a log felled across a swamp. Wondrous tales told of the waters and their speedy dispatch of sundry ailments nevertheless encouraged many of the Schuyler guests to visit the cone-shaped rock and drink and bathe in its bubbling liquids, resting between immersions beneath the white canvas marquee their host had thoughtfully provided.

In August of that year George Washington was induced to make the trip. While waiting for the British to evacuate New York City as a preliminary to the Crown's formal recognition of America's independence, he had relieved the tedium with a tour of inspection of Crown Point, Ticonderoga and other military posts in the north, and had dropped in on Philip and Kitty Schuyler on his way back to the Continental camp at Newburgh. Their enthusiasm for the spring waters intrigued him. His wife had spent a considerable part of her wartime grass widowhood at Virginia's warm springs and he needed little urging to visit High Rock in company with George Clinton, the Governor of New York, and young Alexander Hamilton, who had married the Schuylers' fetching daughter, Betsy.

Impressed by the results of his stay, Washington made inquiries with a view to building a summer home on the land adjoining the spring. Nothing was achieved by these overtures, but his interest in the waters remained firm and his warm praise of their benefits led several of his friends to try them. At least one was disappointed. Visiting the watering place early the following summer with the hope of curing his rheumatism, Brigadier General Otho Williams, the Marylander whose exploits had helped to win the war in the south, wrote to Washington in July:

> They [the springs] are now frequented by the uncivilized people of the back country; but very few others resort to them, as there is but one small hut within several miles of the place. Corporal Armstrong and myself spent one week there which was equal to a little campaign; for the accommodations were very wretched and provisions exceedingly rare. The country about the springs being uncultivated, we were forced to send to the borders of the Hudson for what was necessary for our subsistence.

PUTNAM & THE WOLF.

PUTNAM'S TAVERN
& BOARDING HOUSE

To make the Saratoga watering place more attractive, Gideon Putnam erected a guest house, identified by this sign.

Later, Gideon Putnam laid out a village, which became the village of Saratoga Springs. This early engraving shows Broad Street (later Broadway) in 1815. Putnam's Tavern is at left and at right, facing it, is Congress Hall, a more elegant hotel he built.

The Schuylers refused to let the primitive conditions interfere with their enjoyment of the waters. The canvas marquee was replaced by a two-room cottage and they faithfully journeyed to High Rock each summer.

In 1787 a tavernkeeper, Alexander Bryan, established a public house in the vicinity of the springs to oblige visitors whose thirst ran to something stronger than mineral water, but despite its soothing hospitality a sojourn at the springs continued to vex all but the most dedicated guests. Having made their way to the saline fountains over trails which pained body and spirit, health seekers found no provision for bathing except an open hut with a bench from which they were required to roll into a water-filled trough not unlike the kind used for feeding hogs.

Would no one undertake to make the springs more accessible, their facilities more accommodating? Opportunity knocked loud and clear in the forest stillness, but throughout Saratoga no one answered.

Gideon goes forth   On hearing the call of Lexington in 1775, Major General Israel Putnam had left his plow in a furrow of his Connecticut farm and hurried off to the war. In 1789 his twenty-five-year-old Sutton, Massachusetts, cousin, Gideon Putnam, responded to a different trumpet. With his bride of a few months, Doanda Risley, he journeyed to the Saratoga springs.

Bemused by the wealth of timber surrounding the waters, young Putnam was slow to grasp the prize. He settled beside High Rock Spring, leased three hundred acres and swung his axe with such enthusiasm that he was soon the owner of a sawmill, shipping staves and shingles down the Hudson to New York City. In the next few years so many other colonists were attracted by his success that a small community rose in the vicinity of the springs. The once tranquil watering place became a busy site of falling trees and buzzing saws, and the Hudson was fairly sprinkled with barges carrying lumber from the area to the settlements alongside the river. Gideon Putnam saw that eventually the forest encircling the springs would be exhausted and that the little community which owed its existence to the profits from the timber would disappear.

His thoughts turned to the springs, spouting their invigorating liquids as they had for hundreds of years. Unlike the trees, they promised to run on forever, and with each summer they were becoming better known. Physicians experimented with the waters and published treatises describing their qualities and the benefits which might accrue from their use. Lecturers and writers reported on their visits to the springs in public meetings and popular journals. Unfortunately, their remarks were not always complimentary. Reflecting the general criticism, a New Englander named Elkanah Watson had written:

> I spent a day bathing in a trough and drinking the exhilarating water which gushes from the center of a rock. I met with a

In 1792 a sparkling new mineral spring had been discovered. Named Congress Spring, it was destined to become famous throughout the country. This is the way it looked in 1816. Congress Hall is in the background.

dozen respectable people sojourning at a wretched tavern. The wildness of the region and the excessively bad accommodations made me recur to the condition of Bath in the barbarous ages, when, several centuries before Christ, as the legend says, the springs were discovered by their salutary effect upon a herd of distempered swine wallowing in the mud.

The exasperating conditions of the watering place seemed to offer no greater hope for the future than the vanishing forest, but with the hand of opportunity resting firmly on his shoulder Gideon Putnam began to put the problem in perspective. Unquestionably the springs were valuable, and there was reason to believe that there were many more of them in the vicinity than had thus far been discovered. Two were particularly favored by visitors, High Rock and Red, whose oddly crimson-stained waters had claimed attention three years after Sir William Johnson had revealed the existence of High Rock, but recently a spring had been found that appeared to have more vitality than the others. While pursuing a deer track, Nicholas Gilman had come upon a brook which he traced to a waterfall; below the waterfall was a rock, and from the rock rose a jet of sparkling mineral water. In keeping with its finder's status as a United States Senator, it was called Congress Spring. Gideon Putnam liked the name—indeed, liked everything about the spring. Given the proper accommodations the others had been denied, he was confident that it would not only be a boon to health seekers but would improve his personal prospects and perhaps the community's as well.

He purchased an acre of land beside Congress Spring and cleared it of the tall pines which grew upon it, then hired carpenters to help him build a guest house. Completed in 1803, it was a serviceable frame building seventy feet long and three stories high, with two parlors, a large dining room and a kitchen on the first floor and a plentiful supply of lodgings on the floors above. Gideon put up a sign, boldly inviting—"Putnam's Tavern & Boarding House"—and awaited the seventy guests his rooms would accommodate. The springs had seldom attracted seventy guests during an entire summer, but Gideon was unafraid. Within a year he was so pressed with visitors that he was compelled to enlarge the house.

In the midst of this prosperity Congress Spring perversely refused to flow. For reasons Gideon was at a loss to understand, the rock had been removed from its accustomed place and the effusive waters were silent. He waded into the brook and where it was deepest saw bubbles of air rising in the stream, suggesting that originally the spring had spouted from beneath the bed of the brook. Mustering his assistants, he changed the course of the stream and dug deep into the gravel. Mineral water bubbled among the stones then sprayed into a fountain. To make sure that it would not be lost again, Gideon framed the geyser in a wooden cone buried in the gravel. He then carried his program of reform further by improving the paths leading to the spring and building a bathhouse. As a final touch he put up posters threatening all persons who misused the spring with the full majesty of the law.

In 1805 Gideon's mounting fortune enabled him to add a hundred and thirty acres of land to the acre he had originally purchased and he began to lay out a proper village. Wherever possible he placed each spring in the center of a road so that it could be easily reached and enclosed each fountain in a stout wooden cone driven into the ground in the same manner as he had safeguarded the Congress waters. With the same altruism he planted elm trees * on both sides of the wide thoroughfare he laid in front of his guest house (later it would be named Broadway) and set aside several of his acres for the village to use as sites for a church, a school and a graveyard. His communal spirit was infectious and drew the villagers closer in common cause. There was no need for him to picture the rewards which would follow once the community was made attractive and accessible, for as all could see each summer the springs lured more and more people with money to spend.

Gideon's boarding house grew until it became nearly twice its original size. Another hotel, the Columbian, was built, and as the stream of guests continued to swell, rooms were added to private dwellings. Looking to the future, when these accommodations would also prove inadequate, Gideon determined to build a hotel grandly suited to the village's growing popularity as a spa. He would call it Congress Hall, in tribute to the growing fame of Congress Spring.

In 1811, working along with his carpenters, he saw his imposing design gradually take form, then was forced to halt construction when he was severely injured in a fall from a scaffold. Impatient to continue, he rose from his sickbed before he was fully repaired and summoned the men back to work. Soon he fell ill. On the first day of December, 1812, he died, and was buried in the plot he had presented to the village.

Doanda, his wife, and their five sons and four daughters, carried on and Gideon's grand hotel was completed. As he had anticipated, it became the fashionable gathering place of the spa's guests. The Putnams, however, remained attached to his original dream house, sustaining it with such devoted care that boarders couldn't be sure whether the new name it was given, Union Hall, was meant to celebrate familial unity or the union of states.

Hymn singing and sans souci   During the next few years the community's vision of a golden future began to fade. Although the village could offer a greater number and vari-

---

* With Gideon's example before them, the village trustees in 1827 authorized a reduction of 62½ cents in each landholder's road tax for each tree he planted along the front of his property, thus insuring the elm- and maple-shaded streets which were to become a hallmark of Saratoga's charm.

Putnam's Tavern & Boarding House grew to be a much larger hotel called Union Hall. This drawing of it was made between 1836 and 1844, when Gideon's sons, Rockwell and Washington Putnam, were the proprietors.

In the 1830's Saratoga Springs was not only a popular spa but a fashionable social resort. This view shows guests promenading on the piazza of Congress Hall.

ety of springs than ever before, and there was no lack of moneyed hypo-chondriacs anxious to take the cure, fewer visitors arrived each summer.

The elders who had been entrusted with the leadership of the village following Gideon Putnam's death attributed the declining interest to the increasing host of health resorts. In New York State a plethora of mineral springs, oil springs, nitrogen springs, sulphur springs and salt springs invited the nation to try their therapy, and along the northeastern coast ocean resorts touted the benefits of sea air and sea water. With so many remedies competing for customers, the elders reasoned, it was to be expected that attendance would fall off at Saratoga's springs.

The loss of favor could be traced to other factors too, but the elders were loath to acknowledge them. From the beginning there had been little to attract visitors to the watering place except the praiseworthy waters themselves. Raised with Puritan strictness in stern New England towns, the villagers were suspicious of amusements, and contending with their frowning code of behavior had worked such a strain on guests who sought to enjoy the few pleasures available that in recent seasons many had wan-dered to less confining resorts.

Their departure had been hastened by an enthusiastic evangelist, Dr. Billy J. Clark who, in 1808, had selected Saratoga Springs as the ideal spot on which to establish the country's first temperance society. Members vowed never to touch wine (except at public dinners) or distilled spirits (except when invalided by "actual disease"), and since both in number and weight of opinion they soon were a force to be reckoned with, any hopes for a relaxing of the community's restrictions were quickly dispelled. The village settled into a gloomy routine of hymn singing, buggy riding and drinking and bathing at the mineral springs. Whist, even when played without stakes, was viewed as a form of yielding to Satan and dancing as total surrender. In the hotels and boarding houses the day began, and frequently ended, with a prayer meeting or a Bible reading, and guests were not permitted to arrive or depart on Sunday. The severity of this regimen had unsettled all but the spa's most strait-laced visitors, and so they had started to slip away—a steadily growing portion of them to Ballston, a watering place seven miles south of Saratoga Springs. To the elders of Saratoga, this was the unkindest cut of all.

Ballston had been named for the Reverend Eliphalet Ball, a Presby-terian clergyman and a cousin of George Washington's mother, Mary Ball, who had been persuaded to move his parish to the settlement shortly after it had been established. In time a spring had been discovered several miles distant from Ballston, and later others had been found close to the village.

Ballston had suffered growing pains somewhat more embarrassing than Saratoga's. Visiting the original spring in 1790, the well-travelled Elkanah Watson had decried its accommodations with greater disdain than he had conferred on the conditions at High Rock. Except for the indispensable tavern, there was little to comfort visitors to the waters and still scantier provision for putting them up. Worst of all were the facilities for bathing; Watson had found them both ludicrous and offensive, and said so.

During the next two years, with the assistance of a wealthy speculator, Ballston had spruced up the place and health seekers had arrived in ever more pleasing numbers. Then, determined not to be outdone by Gideon Putnam, who had just improved Saratoga's position with a spacious new boarding house, Ballston had started constructing a hotel that would dwarf its rival in every respect. Its design resembled that of the Palace of Versailles and its cost was estimated at sixty thousand dollars. Built of native pine, it was one hundred and sixty feet long with two wings flung back almost the same distance; piazzas overlooked landscaped grounds; and as a consummate touch, a Frenchman was appointed to attend the whims of the one hundred and thirty expected guests. It was named Sans Souci and was an immediate success.

Content with its own good fortune, Saratoga had regarded the goings-on at Ballston with icy disapproval. Not until some years later would it have reason to wonder why Saratoga's loss was Ballston's gain, but to unprejudiced eyes and uninhibited appetites the superiority of the neighboring resort commenced with Sans Souci. Revisiting the watering place on August 20, 1805, Elkanah Watson had been fairly carried away by the change. He wrote:

> [We] reached the Sans Souci at Ballston amid scenes of elegance and gayety. We seated ourselves at a sumptuous table, with about one hundred guests of all classes, but generally, from their appearance and deportment, of the first respectability, assembled here from every part of the Union and Europe, in the pursuit of health or pleasure, of matrimony or vice. This is the most splendid watering place in America and scarcely surpassed in Europe in its dimensions and the taste and elegance of its arrangements. In the evening, we attended a ball in a spacious hall, brilliantly illuminated with chandeliers, and adorned with various other appliances of elegance and luxury. Here was congregated a fine exhibition of the beau monde. A large proportion of the assembly was from the Southern States, and distinguished by their elegant and polished manners. In the place of the old-fashioned country dances and four-hand reels of Revolutionary days, I was pleased to notice the advance of refined customs, and the introduction of the graces of Paris in the elegant cotillion and quadrille. At table I was delighted in observing the style and appearance of the company, males and females intermixed in the true French usage of sans souci. The board was supplied with the luxuries of more sunny climes. There was a large display of servants, handsomely attired, while the music of a choice band enlivened the festivities.

MORNING   NOON   NIGHT

The weightiest problem on a lady's mind was what to wear.

A visiting French artist supplied this pastoral glimpse of the Spa.

Ballston Springs, Saratoga's closest rival, in 1839.

Other guests were similarly impressed. Soon after the opening of Sans Souci, Ballston was host to an average of two thousand visitors a season.

The medicine man and the chancellor

By 1818 Saratoga Springs was little more than a shadow of its popular rival and the elders were fearful that eventually the resort would die. With this chilling prospect in view, they agreed that they had no alternative but to arrange a truce with Satan, to the extent at least of permitting him a few devices with which to entice summer travellers back to the spa. While the village reluctantly accepted the decision, other voices strongly protested and, as before, Satan was turned away at the township limits.

The township of Saratoga extended fourteen miles east and west and a half dozen miles north and south, and embraced not only the watering place but other communities as well. Apart from their devout respect for the Lord and strict obedience to His ways, the others had few interests in common with the resort. But jealous of their own welfare they were quick to intervene in the affairs of the spa whenever they deemed it necessary— and the decision to cater to pleasure seekers at the springs was one they could oppose in concert. In 1819, however, the village of Saratoga Springs was declared a special township * with the right to govern itself, and the elders were free to act without concern for their neighbors' sensibilities. Following one invitation with another, they made it known that pleasure would enjoy the same standing in the community as piety.

That summer Congress Hall introduced billiard rooms and a little later provided an orchestra to entertain guests in the evening. This innovation paved the way for dancing and flirtation, capped by unchaperoned afternoon drives into the countryside. In the natural course of events gentlemen were permitted to gamble at cards in the privacy of their rooms.

The new freedom at the spa, along with its incomparable mineral waters, drew summer tourists back to Saratoga. To accommodate the influx, old hotels—Union Hall, Congress Hall, the Columbian—were enlarged and improved, and new ones— the Pavilion and Elias Benedict's splendid United States Hotel (which could absorb one hundred and fifty guests)— were built. By 1825 hotels and boarding houses were able to handle a thousand visitors, and the duel with Ballston for supremacy began in earnest.

It was left to a newcomer to Saratoga to deliver the supreme stroke. In 1823, his fiftieth year, Dr. John Clarke had retired to the spa from a vigorous career in New York City, where, as the proprietor of the city's first soda fountain, he had profited handsomely from the popularity of carbonated beverages. He bought acres of land and prepared to live out

* On April 17, 1826, Saratoga Springs was incorporated as a village.

his days as a country squire—a boyhood dream formed in the green fields of his native Yorkshire.

It was not to be. Included in his purchase was Congress Spring, and the riches resting on his doorstep were too tempting for Dr. Clarke to resist. After two years he turned his back on the leisurely life and set up a plant to bottle the sparkling health water. Resembling a commodious shower bath, the peculiar structure seemed to the villagers nothing more than a monstrous eyesore, but its achievements were spectacular. By 1830 Congress water was flowing into containers at the rate of a gallon a minute and twelve hundred bottles of it were being shipped daily to customers in every part of the world. Shrewdly promoted as cathartic, therapeutic and invigorating, useful in curing a variety of complaints ranging from dyspepsia and some species of dropsy to old scorbutic ulcers, depraved appetite and tired blood, the bottled mineral drink became a fixture in thousands of homes, hotels and steamboat salons, and proved to be as indispensable to inveterate overdoers as their after-dinner nap.

With a mixture of perspicacity and community pride, Dr. Clarke declined to sell his unique remedy to Ballston and other resorts regarded as Saratoga's rivals. As the beverage had become increasingly popular, people from all over the Union had visited Saratoga to see and bathe at the celebrated spring from which the Congress waters flowed, and its owner had no intention of letting the spa's competitors trade in on its reputation by supplying them with the elixir that was making Saratoga famous.

Year after year Congress Spring pumped a stream of prosperity into the spa, and Dr. Clarke enclosed the saline fountain in a Doric pavilion befitting its stature as the resort's principal medicinal attraction. He provided new paths to the waters, planted flowers, supplied a platform for promenaders and engaged a band to play concerts at the spring each morning and afternoon. At all times dipper boys stood ready to serve guests who wished to drink the water, scooping it up in tin cups fastened to long sticks.

A half dozen blocks north of the renowned fountain a quite different attraction was also helping to spread Saratoga's name and fame. In the northern wing of a colonial-style house enclosed by a virtual forest of pine trees Reuben Hyde Walworth presided over the Court of Chancery, the highest judicial office in the State of New York, with such wise and witty aplomb that his decisions and opinions were circulated by the nation's press and drew a stream of celebrities to his door.

Chancellor Walworth had settled in Saratoga at the same time as Dr. Clarke, in order to take up his duties as the newly-appointed Circuit Judge of the district, and, five years later, in 1828, had been promoted to his present distinguished judicial post. As the result of his reputation, the modest courtroom in which he sat in his judge's robe and decided the fate of persons and property seemed to tourists a veritable arena where one might glimpse the excitements of real-life drama, and they did their best to attend the cases tried before him.

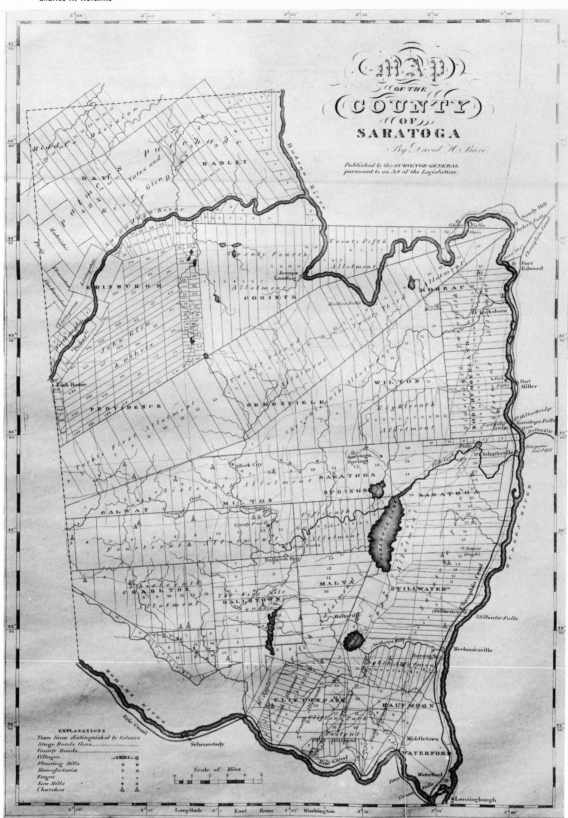

Saratoga County was established in 1791. This map shows it in 1828.

Charles H. Hutchins

Congress Spring (left) and Columbian Spring were the principal attractions of Congress Park, an idyllic oasis in the heart of the village which owed its beauty to the enthusiasm, energy and unstinting largesse of Dr. John Clarke.

Charles H. Hutchins

High Rock Spring during this period.

In 1848 August Kollner drew this scene at the High Rock (left), Iodine and Empire springs.

Charles H. Hutchins

A view of Broadway in 1840. The Grecian pavilion at left shelters Columbian Spring and three of the resort's hotels can be seen: Stanwix Hall (extreme left) and Union Hall, and across the street at right, Congress Hall.

Pine Grove was the home of Chancellor Reuben Hyde Walworth and was the scene of many famous gatherings (guests included the Marquis de Lafayette, James Fenimore Cooper and similar notables). In later years the estate was put to other uses. Said *Harper's Monthly*: "Here [on the grounds] the Indians encamped, sold their bows, canes and baskets, and shot at pennies to show their skill; and here, too, the militia met for drill, armed with umbrellas and broomsticks or, in default of those articles, with cornstalks."

Celebrated visitors also sampled the hospitality of the mansion and grounds, which the chancellor and his wife, Maria, had named Pine Grove. Statesmen, soldiers, authors and artists hitched their horses and carriages in front of the serenely handsome white house, shaded on Broadway by a row of elms but sheltered on either side and in back by lofty pines. They were guests of the Walworths on occasions that usually included dinner, whist and lively discussions in the parlors, on the piazzas and under the arching branches of the trees. In 1828, Walworth's first year as chancellor, the President of the United States, John Quincy Adams, dropped by along with Andrew Jackson, who in the fall election would defeat him and succeed him as the nation's chief executive.

In 1848, the Court of Chancery having been abolished, Chancellor Walworth closed his courtroom and put away his robe, but continued to serve as one of Saratoga's first citizens and most enthusiastic boosters.*

As the century moved into its second half the resort's preëminence as the nation's most popular watering place was virtually unquestioned. Ballston clung to fading splendors, several of its most important springs having disappeared and the worn-out Sans Souci having been converted into a law school, and more distant rivals were hardly a challenge. To Americans Saratoga was Queen of the Spas.

---

* After the chancellor's death Saratoga was shocked by a murder in the Walworth family. Reuben Hyde Walworth's second wife was a widow with three children. In 1852 her daughter, Ellen, was married at the spa to the chancellor's son, Mansfield Tracy Walworth, who was well on his way to becoming a popular novelist. It was not a happy marriage and at long last the two separated; Mansfield Walworth took an apartment in New York City and his wife and children moved into the mansion at Pine Grove, which in 1871 she turned into a private school. Two years later their son Frank called upon his father, accused him of writing insulting and threatening letters to Ellen Walworth, and shot him dead. In 1885 the famous mansion was enlarged to provide more classrooms for the school, and in 1955 it was razed.

PART TWO

"Pray, What Do They Do at the Springs?"

Chapter One

The
astonishment
knew
no bounds

For its metamorphosis from a spa to The Spa, so incontestably America's favorite watering place that it was known simply as the Springs, Saratoga could thank not only Gideon Putnam's vision, Satan's hand-maidens and the far-flung therapy of Dr. Clarke's bottled health water but also an innovation that was transforming the country itself.

Prior to the 1830's the majority of visitors from the north, east and west made their way to Saratoga in canvas-covered stagecoaches. This was a jostling, jolting, nerve-shattering journey during which twelve or more hours a day were spent in travelling forty miles and up to fourteen passengers crammed into each stage were usually enveloped in mutual dislike. Some found relief in proceeding part of the way by canal boat, and visitors from points south of the watering place often came by coastal sloop to New York City, steamboat up the Hudson River to Albany and then completed the trip by stage.

The rich travelled in considerably more comfort and infinitely more style. Wealthy mill-owners, merchants and planters installed themselves and their families in ornate coaches trimmed with brass or gold, frequently with the family crest emblazoned on the doors, and set out for the spa with a retinue of outriders, coachman and footmen. Where stage passengers rode in coaches supported lengthwise by two leather braces which endeavored to alleviate their distress, the carriages of the rich swayed high on suspension springs and their occupants were spared most of the dips, twists and bumps in their paths by the careful ministrations of the outriders and coach-man and the span of six or eight mettled horses they guided.

The progress of each elegant entourage was attended by a succession of crowds who gathered at the post stations along the way to savor the sight. Those that came from the south drew the most admiring audiences, partly because they were large and colorful—each Southern aristocrat bringing a score of Negro servants in splendid livery, including a boy to shine his boots and fan his brow—but mainly because almost every carriage afforded a glimpse of Southern beauty and Parisian fashion. Southern belles were acknowledged to be the fairest in America, a bewitching mixture of grace and charm and an agile, well-educated mind demurely displayed in French couture that the daughters of the Northern rich had not yet been able to match. Many would have been an asset to any court in Europe, as foreign observers were fond of noting in their letters home, and at Saratoga wealthy bachelors fell so completely under their spell that the spa became the country's busiest matrimonial mart.*

In the first third of the nineteenth century the number of vacationists annually transported to Saratoga over the rutted post roads climbed to six thousand; then, in a single season, 1833, it jumped to eight thousand, the result of a spectacular new conveyance that rolled along cast-iron rails laid first from Albany to Schenectady, and then extended to the spa. As originally introduced in 1832, the railway cars that travelled to Saratoga had proved only a little more attractive than the stagecoaches they closely resembled; a single car could accommodate but a dozen passengers and each was drawn by one or two horses at some nine miles an hour to and from a depot on Broadway, Saratoga's main street. But starting on July 3, 1833, three years after the run of the first steam-propelled passenger train in the United States, a gleaming, steaming locomotive puffed into Saratoga Springs pulling a fancy assembly of carriages. The engine, the Fire Fly, had been brought from England and the coaches had been modelled after Europe's compartment-style railway cars.

Stagecoach sufferers switched to the new mode of travel with un-apologetic haste, and in his popular guidebook to the region Gideon M. Davison rejoiced: ". . . a ride to the springs, which was formerly tardy and attended with clouds of dust and much fatigue and lassitude of body, now constitutes one of the greatest sources of novelty and pleasure in a visit to those celebrated fountains of health." Another happy traveller, William L. Stone, wrote: "The cars with horses were a great novelty; but when steam was substituted for horsepower, the astonishment knew no bounds. Every day, on the arrival and departure of the train, 100 to 150 people would go to the depot to see the new wonder of the age; and once, when the cars broke away from their couplings and ran down into Broadway, great was the scattering and consternation." Later he noted: "The speed [of the trains] at first was 15 miles an hour, and . . . fears were expressed at the prospect even of a greater rate being attained. Were the velocity to be doubled, there would be continued apprehensions of danger, in addition to disagreeable sensations of dizziness. But such is not the case now, and the passengers are whirled along in commodious and elegant cars without jolting or any other annoyance, and without the remotest fears for the safety of life or limb."

---

* One Southern beauty's rosebud complexion so unnerved a young Bostonian that he refused to believe it was natural. Pausing to stare at Sally Ward of Louisville, Kentucky, as she passed by on the street, he said to a companion in tones loud enough for her to hear, "She is painted." Pausing too, Sally turned and said, "Yes, good sirs, painted—but by God," and strolled on.

In 1807 Robert Fulton introduced a new mode of travel when his side-wheeler steamship *Clermont* sailed up the Hudson River from New York City to Albany, negotiating the 150-mile distance in 32 hours. Three weeks later his steamer made regularly scheduled trips to Albany in under 29 hours.

Hudson River steamers enabled Saratoga's visitors to journey more comfortably; previously, most vacationists had travelled slowly and painfully to the Spa in stagecoaches. When steamboats plied the Hudson the resort's guests sailed to Albany and then continued to Saratoga by stage. Top: a typical stagecoach in 1818. Bottom: the same in 1828.

STAGE COACH OF 1818.

This sanguine conclusion was not entirely accurate. Steaming between Saratoga and Ballston one summer, the locomotive David Crockett came upon a bull lying athwart the track. Fearless as the frontiersman whose name it bore, the engine plunged ahead and was tossed from the rails together with three coaches. The bull walked off, shaken but triumphant.

There were other mishaps too, but as the speed of the trains increased safety devices were introduced which minimized the dangers of travelling by rail (stubborn bulls were left to wander off the track in their own good time). And as the service improved, the number of vacationists who annually journeyed to Saratoga grew year by year. At the end of the 1830's the spa was host to twelve thousand summer guests, and in the mid-1840's the trains unloaded them at the old brick depot in such quantities as never before.

The arrival of each train was signalled by a bell clanging in the depot cupola, and in a matter of minutes the barnlike station was a scene of cheerful bedlam. Natives hurried to catch a glimpse of the notables and fashionables among the newcomers, and visitors hastened to greet friends and acquaintances. Porters lined up on the platform and as the train whistled and screeched to a halt began shouting the merits of the hotels they represented. Outside, omnibus and hack drivers took up the cry, and the spirited horses waiting with landaus, dogcarts, phaetons and barouches stamped their feet impatiently. From the railway coaches streamed be-whiskered gentlemen in sporty summer suits and bejewelled ladies in Parisian silks and satins, followed by a tidal wave of trunks and boxes. In a few years each stylish lady would replace much of her haphazard assortment of luggage with a wondrous, seemingly bottomless hogshead, iron-bound and curved on top, specially designed to hold a month's infinite change of clothes and named, quite appropriately, Saratoga Trunk. Meanwhile, she was pursued to her hotel by a collection of containers into which she had packed ". . . her white *poux de soie* hats trimmed with green ribbons and lilac branches, her *paille de riz* bonnets with the deep, ear-confining brims, all the fashionable Gimp, Leghorn, Coburg and Jenny Lind models of her day; her parasols of shot silk, with the fringeless, colored borders lined with white Florence, her cambric and muslin dresses with the small bishop sleeves; and her countless needlework chemisettes."

Collision course   Attracted by Saratoga's increasing celebrity as the summer retreat of the fashionable and fun-loving rich, citizens with little claim to wealth or pedigree took advantage of the railway's quicker, cheaper transportation to vacation at the spa and mingle with the elite. The separate backgrounds, interests and aspirations of the seasonal visitors generally led them to the congenial company of their own kind. Patrician descendants of the early

American aristocracy established themselves in Congress Hall. The *nou-veaux riches* settled in the United States Hotel. The Pavilion and the Columbian became equally favored headquarters of middle-class couples on a short holiday, and Union Hall a haven for the elderly and devout. Neither Congress Hall nor the United States catered exclusively to quality, however, and there were no social barriers to separate eminent guests from those who paid to see and be seen with them.

The ease with which amateur social climbers overcame class distinctions and made themselves at home with their superiors was tolerated by most of the latter, but stirred James Silk Buckingham to protest:

> Hundreds who, in their own towns, could not find admittance into the circles of fashionable society . . . come to Saratoga where, at Congress Hall or the United States, by the moderate payment of two dollars a day, they may be seated at the same table, and often side by side, with the first families of the country; promenade in the same piazza, lounge on the sofas in the same drawing room, and dance in the same quadrille with the most fashionable beaux and belles of the land; and thus, for the week or month they may stay at Saratoga, they enjoy all the advantages which their position would make inaccessible to them at home.

While sensitive to such criticism, Saratoga was content to let the situation stand. The prospect of mixing with the rich and sharing their pleasures for a time was attracting far more visitors to the spa in the 1840's than the benefits of the springs, as even the guidebooks noted (said one: "The mineral waters of Saratoga and the healing virtues of the springs are not the only nor the principal objects which draw to its sands the thousands who annually flock thither."). The authorities were loath to take steps which might make the resort less popular with vacationists who looked forward to a holiday fling in which they could emulate the socialites and plutocrats.

Much more disconcerting to the village than the complaints of a few patricians was the reputation it was gaining in the press. Describing the summer-long whirl of activity with more piquancy than truth, journalists gave Saratoga a risqué distinction the facts did not support, but which also served to lure tourists to the spa.

After gingerly opening the door to Satan in 1819 and allowing visitors to amuse themselves with billiards, dancing, unchaperoned drives and private gambling, Saratoga had wavered along a collision course trying to please both the fun-seekers and the God seekers in its midst. Struggling to keep evenly balanced between pleasure and piety, it had resisted efforts to introduce more titillating entertainment and assiduously policed the few liberties permitted. As a result, the majority of guests had become restless again, and in the mid-1820's the elders had anxiously reëxamined the problem to see what might be done to keep them content.

The possibilities, it appeared, were fairly numerous. For guests of the spa, a typical day began with breakfast at eight o'clock, after which there was little to do but sample the waters or sit or stroll on the hotel piazzas and contemplate the seldom-varying life of the village as reflected along Broadway. Dinner, at two o'clock, was followed at each hotel by a prolonged and deliberate march around the veranda in which virtually the entire clientele took part, one couple after another pacing with the same leisurely tread as the munificent midday meal was allowed to settle. When this was accomplished, there again was little to look forward to. One could repair to the flower garden or the shaded walks alongside or in the rear of the hotel, or round up a few intimates and go for a drive—but since the roads leading to the countryside were poor, and better left to undismayed romantics in search of privacy, this meant simply an excursion up and down Broadway and a further glimpse of village life. Supper was served at seven o'clock, and though the hours until bedtime could be whiled away listening to music or dancing they by no means saved the day. Indeed, more often than not the evening pastime was the most vexing of all, so lacking in style and occasion that the ladies took small pleasure in wearing the fashionable gowns they had brought to the resort and husbands and beaux frequently drifted off to a friendly room for a night of poker.

It all added up to a discouragingly uneventful visit, as the elders could agree, and they had set about making the days more satisfying. Old roads had been improved and new ones built to enable vacationists to brighten their afternoons with scenic drives into the country surrounding the spa. Saratoga's hotels had enlivened the evenings by engaging ventriloquists, singers, dancers, comedians and magicians to perform for their guests, and encouraged visitors to amuse themselves with forfeits and other games played in the vast parlors. Those who preferred more substantial diversions were supplied with lectures and concerts, and thirteen bowling alleys were introduced in the village to provide fun on the town. Most gratifying of all, the drab soirees were transformed into elegant balls, at which champagne was served, and less formal but sprightly hops, with the result that the most durable guests danced past midnight—"durable" applying a good deal more accurately to the belles of the entertainments, it appears, than to their gentlemen escorts. Wrote an onlooker:

> The whirl of the dance commences. What a rush and crush of femininity! The thermometer is at ninety in the shade, the gentlemen are exhausted, their shirt collars have wilted, they are in a sea of perspiration, but each beauty is triumphant. She whirls them round until the music ceases, when our model Beaux Brummels seek the air, then their rooms to rearrange their toilet and recuperate, while beauty, unsubdued, rushes into the next dance. So evening after evening is passed until the music stops, the crowd vanishes and the ladies retire to ponder over their new conquests.

Only at Union Hall did things remain the same. There, prayers were said in the parlor every evening and sacred hymns were sung each Sunday night.

By the late 1830's the village had become so emboldened by the success of its program that poker players were invited to step outside their hotels and test their fortunes at faro and chuck-a-luck in the billiard halls and bowling alleys, and a room was fixed up for roulette. In 1842 a professional gambler, Ben Scribner, opened a house modestly but exclusively equipped for gambling off an alley near the United States Hotel, and a few years later a pair of speculators introduced a half-mile trotting track on which races were run three or four days a week during the season and spectators bet on the horses as openly as they pleased.

Inevitably, the change in the spa had aroused the ire of Saratoga's old guard. The public gaming had attracted nimble-fingered practitioners of the art from Western saloons and Mississippi riverboats, and this and other manifestations of the devil had persuaded the strait-laced pillars of the community that the infidels were being permitted to take over their temple of virtue. The dismal fate awaiting the village was forecast from pulpit and lecture platform, and metropolitan newspapers sent reporters to "expose" the "debaucheries" at the "once respectable watering place."

None were more diligent than the employees of the New York *Herald,* whose owner, James Gordon Bennett, was a habitual visitor to the resort. The astute Scot had drawn thousands of readers to the *Herald* with a spicy recipe of crime, scandal and sensation, to which he added a personal fillip in the form of editorials which flayed the hide of persons, places and proposals that incurred his displeasure. His reporters and artists solicited descriptions of the "sinful" goings-on at the spa from servants, chambermaids, porters, grooms and other such witnesses on the periphery of Saratoga's gay new world. As Bennett perhaps knew, articles and drawings for the most part pictured as wickedness that didn't exist, but the *Herald's* readers were enthralled and the stories were continued. In 1844, after the polka—which had so shocked Great Britain's Queen Victoria that she had forbidden it to be danced in her presence—was widely adopted by American society and became a favorite amusement at Saratoga, Bennett stepped up his attack. He wrote:

> Our fashionable circles, who pretend to such extraordinary refinements, are wholly destitute of cultivated taste, polished manners, or moral feelings sufficient to check the introduction of foreign licentiousness and corrupt morals . . . We must say that the indecency of the polka as danced at Saratoga Springs and Newport * stands out in bold relief from anything we have ever witnessed among the refined and cultivated *ton* of European cities. It even outstrips the most disgraceful exhibitions of the lowest haunts of Paris and London.

* The resort town of Newport, Saratoga's Rhode Island rival, was first settled in the mid-1600's.

In 1828 there were experiments with coaches drawn by horses along cast-iron rails.

Two years later, however, locomotives replaced the horses—the result of a dramatic speed-test between Peter Cooper's diminutive locomotive, Tom Thumb, and a horse-drawn car on the Baltimore & Ohio Railroad tracks on August 28, 1830. This sketch reflects the passengers' excitement as the Tom Thumb caught up with and passed its rival.

The first locomotive to draw a train of passenger cars in New York State was the De Witt Clinton. It ran between Albany and Schenectady, and made its ceremonial first run on September 24, 1831. On August 9th, however, the De Witt Clinton in a trial performance gave a foretaste of the comedy of errors that followed the introduction of train travel in America. In his *A History of Travel in America*, Seymour Dunbar describes the trip: "The train started. It did not start all at once, but in sections. The tender was attached to the engine by a chain nearly three feet long made of three large links of wrought-iron; the first passenger coach was attached to the tender in a like manner; the second passenger coach was similarly connected to the first passenger coach; and so on down the train to the very last car. With the first forward jump of the engine the captain was nearly snapped backward out of his seat, but he seized a roof-support and luckily held on. The passengers in the first coach were unprepared for what was about to happen, and those sitting in the front and middle sections were projected backward and piled in a heap against the passengers at the rear. Those in the second car followed suit, and as the slack length of each chain was gathered up by the abrupt forward jerk the succeeding group of passengers was overturned. After the whole train was straightened out it rolled on in good order as far as smoothness of movement was concerned, but a new trouble then manifested itself.

"The fuel of the engine was wood, and the smokestack soon began to belch forth big blazing sparks. These fell among the passengers. The damage done by them in the three covered coaches was not extreme, but the havoc they created on the crowded flat cars was sad indeed. Many of the travellers on the rear cars had carried umbrellas, and those so equipped raised them for protection against the clouds of smoke and rain of fire. As a consequence all the umbrellas were soon in flames and were thrown overboard. Then the clothing of the passengers—a considerable number of whom were women—became ignited by the hot coals, and in a very little while the whole moving company resolved itself into a volunteer fire brigade, each member of which was belaboring the one next to him and trying to extinguish the conflagration in his neighbor's apparel.

"At this point of the interesting journey a further complication ensued. The train was approaching a spot where the locomotive's supply of water was to be replenished, and as it reached the tank the engineer threw a lever designed to apply the brakes and check the train's momentum. The mechanism worked to perfection. The water-wagon came up against the engine with a bump; the first passenger coach hit the tender with a crash; the second passenger coach flew against the first; and so on down the length of the train again, the resultant movements of the passengers being similar to those witnessed at starting, but in the opposite direction."

In spite of these mishaps, the De Witt Clinton covered the 17-mile distance in less than an hour, including all stops, and during part of the journey it rocketed along at a rate of 30 miles an hour.

The popularity of train travel between Albany and Schenectady persuaded railroad builders to lay tracks from Schenectady to Saratoga—and starting in 1832 holiday seekers could take a train to the Spa. As late as the 1850's, however, passenger accommodations left much to be desired. Travellers were obliged to ride in gaudily painted wooden coaches lighted at night by candles or kerosene lamps and heated in winter by small stoves.

The lobby of Union Hall after a train arrived at Saratoga.

The despair of porters was the Saratoga Trunk, a roomy hogshead packed with a whole summer's female wardrobe.

Every lady's luggage contained hoop skirts as a matter of course. They were the rage of Paris couturiers. Gentlemen were apt to view them with no enthusiasm. A French artist compared the effect of a belle walking to a swinging bell.

Four years later he was still on target: "Beautiful Saratoga! Cradle of fashion and intrigue! Rendezvous of lacqueys and jockeys! Seraglio of the prurient aristocracy!"

Whether prompted by indignation or circulation, the many newspaper stories describing Saratoga's *joie de vivre* succeeded at nothing so much as at promoting the spa as the nation's most fashionable pleasure resort. In New York City three hundred wealthy bachelors sought to extend Saratoga's reputation to the U.S.S. *Carolina,* an obsolete warship anchored off the Battery, which they proposed to rename *Saratoga Afloat* and convert into a sea resort whereon guests could dine, dance and lounge on luxurious sofas arranged around the upper deck. Doubtless to Saratoga's relief, the plan was eventually discarded. While it was all to the spa's advantage to have its name bruited about, the village felt more comfortable with less brazen publicity.

A stony gaze, a garland of roses   In late August, 1839, Philip Hone, who had achieved wealth and prestige as perhaps New York City's most enterprising auctioneer, and had used these just rewards to elevate himself to the mayoralty in 1825, wrote in his diary*:

> This is the meridian of the Saratoga season. All the world is here: politicians and dandies; cabinet ministers and ministers of the gospel; officeholders and officeseekers; humbuggers and humbugged; fortune-hunters and hunters of woodcock; anxious mothers and lovely daughters; the ruddy cheek mantling with saucy health, and the flickering lamp almost extinguished beneath the rude breath of dissipation. In a few days this brilliant company will be scattered over the face of the land, and who can tell of how many of them this will be the last season?

Since the season referred to preceded a presidential election year, the question was particularly appropriate; holders and seekers of public office, whose future plans would depend on the whims of the voters, were present in force. From the nation's chief executive, Martin Van Buren, on down they had flocked to the spa to bargain for political support and put themselves on display at the popular resort.

As the Democratic Party's choice to succeed himself, President Van Buren moved through the assembly with pleasant assurance, "as proud and

* Published posthumously, Hone's diary was discovered to be a perceptive though acidulously opinionated account of New York life between 1828 and 1851, gaining for its author a further measure of fame and doubtless adding to the discomfort of persons he had dealt with in its pages. Noting the arrival at Saratoga during the season of 1838 of the commander of the United States Army, a hero of the War of 1812 who had helped to repel the British at Plattsburg, on the shore of Lake Champlain, Hone wrote: "Gen. Macomb came to the fat arms of his expecting wife today; rather warmer work than he had at Plattsburg."

plump and happy as a partridge in the fall," wrote an admirer, "no less attractive to the eyes of the ladies than those of the politicians." Whig newspaper cartoonists took a less charitable view, mocking the little middle-aged leader's curly yellow hair, dandyish dress and delicate posture, which they attributed to the corset he wore. Friends and enemies agreed, however, that his appearance was deceiving; in performance, Van Buren was a master politician and a statesman of greater stature than his actual size implied.

In his ascent to the presidency, Van Buren had contended with De Witt Clinton,* the Governor of New York, for control of the state, and backed by Tammany and the Albany Regency, a political group he had helped form, had deprived Clinton of several important posts. Clinton had returned the blow by winning the governorship for a second time, but had died in 1828 while in office, and Van Buren had been elected in his place. Although the two rivals had become mildly reconciled after Clinton's return to power, and Van Buren had delivered a glowing tribute to his dead foe, the latter's widow was unforgiving. During the period in which he had been required to fight for his political life, her husband had described Van Buren as "the prince of villains" and "a confirmed knave," and she saw no reason to alter this view.

Presiding, as usual, as the dowager queen of Saratoga's elite during the season of 1839, Mrs. Clinton perceived an opportunity to publicly declare her feelings and personally avenge her husband's political reverses in one of the few ladylike ways open to her. As the President of the United States walked toward her across the ballroom floor of the United States Hotel at a ball given in his honor, his face wreathed in a smile, and his hand outstretched, Mrs. Clinton gazed at him stonily until she had the attention of everyone present, then folded her arms and turned her back.

Later, she saw another chance to express her enmity. Henry Clay, one of Van Buren's most formidable opponents in Washington, was expected at Saratoga to advance his candidacy for the Whig nomination in the coming presidential campaign. Although the majority of his supporters were quartered at Congress Hall, Clay had announced that he would stay at the United States, where Van Buren was a guest, and rather than risk a confrontation so early in the game Van Buren departed on "urgent business" on the day of Clay's arrival. Clay was met by a cheering crowd and paused under the great trees in front of the United States to address the throng. At an open window above the hotel's piazza, Mrs. Clinton stood listening with a coterie of friends. Close at hand was a huge garland of roses and hyacinths attached to a silken cord. As Clay finished his speech and started inside the hotel, the floral coronet descended from Mrs. Clinton's suite and gently touched his brow—a well-publicized

---

* A nephew of George Clinton, the first governor of New York State, who, with Alexander Hamilton, accompanied George Washington on the latter's visit to High Rock Spring.

gesture that notified voters in general, and Martin Van Buren in particular, where her sympathies rested.

In the long run the lady's favor made little difference to Clay; locked in a stalemate with Daniel Webster, who also aspired to be the Whig presidential nominee, he was compelled to support William Henry Harrison as the Party's compromise choice. Despite the advantages of a superior Virginia upbringing and education, Harrison was put before the country as a rugged Westerner, a simple backwoodsman who had been born in a log cabin and nourished on hard cider. Van Buren was pictured as a wealthy, effete, "silver-spooned" Easterner, ignorant of and disdainful toward the common man. Since his campaign image precluded Harrison from appearing at Saratoga, the favorite pleasure resort of the rich, Daniel Webster was dispatched to the spa in the summer of 1840 to eulogize his virtues. A parade of supporters, featuring a horse-drawn float on which sat a log cabin with fifty rugged young men and pretty girls arranged around it singing Whig songs, escorted the renowned orator to an outdoors speaking platform. He no sooner mounted it to address the crowd of ten thousand than it collapsed and he fell through the floor. Emerging from the wreckage, Webster held his audience for three hours while he spoke grandiloquently of the needs and duties of the day. A few months later Harrison was elected President, and Mrs. Clinton could sweetly savor Van Buren's defeat.

A parade of waiters, a procession of coaches

Among the improvements in Saratoga's daily regimen were two so elaborately and solemnly ceremonious that together they formed a lengthy, leisurely ritual. It began with the call to midday dinner and ended with the last "tally-ho" of the coachmen's horns on the return to the village of the long procession of carriages from the afternoon drive into the countryside.

Prior to Saratoga's era of enlightenment, the summons to breakfast, dinner or supper at the spa's hotels and boarding houses had produced a scene of exasperating confusion. At each meal guests were fed in one sitting at two long tables at opposite sides of the long dining room, and since the seats were unreserved each family, couple and congenial group was compelled to fence with others for a place to dine together. The continual rivalry had encouraged rude manners, bad tempers and indigestion, the food being absorbed with such haste that breakfast was usually finished in ten minutes and dinner, despite its profusion of dishes, in a half hour.

Now, all was changed. Guests dined in comfort from morning till night and dinner was a highlight of the day. As the midday call sounded, a headwaiter met diners at the door and turned them over to assistants who escorted them to their tables. When all were seated, the headwaiter struck a gong. A corps of waiters formed a double line and marched the length of the room into the kitchen. They reappeared carrying the first course, soup, and at the sound of the gong marched to the tables and deposited a plate in front of each guest. Dishes were removed and replaced by others through the fish and vegetable courses with the same ringing military precision, then the formation was temporarily dissolved while diners were allowed to make their own choice of meat and dessert from a menu. As elaborate as the occasion was, one roguish guest saw a way to make it more so; he asked for baked potatoes with monograms.

During the half hour in which dinner was digested and the diners strolled the piazzas in an impressive formation of their own, a long line of equipages formed in front of each hotel. Many had been brought from as far south as New Orleans, from Boston, Philadelphia, New York City, and from midwestern metropolises beyond the Mississippi River, so that their wealthy owners might make a suitably splendid showing in Saratoga's fashionable and increasingly famous carriage procession. Others had been hired from the local livery stables by visitors who lacked a private coach but enjoyed being part of the parade. And some had been supplied by carriage makers for the convenience of prominent Whips, with the hope that their expertise would draw admiring eyes to the coaches they drove and result in a flood of orders from the spa's elite.

When all were assembled and waiting, gentlemen with twirled mustaches and tall, dun-colored hats escorted ladies with saucy parasols from the piazzas and tucked them into the upholstered seats. Liveried footmen—two if the carriage was especially grand—whisked away footstools, folded away light metal steps or contributed other well-rehearsed ministrations and coachmen, sitting on the high box seats in their tall hats, brass-buttoned coats, skin-tight breeches and top boots, whipped the six or eight matched thoroughbreds harnessed in monogrammed silver and gold. One vehicle following another, the gleaming cavalcade moved with stately grace along Broadway in an unbroken sequence, and then curled away from the village into the adjoining country—"a magical land, picturesque in the extreme," a guest wrote after a typical after-dinner excursion. He continued:

> To the right are fields of white, blossoming buckwheat, pure in color as a bed of new fallen snow, and green corn waving graceful plumes in the breeze; then comes a field of grass, heavy with its perfume of the new-mown hay; beyond, the dark green of the shadowy woods, thick and impenetrable to the sight, and obscuring all further view in that direction. But on the left is a vast plain, dotted over its surface by little lakes and clumps of trees, with a village here and a hill there, but all imbedded in a green that graduates in color to the foot of the hills that go piling themselves up far off in the distance.

So diligently had Saratoga applied itself to the task of making a stay at the spa more diverting that the procession could choose from a half dozen

The celebrated satirist, Honore Daumier, also poked fun at ladies in hoops.

Another comment on the difficulty in coping with the fashion.

A fourth artist suggested a way in which the skirt could be put to more practical use.

Saratoga's most fashionable hotel in the 1840's was the United States, built by Elias Benedict in 1824. For many years the crown had been worn by Congress Hall, but its reign was abruptly terminated when the *doyenne* of the social elite abandoned it for the United States and other socialites followed suit. Distressed by the slight to the Putnams' grand old place, Nathaniel P. Willis, a popular author of the period, wrote: "What is it [United States Hotel] to the leafy dimness, the cool shadows, the perpetual and pensive *demi-jour*—the ten thousand associations of Congress Hall? Who has not lost a heart or two on the boards of that primitive wilderness of colonnade? Whose first adorations, whose sighs, hopes, strategies and flirtations are not ground into that warped and slipper-polished floor . . . ? Lord bless you, Madam, don't desert old Congress Hall!"

The Pavilion Hotel was destroyed by fire in 1843.

scenic drives, but the favorite route led originally to a little ear-shaped lake two miles to the east and later to Lake Saratoga. Surrounded by pyramidal firs, pines and evergreens, and patched at the edges with swamp flowers, the little lake had been named for its owner, who lived beside it, and was called Barhyte's Pond.

Jacobus Barhyte had come to the Hudson River Valley from Germany as a boy of twelve, and at twenty-three had fought with the Continentals in the Saratoga campaign. When the guns were silent, he had been put in charge of a detail of litter-bearers assigned to carry Baron Friedrich von Riedesel, the wounded commander of the Hessians, to Albany, an experience in which he took lasting pride. Of much greater moment to his personal fortunes, however, was a foraging expedition Sergeant Barhyte had made with his detachment into a forest some miles from the battlefield. Climbing to the crest of a thickly wooded bluff beside a little lake, he had been overwhelmed by the autumnal beauty that fed his eye wherever he looked and sentimentally warmed by an excellent view of Bemis Heights, where he and his victorious comrades had been deployed. With un-Teutonic haste, he had at once resolved to build his home on the hilltop.

Promptly after the war was won, he had returned with his wife, made a clearing on the crest of land and constructed a cabin. He had planted corn and vegetables, raised chickens and geese, fished for the trout that leaped in the lake and hunted in the nearby forest for deer, bear, beaver and other tasty game. As the chores increased and a gristmill was added to the farm, he had turned over more and more of the work to his son John and two Negro slaves, and enjoyed longer hours of leisure. In every respect it was as idyllic a life as Jacobus Barhyte had envisioned when he first stood on the little bluff, and at sunset he sat on his stoop and smoked his long-stemmed clay pipe with quiet satisfaction.

Then, to his dismay, visitors began to drop by. Having heard of the frolicsome trout and other delicacies in Barhyte's Pond, Saratoga's sports-minded vacationists journeyed to his farm and asked his permission to fish in the lake. Jacobus looked at them wordlessly, then glumly nodded and gestured to the water.

Perhaps his most persistent guest was a gentleman whose family name was famous, or infamous, over the world. Joseph Bonaparte, brother of Napoleon I and former King of Naples and Spain, arrived at the spa in the summer of 1825 with his sister, Caroline Murat, and drove out to Barhyte's Pond in his coach and six a few days after registering at the United States Hotel.* Captivated by its many charms, Bonaparte offered to buy the lake property, raising his price almost as often as Jacobus stubbornly shook his

* He was preceded as a guest of the hotel in 1824 by a much more distinguished Frenchman, the Marquis de Lafayette. Although he was in his sixty-seventh year, Lafayette still retained his courtly bearing and grace. When Mrs. Benjamin Rush, widow of the physician who had signed the Declaration of Independence and mother of Richard Rush, the newly appointed Secretary of the Treasury, requested a lock of the Marquis' hair as a memento of his devotion to the American cause, Lafayette presented her with a pair of scissors and gallantly lifted his wig while she snipped off three snowy tufts.

head. When it reached $32,000, Jacobus took his pipe from his mouth and spoke. "Sir," he said, "if it's worth that to you, it's worth that to me." And there the bidding stopped. Bonaparte's visits continued, however, and his enthusiasm for the mouth-watering trout drew other eminent anglers to the spot. Then the fairly primitive road to the lake was made much more accommodating, and coachloads of summer guests arrived from Saratoga to enjoy a placid afternoon watching the fishermen and lazing beside the water.

Soon they were present in such numbers* that Jacobus felt obliged to extend them the hospitality of his home. He built a tavern on his farm and stocked it with liquor, and added rooms to his house in which he served trout suppers cooked in his kitchen. When he died, in 1840, little remained of the tranquil life he had prized, but he could look back over many pleasant summers in which he had earned a legion of friends while presiding as Saratoga's first lakeside host.

The popularity of Barhyte's Pond, and the increasingly venturesome excursions into the countryside by the patrons of Saratoga Springs, encouraged James and Hannah Riley to tout the attractions of the great lake four miles from the spa and the advantages of the restaurant they established on its western shore. Lake Saratoga did indeed have a lot to offer. Its waters, eighteen miles in circumference, abounded with trout, black bass, yellow perch, pickerel, muskellunge and other varieties of fish, all of which found their way to the Rileys' tables along with woodcock, partridge, wild duck and assorted vegetables including the Rileys' specialty, creamed potatoes. In addition, there were boating and bathing and a platform for swimmers and divers, shaded by an awning and able to accommodate thirty aquatic enthusiasts at a time, that Riley had erected above seven-foot depths some distance from the shore.

The multiplicity of pleasures the Rileys proffered lured more and more visitors to the lake each season, and as they grew too numerous for the Rileys to handle rival facilities were introduced. Not until Cary Moon opened his soon-to-be legendary Lake House in 1853, however, did Lake Saratoga decisively demonstrate its superiority and displace all other destinations as the late-afternoon goal of Saratoga Springs' daily carriage parade.

The culinary duties at Moon's were shared by Catherine Weeks, generally known as Aunt Kate, and her brother-in-law, George Crum. Dark-skinned with straight black hair and bony features, inherited from the union of a mulatto jockey and a Stockbridge Indian maid, Crum had worked as a guide in the Adirondacks and had been taught the finer aspects of cooking by an epicurean Frenchman who employed him. It was said, frequently by Crum himself, that he could take any edible and transform it into a dish fit for a king, and the eager customers who responded to the call to supper Aunt Kate blew on a fish horn rarely disputed it.

* Among the visitors to Barhyte's Pond were writers, including Edgar Allan Poe. While offering little in the way of evidence, a few historians of the Saratoga region have claimed that in the summer of 1843 Poe worked on his poem, *The Raven*, on the banks of the little lake, and indeed once frightened Jacobus' grandson by hollowly declaiming, "Nevermore."

Congress Park as seen from Union Hall in 1859. Congress Spring is at left, Columbian Spring at right; the shaft in the background is a water tower.

Drinking at the Congress pavilion. Dipper boys scooped up the saline liquids in cups fastened to sticks.

The few who did complain, and returned their orders to the kitchen, were rewarded with the most indigestible substitutes Crum could contrive. It pleased him to watch their reaction, which usually proceeded rapidly from disbelief to indignant departure. In its first season, however, the Lake House was host to a dissatisfied diner who paved the way for its volatile chef to unwittingly create a delicacy of enduring flavor and international fame. Discontented with his French fried potatoes, the guest sent them back to Crum with instructions to fry them longer and slice them thinner. Crum received the request with typical hostility. He sliced some potatoes into paper-thin shavings, bundled them in a napkin and dropped them into a tub of ice water. A half hour later he dumped the chilled slices into a kettle of boiling grease. When they were fried to curly crisps, he took them out, salted them and sent them to the complainer's table—then peered into the dining room to observe the effect. To his astonishment, the recipient was delighted and asked for more. Other diners ordered the crisp potato wafers and found them just as tasty. The next day Crum's potato chips, called Saratoga Chips by the Lake House's tourist-conscious proprietor, were on every table in the restaurant. A few years later they were listed on menus throughout the country. Eventually, they became a favorite around the world, and the French took to them with such enthusiasm that patriotic Paris chefs declared they were an invention of French cuisine.

Anxious to capitalize on his growing fame, Crum opened a restaurant of his own on a low hill at the south end of Lake Saratoga. He kept his expenses down by making waitresses of his five Indian wives, all of whom had remained devoted to him even after each had been replaced in his affections by another. He kept his profits up by charging prices almost as high as his customers paid at the fashionable dining salons in New York City. Since his tables were always crowded, he refused to allow reservations and compelled late-arriving tycoons, socialites and celebrities to await their turn with unprestigious guests.* Objections were muted, for the quality of the food more than repaid both money and patience. William Henry Vanderbilt was so beguiled by the way Crum cooked canvas-backs that he had almost no appetite for them when prepared by less gifted hands, a tribute made still more impressive by the fact that Crum had never laid eyes on the prized species of whitish-backed wild duck until his aristocratic patron brought him one. Still, it had given him no problem. As he later explained, he had simply kept it over the coals for nineteen minutes, the blood following the knife, and sent it to the table hot, and Vanderbilt had told him that he had never eaten anything like it in his life.

The attractions of Lake Saratoga, added to the diversions of Saratoga Springs, made a stay at the spa more indispensable to pleasure seekers than ever before. Each day flowered into a variety of activity, and if anything was lacking the majority of visitors were too busily engaged to take note of it.

* Once seated, Crum's sportier guests passed the time before their orders arrived by playing Fly-Lo, an impromptu form of gambling in which lumps of sugar were dipped in honey and the player whose honeyed sugar attracted the first fly was declared the winner.

For some visitors, sightseeing at the Spa was fraught with peril—such as these Quakers, confronted with a seminude statue.

The young at heart in the 1830's and '40's amused themselves by riding in a self-propelled car on a circular railway.

Forfeits and other games were popular in the vast hotel parlors.

Reflecting the general contentment, a poetic guest supplied an admiring accounting:

Of all the gay places the world can afford,
    By gentle and simple for pastime adored,
Fine balls and fine singing, fine buildings and springs,
    Fine rides and fine views, and a thousand fine things,
(Not to mention the sweet situation and air)
    What place with these Springs can ever compare?
First in manners, in dress, and in fashion to shine,
    Saratoga, the glory must ever be thine!

Eliza and the Knickerbockers

The popular parade of carriages engaged Saratoga's *grande dames* in somewhat less than friendly enmity for the honor of leading the procession. Whoever captured the place at the head of the line reigned as supremely as a queen, and sitting imperiously in their luxurious equipages the great ladies of New York, Boston, Philadelphia and Southern society never tired of competing for the position. Since the post was awarded to the carriage that outmaneuvered its competitors and took possession of it, the start of each day's excursion along Broadway was preceded by a flurry of rivalry in which an unladylike display of guile, determination and gall sometimes proved to be the winning technique. On these occasions the victor usually was an elderly *élégante* who had employed the formula with conspicuous success throughout her career and who enjoyed her triumph all the more because it enabled her to lord it over the Knickerbocker dowagers who had persistently stood in the path of her recognition by the social elite.

On the surface Madame Stephen Jumel's eligibility for society seemed beyond cavil. She was rich, regal in manner and appearance, and still showed a trace of the legendary beauty of her youth. She lived in one of New York City's finest mansions, spent each summer in an elegant house in Saratoga and rode in a sumptuous gold-colored coach equal, if not superior, to any other vehicle displayed at the spa. She had mixed intimately with royalty and nobility as a favorite of the French Court and had been married to a former Vice-President of the United States. All of this, however, was insignificant in the view of the arbiters of Knickerbocker society when compared with the circumstances of the lady's birth and upbringing and her numerous romances before and after she became Madame Jumel.

Unfortunately for her future aspirations, Madame had been born to a sailor and a prostitute. Named Elizabeth Bowen, she had spent her childhood in Providence, Rhode Island, trailing after her mother while the latter plied her trade and performing chores in the workhouse during the frequent intervals when her mother was sent to jail. In the course of this vagrant existence

So, too, were Bible meetings, at which prayers were read and hymns were sung.

Guests of Union Hall could also lounge in the gardens, gossip and listen to band concerts.

In 1839 the President of the United States, Martin Van Buren, turned up at the Spa.

Also present was Mrs. De Witt Clinton, the *grande dame* of the resort and the widow of one of Van Buren's most outspoken political rivals.

"The Cut Direct": at a ball given in his honor at the United States Hotel, Mrs. Clinton turned her back on the President.

A hallmark of the Saratoga season was the afternoon drive into the countryside in fashionable equipages. The favorite destination of the procession was Lake Saratoga, shown here in 1848.

Cary Moon's Lake House was the goal of most coaches and carriages. It overlooked Lake Saratoga from the top of a sloping hill. "Moon's miraculous dinners," a guest noted in 1862, "run the gamut of delicacies from fried potatoes to green figs, the intermediates being trout fresh from the pond, bass boiled to a nicety, woodcock, snipe, quail, partridge, in fact game in such endless variety that Audubon himself would take a week to describe them ornithologically. Then there are fresh figs, pineapples, tamarinds, pomegranates, lemons, peaches, apricots—in brief, all the gifts of Pomona. In addition, the table is ornamented with a *bijou* grapevine, loaded with the most luscious fruit, the root of which is cased in an elegant porcelain vase." Visitors to the lake also took pleasure in sailing to White Sulphur Spring on the steamer, *Addie Smith*.

she had acquired a willful disposition and a blunt vocabulary to express it. She had also developed into a remarkably pretty girl.

At eighteen she flowered into a stunning young woman with red-gold hair, deep blue eyes, a piquant, upturned nose and a curvaceous figure. She was called Betsy Bowen now, and was one of the more arresting sights on the streets of Providence. Shrewd and ambitious, she decided to move to New York City, where she could use her assets to greater advantage, but was delayed by expectant motherhood. Betsy abandoned the child promptly after it was born, and entered New York on the arm of Captain William Brown, a seafaring man with a family. She settled close to Bowling Green and changed her name to Eliza Brown.

But not for long. Soon afterward she met and married a French ship-master, Jacques de la Croix, and accompanied him on his voyages across the Atlantic. When these became wearisome, she parted with her husband and reëstablished herself in New York to await something more interesting. It turned up in the person of the handsome, gifted lawyer-politician, Aaron Burr, who gave her a taste of social pleasures which previously had been beyond her reach. Dazzled by her glimpse of the world of high society, Eliza cast about for a means of entry and chose one of Manhattan's most eligible bachelors, to whom she had once been introduced, Stephen Jumel.

A wealthy importer of wines, brandies, cordials, spirits and other fine liquids, Jumel was a singularly attractive Frenchman whose forty-five years rode easily on his tall, muscular frame. He dressed impeccably, conversed with Gallic wit and charm, and was thoroughly at home among the books and *objets d'art* in his yellow-brick mansion. Drawing from her excellent stock of feminine wiles, Eliza placed herself in the merchant's path and sought to capture his interest. The vivacious French mannerisms and hesitant French phrases she had picked up in her trips to France with De la Croix, and her youth and beauty, intrigued him, and he made her his mistress.

Strongly disapproving, Jumel's patrician friends turned their backs on Eliza. Although they were as ignorant of her past as Jumel at this point, she struck them as more raffish than refined and as unworthy of both their acquaintance and his. Angered by their rebuffs, Jumel took Eliza to France aboard one of his brigs and introduced her to Paris society. His Paris friends were as intrigued by her beauty and vivacity as he, and Eliza made the most of every invitation to educate herself in the social graces. When they sailed home, she was schooled in etiquette, possessed an extensive wardrobe of French gowns and exhibited a genteel sophistication acquired from frequent tête-a-têtes with French intellectuals in the salon of Madame Jacques Récamier, where she had been a favored guest.

Jumel installed her in his mansion and gave a succession of dinner parties at which she displayed faultless grace and charm. He bought her an expensive carriage in which she rode through New York City's fashionable streets, sitting demurely behind her blue-liveried coachman and two black horses. Neither succeeded in persuading the strait-laced Knickerbocker socialites to accept Eliza. They consigned her invitations to the waste-basket and stared with open hostility when she promenaded past their doors.

Despairing of ever achieving recognition as long as she remained Jumel's mistress, Eliza took advantage of his absence on a business trip to pretend to her doctor that she was deathly ill. Hastily summoned to her bedside, Jumel also fell under the spell of her performance. When she whispered that her dying wish was to become his wife, he did the gentlemanly thing and married her on the spot. A few days later she was up and about with her customary vigor and a new radiance engendered by her status as Madame Jumel. The change in no way improved her social position, however; New York's staid aristocrats continued to ignore her as before.

Eliza endured their indifference for six years, then made a final bid for their favor. She persuaded her husband to buy the once magnificent mid-Georgian mansion Roger Morris had built for his bride on the heights of upper Manhattan in 1765. For a time, during the War of Independence, it had been George Washington's headquarters, and while most recently it had served as a tavern Eliza was confident that it could be restored to its former splendor. Sparing no expense, Jumel generously did as she asked, and when the two-story, nineteen-room house was completely renovated turned it over to his wife as a gift. The party they gave to show off their grand mansion was one of the most lavish New York had seen, and the promised munificence together with a desire to see what Eliza had done to the famous place induced several of the city's haughtiest socialites to attend. But in the months that followed they characteristically refrained from inviting the Jumels to their own entertainments.

A few years later their resistance solidified when Eliza's early history was publicly disclosed by an old acquaintance of her Providence days. Jumel too was shocked by the revelations, and Eliza put aside her social ambitions and concentrated on saving her marriage. She succeeded so well that Jumel took her on another visit to France. His brig arrived just as Napoleon, who had returned from exile to Elba only to be crushed at Waterloo, was seeking a means of escaping capture by the British. Jumel agreed to take him aboard his ship as a secret passenger and sail back to America; British frigates blockaded the harbor, but it seemed likely that an American ship would be allowed to slip through. The hour set for departure passed, however, without a sign of the emperor. He had decided to deliver himself to the British with the hope that they would grant him asylum in England. But in appreciation he sent the Jumels his travelling carriage and to Madame, personally, a clock and his military chest with its secret lock and distinctive gold key. Word of the Jumels' efforts to rescue the emperor spread through the Paris salons, and they were courted so assiduously by the Napoleonic aristocracy that they lingered in France for ten years, a glittering decade through which Eliza moved serenely from one social triumph to another. The extravagance of their life, together with several financial misfortunes, drove Jumel to the

Other popular restaurants on the shore of Lake Saratoga included Glen Mitchell Hotel (top), Lakeside House (center), and Cedar Bluff House.

William Henry Vanderbilt was beguiled by the skill of Moon's chef, George Crum.

The most controversial visitor to Saratoga Springs in the 1830's and '40's was Madame Jumel. Saint-Mémin's portrait shows her in 1797, when she was Madame de la Croix.

As the wife of Stephen Jumel, Madame Jumel was the mistress of the magnificent mansion Roger Morris had built in New York City.

In 1833, after Jumel's death, Madame married
Aaron Burr; he was 77, she 59. They were divorced
three years later.

border of bankruptcy. While he remained in France to try to recoup his losses, Eliza settled again in her mansion in New York.

During the years she had been away the city had blossomed with prosperity. Golden opportunities awaited citizens with sufficient imagination and capital to seize them. Armed with her husband's power of attorney, Eliza swiftly pyramided his meager assets in America into cash and holdings several times their original worth. When Jumel returned home, after three years, he discovered that he was supremely wealthy; or more accurately, his wife was. In his absence she had put all of their property in her name.

Also during his absence she had indulged in a few amorous adventures, and when Jumel died in 1832 a persistent swain entreated her to marry him. Aaron Burr had crowned a promising career by serving as Vice-President of his country and had then plunged to his political death by fatally wounding Alexander Hamilton in a pistol duel. Later misadventures had further diminished his reputation. Nevertheless, his name was still of some importance. As Madame Burr, Eliza reasoned, she might enjoy greater prestige. A year after Jumel's death she agreed to become his wife. Burr was seventy-seven, Eliza fifty-nine.

It was one of her few mistakes. Burr spent her money with a prodigal hand and was unfaithful to his most solemn marital vows. After a series of quarrels, Eliza locked him out of her house and divorced him shortly before he died in 1836.

Although Madame Jumel's popularity in the Paris salons and frequent appearances at the French Court had not passed unnoticed in New York's social circles, they had produced no change in society's attitude toward her. The stately dowagers she sought to impress after her return remained stiffly aloof. Since she determinedly pursued the same paths and pleasures, however, she was hard to avoid, particularly in the fairly compressed area of Saratoga Springs. Each summer she journeyed to the spa in a luxurious coach and eight, attended by liveried footmen, coachman and outriders. Shortly after Jumel's death she had purchased a mansion on Circular Street and made it her summer home. It was an impressive white house in the Greek Revival style, with tall columns carrying the roof forward in the manner of Greek temples, and with fond memories of the palace in Paris where she had been warmly received she had named it Les Tuileries. It attracted few visitors, however, and from time to time Eliza varied her stay by taking a suite at one of the spa's fashionable hotels. The piazzas and balls enabled her to mix with her adversaries, recount her triumphs in Paris and preen her still well-turned figure in her Parisian gowns. Most vexing of all to the ladies, the daily promenade of coaches gave her numerous opportunities to reign as queen of the occasion, and through bold, determined stratagems she frequently won the role.

In the summer of 1849 they gained a measure of revenge. Descending from the veranda of the United States Hotel, Madame Jumel seated herself in her gold-colored carriage behind four black horses and looked on with pleased surprise as her coachman and outriders maneuvered to the head of the assembling procession with scarcely any opposition. When the line was complete, she led the way along Broadway toward the road to Lake Saratoga, bowing and gesturing with her familiar ostrich fan. The response was disconcerting; instead of politely acknowledging her leadership, as they normally did, the sidewalk spectators broke into laughter, slapped their thighs and pointed. Eliza looked back. Only a single coach followed her carriage. It was painted a gleaming yellow to resemble the golden coloring of her equipage, and was drawn by four bony horses. A village cut-up in coachman's livery sat in the driver's seat and another prankster in footman's uniform rode high in back atop an overturned clothes-basket. Inside the carriage Thomas Camel, formerly one of Jacobus Barhyte's Negro slaves, languidly postured in a low-necked gown, fanning himself with a fan very much like Madame Jumel's and bowing and waving in an exaggerated parody of her mannerisms.

White with anger, Eliza returned to the hotel. The next day her carriage again moved to the head of the procession, again without opposition and with no attempt made to ridicule her. In full view of everyone she carried a pistol.

After that summer she stayed away from Saratoga and confined herself more and more to her mansion in New York City. In 1865, her ninetieth year, she died in her Napoleonic bed.

Bonfires and handkerchiefs By mid-century the gayety and frivolity at Saratoga were a favorite summer topic in the country's illustrated weeklies, and public curiosity about the Spa or the Springs, as the resort was more and more familiarly called, grew steadily. Since most of the stories were embroidered with considerable fancy, readers thirsting for the truth would have done better to turn to the recital of a typical day's activities John Godfrey Saxe addressed to a curious inquirer in his *Song of Saratoga:*

> "Pray, what do they do at the Springs?"
> The question is easy to ask;
> But to answer it fully, my dear,
> Were rather a serious task.
> And yet, in a bantering way,
> As the magpie or mocking-bird sings,
> I'll venture a bit of a song
> To tell what they do at the Springs!
>
> *Imprimis,* my darling, they drink
> The waters so sparkling and clear;

Though the flavor is none of the best,
  And the odor exceedingly queer;
But the fluid is mingled, you know,
  With wholesome medicinal things,
So they drink, and they drink, and they drink,
  And that's what they do at the Springs!

Then with appetites keen as a knife,
  They hasten to breakfast or dine;
(The latter precisely at three;
  The former from seven till nine.)
Ye gods! what a rustle and rush
  When the eloquent dinner-bell rings!
Then they eat, and they eat, and they eat—
  And that's what they do at the Springs!

Now they stroll in the beautiful walks,
  Or loll in the shade of the trees;
Where many a whisper is heard
  That never is told by the breeze;
And hands are commingled with hands,
  Regardless of conjugal rings;
And they flirt, and they flirt, and they flirt—
  And that's what they do at the Springs!

The drawing-rooms now are ablaze,
  And music is shrieking away;
TERPSICHORE governs the hour,
  And FASHION was never so gay!
An arm 'round a tapering waist—
  How closely and fondly it clings:
So they waltz, and they waltz, and they waltz—
  And that's what they do at the Springs!

In short—as it goes in the world—
  They eat, and they drink, and they sleep;
They talk, and they walk, and they woo;
  They sigh, and they laugh, and they weep;
They read, and they ride, and they dance;
  (With other unspeakable things;)
They pray, and they play, and they *pay*—
  And that's what they do at the Springs!

Early in the 1850's Saratoga's summer citizens pursued the resort's pleasures with somewhat less abandon. The hostility that had developed between the North and the South over slavery was reflected at the Spa in a growing coolness between Northern and Southern guests, and as events marched toward a showdown Southern planters chose to vacation with their wives and daughters and Negro servants at watering places in Georgia, Virginia and along the Gulf of Mexico.* The atmosphere was strained still more when, in 1856, Harriet Beecher Stowe's *Uncle Tom's Cabin* was performed at the Springs before a packed house in which there didn't appear to be a dry eye.

Stephen A. Douglas visited the resort in the summer of 1860 to strengthen his bid for the presidency, and a parade of sympathizers followed his flag-draped carriage to hear him speak. Among his listeners was young Baron Salomon de Rothschild of the Paris branch of the world's most famous Jewish family. He was in America on business for his family's bank and was seeing Saratoga for the first time. A few days after leaving the Spa he wrote in a letter home:

> The evening before my departure there was a big meeting in favor of Douglas, in which the speakers called the people of the South a rabble, traitors, etc. To show still more enthusiasm, the partisans of the "little giant" put a barrel of tar and resin in the street and set fire to it. The flames were going splendidly when up came a stage-coach driven by a coachman of a different political party. In this country coachmen are knee-deep in "politics." This one drove his carriage straight at the barrel, which he knocked over and broke to pieces. In a second the inflammable material spread, causing a fire that the people at the "meeting" had to put out themselves.

Guests who ignored the temper of the times enjoyed their stay at the Springs in spite of such incidents. Elsewhere in his letter the twenty-five-year-old baron wrote:

> Every day the young girls put on new dresses in order to attract admirers. When one of them has several around her, she encourages them all until she has made a decision in favor of one of them. I was present several times as a confidant at these intrigues and it is quite diverting, I assure you. The girls give their handkerchiefs, their gloves, even their slippers; it binds them to nothing. The married women are less generous, although they make an exception for some people. I have to my credit a pretty collection of pocket handkerchiefs, for I never ask for anything else.

---

* In June, 1862, when the North and South were at war, *Leslie's Weekly* attempted to minimize the loss of Southern comfort at the Spa with what seems to be a bit of whistling in the dark: "Although we shall probably miss in the ensuing season those very charming Southern ingredients to this most *piquant* of social salads [Saratoga Springs], the belles of Charleston, Savannah and New Orleans, we may yet have amends in the greater intellect and earnestness of our Northern ladies. The society of Saratoga may lose somewhat of its *vim* and vivacity, but it will gain in intelligence and power."

In November of that year an uncompromising opponent of slavery, Abraham Lincoln, was elected chief executive of the land, and the following April, 1861, the quarrel between the Northern and Southern states flared into open battle in the harbor of Charleston, South Carolina, and a civil war began.

Chapter Two

Old
Smoke

The new war in North America was but a sound of distant thunder in the valley of the springs at the southernmost spur of the Adirondacks and scarcely interfered with the natives' habitual pursuits. Well out of harm's way, the village of Saratoga, indeed, suffered the hostilities most pleasantly. Hardly had the guns of Fort Sumter echoed throughout the Union and the blue and gray clad battalions taken the field than throngs of noncombatants descended on the Spa seeking respite from the news and moods of the conflict and eager to savor any and all pleasures the resort could provide. The most popular of these were supplied by a brash and boldly handsome newcomer named John Morrissey.

A six-foot, broad-shouldered, deep-chested, two-fisted, black-browed and fully-bearded thirty-year-old Irishman, Morrissey was the most notoriously prosperous gaming-house proprietor in New York City. The golden opportunities awaiting one of his calling at the upstate resort had tempted him for some time, and in midsummer of 1861 he moved an assortment of gambling paraphernalia, dealers and bouncers into a house on Matilda Street,* just a short stroll from Broadway and the best hotels, and prepared to cater to the Spa's war-fatigued, well-heeled vacationists' craving for amusement.

The presence of the new gambling emporium filled the village fathers with gloomy foreboding. Thus far the transgressions of fun-loving summer visitors had left Saratoga's bulwarks of decorum unshaken; devout and soberly respectable citizens continued to enjoy a sojourn at the Springs as well as the pleasure seekers. But from all that was known about John Morrissey, it looked as though the village was in for a troublesome time.

Transported from Ireland to Troy, New York, when he was three, Morrissey had spent most of his undisciplined youth in the streets. As the leader of a teen-age gang, he learned and used the artful tricks of gutter fighting—attacking head-on with butting skull, maiming knee, bared teeth

* Later, it was named Woodlawn Avenue.

and thumbs at the ready to gouge out his adversary's eyes. Before he was eighteen he was indicted twice for burglary, once for assault and battery, once for assault with intent to kill, and spent sixty days in jail. He was nineteen before he learned to read and write.

Thus equipped he journeyed to New York City and offered his services to Tammany Hall. Impressed by the confident, well-muscled young giant and his reputation as a brawler, the sachems turned him over to one of their number, Isaiah Rynders, who taught him how to improve his pugilistic skills and placed him in charge of the organization's band of toughs, the Dead Rabbits gang. With Morrissey at their head, the Rabbits routed a rival political gang and insured victory for Tammany in a vital election. The bully boy's star began to rise.

While in Troy, Morrissey had worked briefly as a deckhand for a Hudson riverboat captain and had fallen in love with the captain's daughter, Susie Smith, a radiant and respectable girl whom, unlike others who attracted his eye, he was content to admire at a respectful distance. In no way bound by this devotion, he took advantage of his bold good looks and growing importance in New York City's political circles to make love pretty much as he pleased, a pastime which in one instance almost cost him his life.

In the course of his conquests Morrissey endeavored to supplant a prominent hoodlum, Tom McCann, in the affections of his mistress, Kate Ridgely, the madam of a brothel, and the two suitors met in a saloon to decide with their fists which one would henceforth enjoy the lady's favors. The clash knocked over a stove and McCann knocked Morrissey on top of the hot coals which rolled out of the firebox onto the floor, then flung himself on his fallen foe and held him prostrate until Morrissey's flesh began to burn. Squirming in agony, Morrissey at last wrenched himself from the coals and beat his rival unconscious. In tribute to the circumstances which produced the victory, he was nicknamed Old Smoke. Morrissey moved in with Madam Ridgely; having paid for her with a bit of his person she was pleased to support him with her own earnings of the flesh.

The gold rush, with its arch promise of quick riches, lured Morrissey to San Francisco, but after weighing the months of effort a search would require he was persuaded to become a partner in a small gaming house. The following year, 1852, twenty-one years old and still sound of wind and limb, he made his debut as a prizefighter at Mare Island, California, disposing of a clever boxer named George Thompson in eleven rounds, sixteen minutes to win a purse of $4,000 and a side bet of $1,000. Spurred by the easy money, Morrissey challenged the American heavyweight boxing champion, Yankee Sullivan, to a title match—a stand-up, bare-knuckle fight for the championship of America under the London Prize Ring Rules.

The London Rules approved of both punching and wrestling. A round ended when one of the combatants was knocked off his feet, and if his seconds could not revive him in the thirty-second rest period, or if he failed to come to the center of the ring at the referee's call of "Time," he was declared the loser. The winner took all of the prize money, and that plus a title, if a championship was at stake, was his sole reward. Physically, he was frequently worse off than the loser, his hands having taken more punishment. Since the bouts were fought to a finish, both fighters were apt to leave the ring with broken fingers or knuckles, a torn tendon or fractured limb, and disfigured features. There was also the possibility that they would be tossed into jail. It hardly seemed a profitable venture even for the victor.

Nevertheless, his original challenge having been ignored, Morrissey kept after Yankee Sullivan, pressing his candidacy for the heavyweight title with a few choice barbs directed at the champion's nickname. An Englishman who had escaped from an Australian penal colony, Sullivan insisted on showing his appreciation to the country of his asylum by wrapping himself in the American flag each time he entered the ring. It was a noble gesture, Morrissey submitted, but it still left Sullivan considerably short of being a Yankee.

Stung by the gibes, Sullivan assented to the match, and on October 12, 1853, champion and challenger met at Boston Corners, New York, a hundred miles north of New York City. Morrissey began confidently. He was taller than his opponent, almost thirty pounds heavier and twenty years younger. But the blunt technique he had perfected in street fighting was outclassed by the other's professional finesse. Through the first twenty rounds Sullivan cut him to ribbons. Morrissey hung on, and as the bout progressed the champion began to tire. The atmosphere outside the ring grew almost as heated as the activity inside. In the thirty-eighth round Sullivan stepped through the ropes and mixed it up with one of Morrissey's seconds. Being so busily engaged, he failed to respond to the referee's summons for the next round, and Old Smoke was declared the winner and new heavyweight boxing champion of America.

Tammany beckoned. The sachems had picked the rich and unscrupulous opportunist, Fernando Wood, as their candidate for Mayor of New York City, and Morrissey's peerless leadership of the Tammany gang of toughs was needed to help sell him to the voters. Morrissey returned to his old post and Wood was elected, obliging his supporters by presiding for two unstintingly corrupt terms. In the midst of these a battle for political supremacy broke out in the high council of the organization and the sachems divided into two hostile camps. Morrissey cast his fortunes with the "old guard" and went on using his fists with excellent results at the polls. When the "old guard" won the dispute, he was assured that his street brawling days were over and that a more peaceable and profitable future awaited him.

In October 1858, he stepped into the ring for the last time, defending his title at Long Point, Canada, against the ambitions of John C. Heenan, popularly known as the Benicia Boy. Later, Heenan was to become the heavyweight champion and the first of four husbands of the vivacious, violet-eyed, sometime actress and all-time seductress, Adah Isaacs Menken, whom he taught to box and who rewarded him by hanging a mouse under his eye when she connected with a solid right to the head during a quarrel. Against Morrissey, he fared a good deal worse. When he was unable to come from his corner for the twelfth round, Old Smoke tucked away the prize money, his championship belt and a $5,000 side wager he had won and announced that he was retiring from pugilism. Having recently married his true love, Susie Smith, whom he had been courting for some time, and basking in the warmth of Tammany's affection, he was ready to mix with a more sociable and respectable group.

While the police dutifully looked the other way, he opened a gambling house in New York City; then a second, then a third. His public games were skin games, designed to cheat gullible bettors, but in private poker sessions with friends Morrissey, an expert at cards, was scrupulously fair. Such was the opinion of his friends, at any rate, and those who questioned a play by their host were usually favored with the same disarming defense: "No man can say that I ever turned a dishonest card or struck a foul blow."

Fair and foul, the profits from the three gaming houses were highly gratifying and established Old Smoke as the king of gamblers in New York City. Casting about for a new world to conquer, his eye had fixed on the lively and affluent summer resort one hundred and seventy-five miles or so to the north, Saratoga Springs.

The most classic course   The new casino at the Spa was an instant success, and to insure its flow of wealth John Morrissey set about laying Saratoga's misgivings to rest. The village fathers had suffered further qualms when a Boston newspaper described the Matilda Street emporium as a "gambling hell," confirming their worst suspicions and rousing a few outspoken members to call for action. A younger, brawling Morrissey would have met the opposition head-on, but Tammany's slick political machine had smoothed down most of his rough edges and as a gaming-house proprietor he had learned the advantages of diplomacy and Irish charm. He quickly demonstrated his civic pride by donating generously to Saratoga's charities. Chairladies in need of capital to finance community social functions discovered that just a hint of their predicament dropped in Morrissey's presence swept their troubles away. He was careful not to draw attention to his gaming house, and to avoid damaging publicity he operated the games with uncharacteristic honesty—a procedure which proved to be far less costly at the tables than his croupiers feared. Such were the odds against the players, and such was the number of plungers at the Spa, that rich plums fell into his lap without his employees furtively shaking the tree. His personal behavior was equally circumspect. Street fighting was behind him, and married to a lovely woman he adored he was a faithful husband. After a period of hesitation, Saratoga accepted John Morrissey and his Matilda Street casino as part of the resort scene.

Prior to the Civil War, Saratoga was famous as a health and social resort. After the war, gambling and sports added to the Spa's renown. Largely responsible was a brash Irishman named John Morrissey, who introduced the Club House and a race track. This portrait shows him soon after he settled at Saratoga in 1861. In his shirt he wears a diamond stud.

In 1853 Morrissey had become the heavyweight boxing champion of America by defeating Yankee Sullivan.

Morrissey's last ring opponent was John C. Heenan, called the Benicia Boy, whom he fought at Long Point, Canada. Morrissey won in 11 rounds, 22 minutes.

In 1865 the celebrated artist, Winslow Homer, captured the suspense among the spectators at the Saratoga races in a drawing published in *Harper's Weekly*. The gentleman with the mustache and pince-nez in the middle foreground is the artist's favorite brother, Charles Savage Homer.

The success of his initial venture at the Springs encouraged Old Smoke to look for other profitable ways of amusing the free-spending summer guests and, the authorities agreeing that it would be a pleasing addition to the resort's attractions, he began to build a track on which thoroughbred race horses could compete. When it was finished in 1863 he announced a program of four days of racing, two races a day, starting on August 3rd.

To most horse lovers it seemed unlikely that the meeting would take place. One month previously the Union had fought and won two of the bloodiest battles of the war at Gettysburg and Vicksburg, and to press on to ultimate victory the army had requisitioned every healthy horse it could find. Where could the track obtain blue-blooded steeds in sufficient numbers to introduce racing at the Spa that summer?

Morrissey laid the problem before three turf experts: William R. Travers, a wealthy stockbroker, clubman and New York society's favorite wit; John R. Hunter, a prominent sportsman; and the lawyer, horseman and yachtsman, Leonard W. Jerome, whose daughter Jennie was to become Lady Churchill and make him the grandfather of a future world-famous soldier, statesman and author, Winston Churchill. They formed a racing association, produced twenty-six horses to compete in the eight events, and the track's opening program was held as scheduled. On a shimmering summer day an elegant crowd saw Lizzie W., a three-year-old filly with a one-eyed jockey in the irons, gallop three miles to beat a colt named Captain Moore in the first running race at the Spa. When the four-day program was over the enthusiasm of all who witnessed it was reflected in a front-page story in *Wilkes' Spirit of the Times,* which began:

> The meeting at Saratoga was a great success . . . It must have laid the foundation for a great fashionable race meeting at the Springs, like that at Ascot in England, where the elegance and superb costumes of the ladies vie with the blood and beauty of the running horses and the neat but splendid appointments of the various riders. It is now established that of the many thousands of people to be found at Saratoga this season of the year, there are but few who will not eagerly avail themselves of the opportunity for such amusement and interest as the sports of the turf afford.

There were rumbles of discontent, even so. The grandstand was too small, it was pointed out, and the track too narrow. Unwilling to settle for less than perfection itself, the racing association purchased one hundred and twenty-five acres across the road from Morrissey's track, landscaped them with a lavish hand and installed more elegant and elaborate appointments. The result so filled Saratoga with pride that its brochures picturing the Spa's attractions virtually rang with praise: "The Most Classic Race Course in This Country, Located Among the Pines, Beautiful to the Eye, Rejuvenating to the Horse."

The new track was inaugurated with a four-day program commencing on August 2, 1864, and although the war was far from won it cast no visible shadow over the gay and fashionable crowd. During the meeting, in tribute to the president of the racing association, William R. Travers, a special event was introduced, the Travers Stakes, and appropriately enough was won by Kentucky, a colt carrying Travers' colors.

The following season saw the first running of another race destined to become a turf classic, the Saratoga Cup Stakes. Then steeplechase races were added to the program. Attendance swelled. In a few years it frequently reached ten thousand spectators a day.

While the abandonment of his original race course* had removed his hand from the gate receipts, John Morrissey had seized other money-making opportunities the track provided. Wealthy sportsmen who differed on the merits of the horses and elected to support their opinions with sizable bets found him ready to act as stake-holder. Also, in advance of each day's races he conducted an auction pool on the outcome of each event. In both instances he subtracted a substantial commission for his services. Since private bettors frequently entrusted him with as much as $200,000 a day, and the auction pools sometimes rose to astronomical heights, the total commissions were no little part of Old Smoke's seasonal profit.

Later on he saw another chance to spread Saratoga's name, lure patrons to the Springs and earn a suitable recompense for himself. Boat racing having become one of the public's favorite sports, he offered attractive prizes to the winners of contests rowed on Lake Saratoga. The famous boat clubs of Boston, New York, Philadelphia, Baltimore and other cities favored with waterways came with their light, narrow racing shells backed by an army of supporters bearing pennants and betting money. Their enthusiasm for the resort induced college oarsmen to hold their regattas on the lake. Soon the Spa was a popular sports center—precisely what Morrissey had hoped for. Sportslovers, being the same everywhere, whiled their evenings away in his gambling casino, usually losing the sums they had won wagering on the races and repaying Old Smoke's prize-money awards to the victorious boat clubs many times over.

Vision of conquest   In the spring of 1865 the long war ceased, and during the following summers Saratoga was host to a teeming *mélange* of profiteers newly enriched by a carpet-bag tour of the South, Eastern financial titans, Western bonanza kings, transportation tycoons, statesmen and politicians, society dilettantes, sporty members of the burgeoning turf aristocracy, and a swarm of lesser mortals who came to mingle with the mighty and emulate their antics within the limits imposed by their considerably less bountiful capital.

* Named Horse Haven, the Morrissey-built race course was used as a training track.

The winner of the first Travers Stakes and the first Saratoga Cup (historic races today) was the great bay colt, Kentucky, who appears here as painted by Edward Troye.

Weighing the jockeys.

Going to the races in the early 1870's was a colorful and spirited ceremony in which all of Saratoga's fashionable guests participated. These sketches show a typical stream of coaches and carriages flowing past Morrissey's Club House and, some 20 minutets later, emptying their occupants at the entrance to the grandstand.

Inside the race course, the scene was charged with excitement. Top: the start of a mile and three-quarter dash. Bottom: the horses at the judges' stand, D'Artagnan winning.

The success of thoroughbred racing at the Spa led to boat racing on Lake Saratoga. Professional scullers and college oarsmen competed. This drawing depicts the crush on Broadway as boating enthusiasts started for the lake to witness an intercollegiate regatta.

Saratoga's resident population jumped to ten thousand as new arrivals settled down to cash in on the summer opulence.

Gazing upon the expanding pageant of eager spenders, John Morrissey entertained a new vision of conquest. His original move in establishing a gaming house at the Spa had been partly prompted by tales he had heard of a Parisian waiter, François Blanc, who had selected a fashionable German watering place, Baden-Baden, as the setting for a casino and had picked up several fortunes squandered by European rakes. Recently, Blanc had moved to the French Riviera and on the rock of Monaco had introduced a deluxe Monte Carlo casino that enthusiastic patrons declared was the world's best. In Old Smoke's view, there appeared no reason why he should not establish an elegant new gambling emporium of his own.

He purchased some thirty acres of land adjoining the Congress Spring estate of Dr. John Clarke, landscaped the property and placed an impressive red brick Club House on the elm-shaded, terraced lawn. In 1869, when everything was to his satisfaction, he opened the casino's doors and a glittering crowd surged into its richly appointed, softly carpeted rooms. A great public gaming room on the first floor enabled modest bettors to test their luck at faro and roulette, and heavy plungers were invited upstairs to private rooms, one of which was reserved for poker, where they could indulge themselves with escalating stakes and uninterrupted play for as long as their money lasted. Upstairs and downstairs, gaming was open only to patrons in a position to risk their cash; no credit was given.

With an eye still on the local proprieties, Morrissey welcomed women to the handsomely chandeliered dining salon and amused them with sweets, ices and other refreshments, but barred them from the gaming rooms. As expected, the ladies regarded the barrier as a personal affront and assaulted it with pleas and cunning and, when these didn't succeed, marched directly against the guarded entrance on the arms of their male escorts. Regardless of the strategy employed, Morrissey held firm. In addition, he ruled that no resident of Saratoga would be permitted to gamble at the Club House, and thus eliminated the possibility of local "sore losers" mounting a hostile community action against the new casino.

A social as well as a financial triumph, the Club House soon commanded all of Morrissey's attention in season at the Springs. He gave up his Matilda Street establishment and announced his retirement from politics (prior to envisioning his new casino he had been elected to a four-year term in Congress, but this was coming to a close and he was under no pressure to extend it, his most notable proposal to the august body of lawmakers having been an offer—wisely declined—to whip any ten men in the House of Representatives).

Morrissey devoted himself to his new responsibilities with pride and zeal. He enjoyed his importance as the proprietor of the fashionable Spa's fashionable casino and took advantage of it to mingle freely with his rich and well-born guests. In the affable atmosphere of the Club House they

In 1874 Frank Leslie, the well-known publisher, who owned a 92-acre summer estate called Interlaken on the northwest shore of Lake Saratoga, presented this trophy, shaped like Cleopatra's barge, to the winner of an international amateur race.

received him with unpatrician familiarity, and encouraged by the informal good fellowship Morrissey saw no reason why he shouldn't win their social recognition as a gentleman. In pursuit of this goal, he cultivated an urbane manner and made his nightly appearances at the Club House tastefully dressed in black broadcloth and white linen with a $5,000 diamond stud in his shirt as the single badge of his success. The gay whirl of the hotels and promenades found him in livelier attire: beaver hat, swallow-tailed coat, striped trousers, patent-leather boots, white kid gloves and accessories, which usually consisted of diamonds flashing from his scarf, cuffs, rings and watch-chain. At his side was an equally arresting sight, lovely Susie Morrissey. Great black eyes, a queenly form and a sparkling personality had won her a reputation as one of New York City's most stunning women and she enhanced her beauty by the magnificence of her dress. Such was her fame that visitors to Saratoga had scarcely been tucked into the carriages which were to take them from the depot to the hotels before they asked that Mrs. Morrissey be pointed out to them.

In common with her husband, Susie Morrissey could lay small claim to good breeding and education, but she had acquired poise as well as style and she was as determined as he to join the social elite. The one thing missing from their credentials seemed to be a suitable home in which to entertain. The socialites maintained fine mansions in cities wherein their lineage had flourished for generations: Boston, New York, Philadelphia, Baltimore and so on. Saratoga, delightful as it was, was a summer respite from the regular social season and offered the Morrisseys little opportunity to bid for social recognition.

With Susie's approval, Old Smoke decided to build a mansion in Troy, the city which had been his home through the years of his youth. To his puzzled surprise, his efforts to purchase a desirable tract of land on which to put the house were repeatedly rebuffed, though the price he offered was increasingly generous. At last he was told why. Troy society, a mixture of the descendants of the Hudson River aristocracy and the industrial rich, didn't want a professional gambler, particularly one with such a notorious past, living alongside them, and had agreed to resist all his attempts to settle in their fashionable section. Cut to the quick, Morrissey struck back. Close to the select residential area were several vacant lots over which a stiff breeze frequently blew from the river toward the posh homes. Morrissey bought the lots and erected a soap factory on the property. The soap it produced was not in the least pleasantly scented—and every breeze carried its odor to Troy's most sensitive nostrils.

With the hope that it would be more hospitable to their social ambitions, the Morrisseys returned to New York City, and to improve their chances for advancement Morrissey ran for the New York State Senate. He won, but the ring into which he had cast his hat, the Fourth District, had been the most compliantly corruptible election area bossed by the deposed Tammany grand sachem, William Marcy Tweed. Honest John Kelly, the

Yale, Harvard, Dartmouth, Princeton, Columbia, Cornell and other leading colleges were represented in the intercollegiate regatta of 1874, the first held on the lake. Cheering spectators in the arbor and grandstand saw Columbia win.

After the regattas, the fashionable audience frequently repaired to the lake houses for supper. Briggs House was among those favored.

The public gaming room in the Club House.

The Honorable John Morrissey. At the same time that he conducted Saratoga's most prestigious and profitable gambling casino, Old Smoke was a member of Congress.

Morrissey's previous accomplishments as a street brawler and political hack for Tammany Hall made him a favorite whipping boy of newspaper cartoonists. Drawing at left is by Thomas Nast.

Commodore Cornelius Vanderbilt, a frequent patron of the Club House, was the richest man in the country.

new Tammany chief, with whom Morrissey had quarreled, promptly announced to the press that only such a delinquent district could have shown contempt for the dignity of the state legislature by electing to it "a vicious thug, a rowdy prizefighter and a notorious gambler." Furious, Old Smoke ran again for the Senate, this time as a candidate from the Seventh "Silk Stocking" District. After a savage campaign in which William Cullen Bryant, Peter Cooper and other notables lent their support, he scored a narrow victory.

Morrissey was elated. As the ambassador of New York City's best people to the state capital, there would seem to be no question now of his and Susie's eligibility for society. In anticipation of their triumph, he bought his wife a pair of opera glasses, the costliest in America. Priced at $4,500, they were made of gold set with diamonds and bore Susie's initials interlaced in pearls.

As time went on the opera glasses turned from a token of victory into a memento of failure. New York's socialites ignored Old Smoke's new eminence, and the invitations to their fashionable entertainments omitted the Morrisseys as before. To cap their dejection, the election campaign he had fought so hard to win had dealt severely with Morrissey's resources, physical as well as financial.

He could more easily withstand the blow to his purse than the strain on his health. While he was considerably less wealthy than he had been in earlier days, the income from his various gaming establishments was still robust. Both the upturn and the downcurve of his fortune had commenced in the same year, the summer in which he had opened his new casino at Saratoga. Morrissey had been a millionaire when he built the Club House, and in two seasons it had repaid his $190,000 investment with a $500,000 profit. He looked forward to still greater rewards from his gaming tables, but a formidable shadow fell across the light of his future in the person of Commodore Cornelius Vanderbilt. A titan of titans, the richest tycoon in America and a gentleman who had lifted himself to this lofty pinnacle by his own bootstraps, Vanderbilt obviously was one to admire, and Morrissey had been greatly flattered by his favors at the Club House. With the Commodore's encouragement he had plunged in New York Central Railroad stock and in a single eventful day, Black Friday, 1869, had been cleaned out of $800,000. Jolting as this was, Morrissey's faith in the great man's judgment had not wavered. Acting again on Vanderbilt's advice, he had loaded himself with Harlem Railroad stock and lost again, dropping $200,000 during a Wall Street manipulation in which the Commodore added another handsome profit to his own exchequer. As a result of these unlucky forays into the market, Morrissey had let debts accumulate and now old creditors, as well as new ones he had inherited from the closely fought election campaign, were pressing him for their money.

But dwindling finances gave the Morrisseys a good deal less cause for concern than Old Smoke's fading health. The years of affluence and an undisciplined appetite had divested him of his once proud physique, and lately his stomach and kidneys had begun to rebel. Asthma thickened his voice and his throat became infected.

With Susie, he spent a restless summer at Saratoga. In a half mocking, half serious gesture which compelled his socialite patrons to acknowledge him as an equal on his own property, if not on theirs, he stood day after day at the entrance to the Club House grounds and, with a green umbrella as his semaphore, directed their carriages as they arrived at his driveway, halting each stylish equipage and keeping it waiting whenever it pleased him. When the season was over, he went south with Susie, hoping to regain his vigor, but fell ill with pneumonia on his return to the Spa.

He died on the first day of May 1878, in his forty-seventh year, and his widow was comforted by a show of respect greater than any he had received while alive. The aristocrats of New York City newspapers, the *Times* and the *Herald,* devoted a dozen columns to his obituary, and other journals also described him at flattering length. The flag on New York's City Hall was flown at half-mast. And in Troy, nineteen thousand citizens followed his body in a downpour of rain to a grave not far from the social fortress he had succeeded in penetrating only as an odor of soap.

Chapter Three

A
quite momentous
spectacle

In the summer of 1870 a twenty-seven-year-old author whose essays and short stories had put him well along the path to literary eminence came to see the legendary resort and observe the new American privileged class in the process of enjoying its leisure.

Henry James was much more at home in Europe than in his native land. He had spent a good deal of his youth touring the Continent with his father, a firm believer in the educational benefits of foreign travel, and just a year ago had made his first trip abroad alone. He had returned exhilarated by the experience, and had thought more and more seriously of abandoning the country of his birth and establishing himself permanently in Europe. Both his tastes and ambitions would be better served in the Old World, he felt, particularly in Paris, which had so much to offer expatriates.

But this was still a decision of the future. For the present there was Saratoga Springs. With perceptive eye and fluent pen, young James set out for the Spa bent on capturing postwar America's changing social order in its most popular milieu. Despite his many talents, it was a task to which the author was unsuited. His enthusiasm for Old World culture and customs prejudiced his judgments, and his fastidious nature recoiled from the raw thrust of the new society*. By the best American standards Saratoga was ostentatious and frequently raffish, and to Henry James, thoroughly committed to European tastes and manners, it appeared doubly so. It is unlikely that any other tourist ever looked at the Springs with so hostile an eye. Nevertheless, the young writer cut to the heart of his subject with shrewd insight and surgical skill. One may quarrel with his opinion of the Saratoga scene, but not with what he observed and reported that summer of 1870 in his article in *The Nation*.

* Years later W. H. Auden pinpointed James' inflexible social posture with this comment: "I have read somewhere a story that once, when James was visiting a French friend, the latter's mistress, unobserved, filled his top hat with champagne, but I do not believe it because, try as I will, I simply cannot conceive what James did and said when he put his hat on."

In 1870 Saratoga's reputation as America's favorite summer reso induced a 27-year-old author, Henry James, to visit the Spa. He shown at about 20, photographed at Newport (left) and Gene

The most formidable attraction at the Springs at this time was the Union Hotel, which had metamorphosed from Union Hall after the Putnam place was purchased by the Leland brothers in 1864. Original enlargements and improvements produced this view.

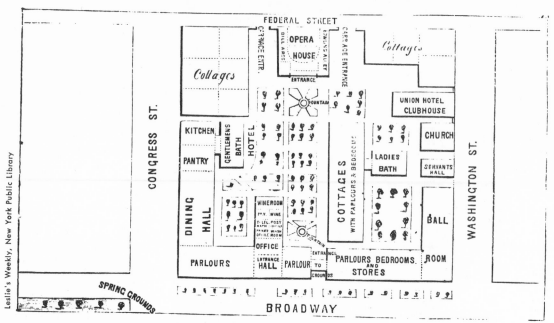

In 1865 the transformation was even more magical and immense. As the diagram shows, private cottages and an opera house were among the Union's additional comforts.

The interior court of the grand new Union Hotel was a park shaded with elm trees. In this sketch the opera house appears in the background, bathhouses and cottages at left and right.

Arriving at the Spa, James was at once offended by the architecture which met his glance: a romantic extravagance of turrets, towers, cupolas, balconies, bays and other excrescences wreathed with gingerbread fretwork. He singled out the largest hotels as particularly unsightly, characterized them in his essay as "two monsters which stand facing each other." One was the Union Hotel. The other, across Broadway—the wide main street softly shaded by rows of wine-glass elms—was Congress Hall.

The Union Hotel originally had been Union Hall, and had been re-named by the new owners when they purchased it from the Putnam heirs in 1864 and subsequently enlarged and improved it. It could look back with pride on two occasions when it had received Ulysses S. Grant with ap-propriate largesse: a grand ball tendered the conquering hero in 1865, a brilliant reception given the nation's chief executive in 1869. Congress Hall, Gideon Putnam's fateful and grandiose venture, had been destroyed by fire in 1866, as had another hostelry, the Columbian, and a new Congress Hall of brick with brownstone trimmings—only slightly smaller than the Union Hotel and boasting piazzas almost as impressive—had risen in its place. Since the United States Hotel had been levelled by flames in 1865, the rivalry between Henry James' "two monsters" was brisk. But the Clarendon, a picturesque refuge of white woodwork and green shades which had moved into the lead while the Congress and the United States lay in ashes, re-mained the favorite retreat of the social elite despite its refusal to modernize.

James also bridled at the boastfulness of the cocky newly rich, per-sonally relishing the reserved and understated style of the English. Sara-toga's foremost attractions, he was repeatedly told, were the largest (piazzas of the Union Hotel) or the finest (Congress Spring waters, Morrissey's casino) in the world. James could find no fault with the waters; they were, he wrote, "excellent in the superlative degree"; but the high praise for the Club House induced him to put tongue in cheek. "I bowed my head sub-missively . . . but privately I thought of the blue Mediterranean, and the little white promontory of Monaco, and the silver-gray verdure of olives, and the view across the outer sea toward the bosky cliffs of Italy." He conceded that the Broadway promenade of the Union Hotel might well be the biggest of all piazzas, though it was no beauty, and that—as could also be said of the facing piazza of Congress Hall—it afforded impressive space for an immense number of persons to sit or stroll in the open air. More helpful still, particularly to the purpose of his visit, the great porches were the best places from which to observe the wondrous world of Saratoga. He wrote:

> Seeing it for the first time, the observer is likely to assure himself that he has neglected an important item in the sum of American manners. The rough brick wall of the house [Union Hotel], illumined by a line of flaring gas-lights, forms a natural background to the crude, impermanent, discordant tone of the assembly.

A bit later:

You are struck, to begin with, by the numerical superiority of the women; then, I think, by their personal superiority. It is incontestably the case that in appearance, in manner, in grace and completeness of aspect, American women surpass their husbands and brothers.

Casting his eye over the men he found them, nevertheless, worthy sons of the Republic:

They suggest to my fancy the swarming vastness—the multi-farious possibilities and activities—of our young civilization. They come from the uttermost ends of the Union—from San Francisco, from New Orleans, from Alaska. As they sit with their white hats tilted forward, and their chairs tilted back, and their feet tilted up, and their cigars and toothpicks forming various angles with these various lines, I seem to see in their faces a tacit reference to the affairs of a continent. They are obviously persons of experience—of a somewhat narrow and monotonous experience certainly; an experience of which the diamonds and laces which their wives are exhibiting hard by are, perhaps, the most substantial and beautiful result; but, at any rate, they have *lived,* in every fibre of the will . . . They are not the mellow fruit of a society which has walked hand-in-hand with tradition and culture; they are hard nuts, which have grown and ripened as they could. When they talk among themselves, I seem to hear the cracking of the shells.

Then, with enthusiasm:

If the men are remarkable, the ladies are wonderful. Saratoga is famous, I believe, as the place of all places in America where women adorn themselves most, or as the place, at least, where the greatest amount of dressing may be seen by the greatest number of people . . . Every woman you meet, young or old, is attired with a certain amount of richness, and with whatever good taste may be compatible with such a mode of life. You behold an interesting, indeed a quite momentous spectacle; the democratization of elegance. If I am to believe what I hear—in fact, I may say what I overhear—many of these sumptuous persons have enjoyed neither the advantages of a careful education nor the privileges of an introduction to society. She walks more or less of a queen, however, each unitiated nobody.

James noted with pleased surprise that quite often in their dress the ladies at the Spa displayed an instinct for elegance, for what the French called "chic." Not infrequently, this resulted in a figure so exquisite it

The Union dining room was a vast hall in which 1,000 guests were served at one time (400 more were accommodated in an auxiliary dining room on the north piazza) by 100 waiters.

seemed shameful that it should have, in Saratoga, "so vulgar a setting"; until, on second thought, even this struck him as a welcome change from Europe's "dreary social order in which privacy was the presiding genius and women arrayed themselves for the appreciation of the few." Still, it saddened him that the daily public display was so ungratifying to the performers . . .

that these conspicuous élégantes adorn themselves, socially speaking, to so little purpose. To dress for every one is, practically, to dress for no one. There are few prettier sights than a charmingly-dressed woman, gracefully established in some shady spot, with a piece of needlework or embroidery, or a book. Nothing very serious is accomplished, probably, but an aesthetic principle is recognized. The embroidery and the book are a tribute to culture . . . But here at Saratoga, at any hour of morning or evening, you may see a hundred rustling beauties whose rustle is their sole occupation. One lady in particular there is, with whom it appears to be an inexorable fate that she shall be nothing more than dressed . . . every evening for a fortnight she has revealed herself as a fresh creation. She, especially, has struck me as a person dressed beyond her life and her opportunities . . . her beautiful hands folded in her silken lap, her head drooping slightly beneath the weight of her *chignon,* her lips parted in a vague contemplative gaze . . . her husband beside her reading the New York *Herald.*

The author was similarly affected by the sight of couples who were isolated from Saratoga's social whirl. They were proud little islands in a busy sea of activity; people who had money, finery and expensive accouterments but lacked friends at the Spa, and so were left to themselves in lonely grandeur. He wrote:

Women, of course, are the most helpless victims of this cruel situation, although it must be said that they befriend each other with a generosity for which we hardly give them credit. I have seen women, for instance, at various "hops," approach their lonely sisters and invite them to waltz, and I have seen the fair invited surrender themselves eagerly to this humiliating embrace. Gentlemen at Saratoga are at a much higher premium than at European watering-places. It is an old story that in this country we have no "leisure-class"—the class from which the Saratogas of Europe recruit a large number of their male frequenters.

The role played by children in the resort's social life seemed to James another instance of "the wholesale equalization of the various social atoms which is the distinctive feature of collective Saratoga." Not only did the youngsters mix freely with the adults, he noted, but they took part in the latter's diversions and entertainments, and indeed, with "unfaltering paces," usually opened the hops. "You meet them far into the evening," he wrote, "roaming over the piazzas and corridors of the hotels—the little girls especially—lean, pale, formidable. Occasionally childhood confesses itself, even when maternity resists, and you see at eleven o'clock at night some poor little bedizened precocity collapsed in slumber in a lonely wayside chair."

Young James followed his stay at the Springs with a visit to Newport, the Rhode Island resort which was closely contesting Saratoga's position as society's favorite summer haven, and there among "the villas, the beautiful idle women, the beautiful idle men, the brilliant pleasure-fraught days and evenings" found a European-flavored atmosphere in which he could feel at ease. Five years previously *Godey's Lady's Book,* indignant at the fashionable use of mascara by the ladies of Saratoga and Newport, had paired the two resorts as "the Sodom and Gomorrah of our Union." James saw little resemblance between them whatsoever. "There is, indeed, in all things a striking difference in tone and aspect between these two great centres of pleasure," he wrote. And continued:

> After Saratoga, Newport seems really substantial and civilized. Aesthetically speaking, you may remain at Newport with a fairly good conscience; at Saratoga you linger under passionate protest. At Newport life is public, if you will; at Saratoga it is absolutely common. The difference, in a word, is the difference between a group of undiscriminating hotels and a series of organized homes. Saratoga perhaps deserves our greater homage, as being characteristically democratic and American; let us, then, make Saratoga the heaven of our aspiration, but let us yet a while content ourselves with Newport as the lowly earth of our residence.*

Five years after rendering these judgments, Henry James settled in Europe permanently. Time, distance and his experiences abroad matured his perspective and made him much more favorably disposed to America's burgeoning "vulgar" democracy, of which Saratoga was so splendidly accurate a cross section. In 1903, when he was sixty, James wrote to a friend, "Europe has ceased to be romantic to me, and my own country, in the evenings of my days, has become so." The next year he returned to his homeland and wrote a fresh appraisal of it. While still critical, his observations on the new American breed of society were suffused with understanding and affection.

* In preferring Newport to Saratoga, Henry James stood virtually alone among commentators on the American social scene. The popular view was upheld by such voices of opinion as *Harper's Weekly,* which said: "Saratoga reflects our national traits to a degree not true of Newport. The latter has an air of aristocratic exclusion and leisure far less lively than that engendered by the commingling of classes at Saratoga. Beyond any other American resort, Saratoga is a social microcosm."

The new opera house was opened on July 4, 1865, when General Ulysses S. Grant was the guest of honor at a military ball.

By no means as imposing as the Union or Saratoga's other mammoth hotels, the picturesque Clarendon nevertheless attracted its share of the Spa's elite (one frequent guest was the popular poet, John Godfrey Saxe).

The approach of summer was a nationwide signal for holiday preparations, which, in the words of *Leslie's Weekly,* meant "packing that indispensable traveling companion, the Saratoga Trunk, with Saratoggery." These three drawings, published in 1873, reflect both the preparation and the anticipation that invariably accompanied spring. The first, from *Leslie's,* shows "three open-mouthed monsters of summer campaigns, waiting for the gems of summer attire to be buried within them." *Harper's Weekly* pictured a pensive belle with her Saratoga Trunks packed ("Prepared for the Campaign—a Reverie of the Coming Summer," said the caption) and stepping out, as from an Easter egg, in her most elegant finery at the resort of her choice.

For most fashionable belles in the early 1870's, Saratoga was first on the list of preferences. Here a few make some last-minute adjustments in the ladies' parlor of the Union Hotel before starting for the races.

An artist's comments on the trends in feminine fashion of the period and what might be expected in the future.

Charles H. Hutchins

The Grecian Bend, a popular ballroom-walk of the day, was introduced Saratoga by Celia Wall—an aunt of Berry Wall, who would make an arre ing impression on the Spa some years later. As this songsheet portrait of h suggests, the Grecian Bend was at least partly the result of an attempt balance the bustle.

In the late '70s, Congress Spring boasted a new pavilion. "The new Fountain Hall is a thing of beauty," wrote an admirer. "Its walls are fretted and arabesqued, and inlaid and dadoed after the most aesthetic fashion. Stained glass windows pour floods of varied rainbow hues on the tiled floor; the counters make one feel as if the elbows were specially constructed for leaning upon them; tables and chairs of elaborate pattern are scattered here and there, while baskets of flowers hang suspended from every available carved beam in the groined roof. Everybody comes here to drain what Artemus Ward called 'the flowin' bole,' the water being drawn by elaborate pulleys from the well and served up *au naturel*. This is the very refinement of health-imbibing."

Although the Congress waters were the most famous and the most favored, Saratoga's other mineral fountains attracted their own loyal following.

High Rock Spring.

High Rock Spring (interior view).

Columbian Spring.

Hamilton Spring.

Pavilion Spring.

Red Spring.

Empire
Spring.

Triton Spring.

Excelsior
Spring.

Saratoga Star
Spring.

Geyser Spring.

Glacier Spring.

Congress Spring
(interior view).

Not long after it felt the sting of young James' acidulous portrait in *The Nation,* Saratoga's spirits were revived by a devoted and extraordinarily wealthy summer guest who promised to provide the Spa with the largest and most lavish hotel in the world. The immensity and extravagance proposed were such that, should he ever return, Henry James would have to find a new word to describe it; "monster" would be inadequate.

Alexander Turney Stewart was an undersized Scotch-Irish immigrant who had wooed the American dream with Irish laces and been rewarded in his fifty-ninth year, in New York City, with the world's largest retail store (after his death, it would eventually be sold to John Wanamaker). In 1872 he bought the Union Hotel for $532,000, changed its name to the Grand Union and spent an additional half million dollars enlarging and furnishing it. In 1874, when it was ready to receive visitors, it was everything Stewart had promised.

Its elaborate, five-story brick contour flowed over seven acres, facing Broadway for 450 feet and then folding back in two wings each nearly a quarter of a mile long. Between the wings lay elm-shaded, landscaped gardens. There were 824 guest rooms, all of them spacious and many of them suites to accommodate families, a dining room capable of serving 1400 guests at a sitting, a mile of piazzas (including a spacious piazza overlooking the gardens), two miles of corridors, twelve acres of carpeting and an acre of marble apportioned between the tiled lobby and ballrooms and marble-topped bureaus in the bedrooms. Crystal chandeliers glittered over the guests while they dined and danced, black walnut staircases and a steam-engine elevator installed by the Otis brothers carried them from floor to floor, and if one could afford the best one could retire to the splendid privacy and solid comfort of a mahogany cottage suite.

The most striking decoration was one which came to rest in the main ballroom of the Grand Union almost by accident. In 1870 Stewart had commissioned a painting from a French artist, Adolph Yvon, which he planned to hang in his Fifth Avenue mansion. When it was completed two years later the price, $110,000, seemed in proportion but the size of the work was so out-of-hand, 18 by 29½ feet, that Stewart could find no place in his mansion big enough to accommodate it. And so he had shipped the painting to his new hotel, where it covered the entire west wall of the ballroom from floor to ceiling. Owner and guests viewed it with pride. Entitled *The Genius of America,* it depicted the richly endowed young nation as a lush Amazonian beauty dispensing largesse to the world from a horn of plenty.

At the same time that Stewart went to work on the Union Hotel, a new, grandiloquent United States Hotel began to rise from the seven-year ashes of its predecessor and opened in the summer of 1874. It too was a million-dollar ode to the mid-Victorian mode.

U-shaped, as was the Grand Union, and encompassing another seven choice acres, the five-story brick United States confronted Broadway for

233 feet and then winged back for an eighth of a mile on one side and somewhat less on the other, almost completely enclosing a pretty three-acre park where arching elms spread their foliage over a bandstand. There were 768 guest rooms and an abundant supply of cottage suites; all were equipped with marble washstands and cold running water (hot water had to be ordered and was brought by a chambermaid in a covered container), but only the suites could offer a private bath.

The decor was pretty much the same in all the visiting quarters regardless of the rental fee: elaborately carved black walnut furniture, heavily-flowered carpets, thick Brussels lace curtains festooned over the tall windows—and the inevitable coil of knotted rope, one end firmly stapled to the wall, which in all Saratoga hotels was the fire escape, and which practical-minded ladies with insufficient closet space stretched across the room and used as a clothes-hanger.

The United States could boast too of a superbly appointed drawing room, ballroom and dining room, which could seat a thousand guests, and in the vast cellar was a large wine chamber and a still larger meat chamber. Before each social season Saratoga's farmers would drive herds of cattle and sheep into the cellar, where they would be slaughtered and the meat stored for the kitchen.

At both of the Spa's magnificent hotels mid-afternoon dinner was a major event of the day. "Breakfast had pretty thoroughly covered the field of comestibles,* and what was called a 'light luncheon' but was a good-sized meal was served early for the racing public," wrote a guest years later with sweet remembrance, "but dinner was a challenge to longevity. There were eight courses of many choices—all bountiful and extravagant. It endured for two hours, and after dinner the hotel was engulfed in contented lethargy."

Two hundred and fifty Negro waiters attended the guests in the dining room of the Grand Union and almost as many served at the United States, and at each hotel an aging Negro headwaiter ruled with aloof authority and overpowering panoply. "He will, in an extraordinary emergency, hand a lady a spoon or, with his own hand, will replenish her cup; but seldom will he drop from his lofty range of thought to perform these slender services for a man," reminisced Joseph Smith, head usher at the United States. Table waiters were not easily intimidated either, as illustrated by a verbal exchange Smith overheard between a ruffled guest and his unruffled attendant:

"Waiter, didn't I give you a dollar when I came in?"

"Yes, sir."

"And yet you've kept me waiting here nearly three quarters of an hour."

* A typical breakfast served at the Grand Union and the United States began with cereal and progressed through fish, omelet, griddle cakes, a choice of cutlet or chop, cold ham or beef, fried potatoes and chocolate, coffee or tea.

Charles H. Hutchins

Charles H. Hutchins

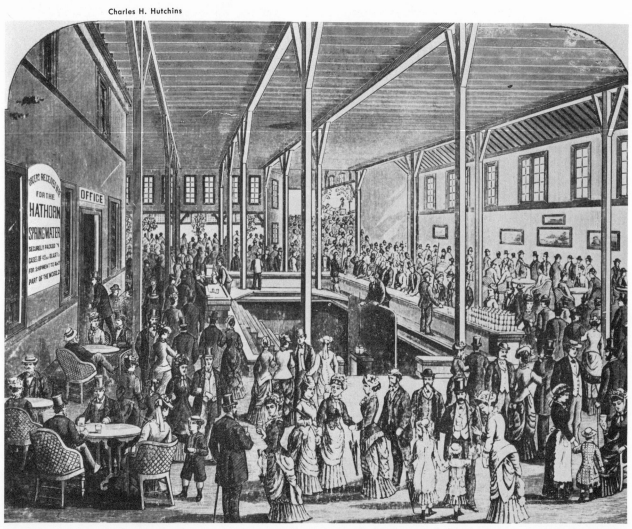

orn Spring, a latecomer to the Spa, was particularly well patronized. It possessed ater abundance of minerals than any other Saratoga water. Discovered by work in 1866 while digging a foundation for the ballroom of the new Congress Hall original hotel, built by the Putnams, had been destroyed by fire), the spring was d for the hotel proprietor, Henry H. Hathorn.

In 1870, seeing Saratoga for the first time, Henry James criticized the resort's architecture—and indeed it was a fussy panoply of turrets, towers, balconies, bays and other architectural frosting mainly borrowed from popular European styles. The fanciful and frequently ostentatious extravagance of Saratoga's homes and hotels, however (as James perhaps knew, but didn't say), was an index of not just Saratoga's character but of the exuberant and expansive personality of post-Civil War American society as a whole. Discarding the simplicity of the Greek Revival style, which had dominated American architectural taste until 1840, Saratoga, along with the rest of the country, had embraced a variety of flamboyant fixtures exhibited by French chateaux, Swiss chalets, Italian villas and the like which seemed to better express the young nation's rapidly mounting wealth and confident mood; during the lush Victorian era it easily persuaded itself that ornament and design were identical. The following five sketches show that Saratoga's architectural extravagance was in keeping with the florid style of New York City's famed Vanderbilt mansions, completed in 1880, and New York *Herald* publisher James Gordon Bennett's much-admired villa on Washington Heights overlooking the Hudson River.

George Sherman's residence.

Mrs. G. R. Putnam's residence.

Charles Reed's residence.

The Medical Institute.

Seymour Ainsworth's residence.

The Vanderbilt mansions. Top: William Henry Vanderbilt's sumptuous home consisted of two houses (one occupied by Vanderbilt and his wife, the other by their two married daughters) and by at least one commentator was considered "an edifice that would not look out of place among the *palazzi* in northern Italy." Bottom left: William K. Vanderbilt's home was a mixture of French chateau styles. Bottom right: Cornelius Vanderbilt II's richly carved mansion with its projecting round towers owed its design to the Dutch Renaissance.

By 1875 a swarm of Eastern resorts beckoned to holiday seekers—Long Branch, Cape May, a plethora of summer havens in the Catskills, the Berkshires and elsewhere—but only Newport, "the feted, petted and caressed," seriously challenged Saratoga's claim to supremacy. Pinpointing the principal difference between them, *Harper's* noted: "The society at Newport is severely exclusive. Everybody knows everybody else, and outside that charmed circle the casual visitor is a pariah." And *Leslie's*: "The hotels of Saratoga are perfect villages. Unlike Newport, where the most fashionable seek a residence in cottages, here they all reside at the hotels." These vignettes of fashionable life at Newport appeared in an 1877 issue of *Leslie's* and were captioned as follows: 1. Arrival of summer cottagers at the hotel on a hop evening; 2. Afternoon scene on Bellevue Avenue Drive; 3. The old stone mill, a favorite retreat of children; 4. A cozy chat on the beach; 5. A morning airing on the beach; 6. An afternoon game of polo at the Westchester Club.

"Yes, sir. I did that, sir, to show you that I couldn't be bribed, sir."

A distinguished feature of the United States was a thirty-foot-wide veranda overlooking Broadway. It swept full across the face of the hotel, with twelve ornamented wooden pillars soaring fifty feet to flower into a veritable jungle of Victorian scrollwork which supported a roof. The piazza facing the park was but a slightly smaller version of the one in front, the two porches combined extending over more than an acre. On them stood a thousand wicker rocking chairs (supplied by Alexander T. Stewart's department store, which had placed them on the Grand Union piazzas as well) which in company with the waters, the races, the gaming and the Spa's three social worlds—the *haut monde, beau monde* and *demimonde*—were to make Saratoga a national word. For the majority of Americans, a front porch and a rocking chair were indispensable props of an active social life, affording an eyeful and an earful of all the goings-on about town. But the porches they were used to in no way prepared the Spa's provincial guests for the vast verandas of the hotels, stretching as far as the eye could reach, or for the spectacle of hundreds of people gossiping, reading, sipping fruit ices or watching the parade of passersby on Broadway while they rocked in the wicker rocking chairs and the diamonds they wore sparkled in the sunlight. This was front-porch life without peer.

Diamonds were a badge of distinction—the bigger and bolder the more deserving the wearer of recognition and esteem, their popularity implied. Tiffany's established a branch at the Springs and other famous dealers in fine jewels followed suit. As time went on and America distributed its wealth with increasingly munificent gestures, more and more visitors to Saratoga wore diamonds who had never worn them before. Joseph Smith, in his diary, took note of a few. The horny hand in which a tall Texan held a glass of spring water was adorned with three diamond rings, and a diamond-and-sapphire pin gleamed from his white satin tie, loosely knotted to show the immense solitaire which served as a collar button. On another page he observed:

> A Mrs. Blood from Boston had a whole fortune in diamonds upon her at the last hop. Among her jewels was a necklace of great solitaires which clasped the white marble of her neck like balls of fire. She had a great diamond star on her head and her hands fairly blazed with rings set with precious stones. A very pretty blonde girl wears two earrings as big around as a silver quarter, formed by a wide circular band of diamonds. There are pearls and diamonds in such quantity as would put the fabled riches of Croesus to shame.

More substantial evidence of wealth than a dazzling display of gems was necessary, however, for one to win entree to the elite circle which casually claimed the north piazza of the United States Hotel. This was the retreat of the very rich, men who used at least seven ciphers in the figures which represented their worth. Lacking this sum, one had to be content with gaping to see if Jay Gould, J. Pierpont Morgan, John D. Rockefeller and other titans looked as colossally wealthy as they were.

Nieces,
cousins
and secretaries

In deference to the rich, who often brought their families and servants to the Spa for the entire summer, the United States had allotted the shorter of its two wings to cottage suites. These had originated in the 1820's, when the larger hotels had tucked a few actual cottages in the rear to accommodate an overflow of guests. Over the years their seclusion had made them so popular that both the Grand Union and the United States had included in their blueprints apartment suites which would offer cottage privacy with the solicitude and service of an elegant hotel. They were everything their proprietors claimed. At the United States each elaborate suite contained a large parlor, one to seven bedrooms and a private bath. Visitors were announced by card, carriages were brought directly to the door and, if desired, breakfast, luncheon or dinner was delivered to the occupants in their suite or on the apartment's porch.

The seclusion, size and superior comforts of the cottage suites inevitably attracted loving couples of the sort a respectable family gathering was not apt to include. Since their intimacies were discreet, neither the hotel managers nor the village trustees were unduly disturbed. Indeed, by looking the other way, which they resolutely did, love in the cottages could be viewed as the best solution to an ever-nagging problem.

Each summer's invasion of the Spa brought a number of wealthy bachelors, and family men with wives and children vacationing in Europe, who relished a delectable liaison as a nightcap to a day of betting on the horses and gaming at the Club House. Prior to the cottage suites, their arrival had produced a difficult dilemma all around. Rich sporting bloods disdained the local brothels and the village fathers resisted attempts to introduce bordellos lushly appointed to their tastes, a stand-off which tried the patience of a good many free-spending guests and aroused concern among the natives that they might abandon the Spa and transfer their largesse to a more hospitable resort. In the face of this voluble discontent the pillars of the community stood firm. Fashionable bordellos were inimical to Saratoga's best interests and would not be allowed, the trustees ruled.

There was nothing the authorities could do to prevent ladies of the evening from socializing at the Springs, however, and many did. At the start of each season Grace Sinclair, Hattie Adams and other renowned madams installed their most beguiling nymphs in well-provisioned mansions where they presided nightly at "open house." During the day the girls were displayed at watering place, race track, casino and lake. To male eyes there was none so tantalizing a sight as the madams' fairest flowers passing by in the carriage parade, each cluster perched atop a fancy coach and smil-

Alexander T. Stewart owned the world's largest retail store. In 1872 he purchased the Union Hotel, renamed it the Grand Union, and enlarged and improved it until it was the world's largest and most lavish lodging house.

The most dramatic change in the Union transformed the hotel's interior court. A new wing was added and the gardens were rearranged with greater elegance.

The billiard hall was reserved for the amusement of gentlemen only.

Ladies and gentlemen both highly enjoyed the Grand Union's new main ballroom. Crystal chandeliers hung from the ceiling and one whole wall was devoted to a 3,000-pound allegorical painting by Adolph Yvon which was called *The Genius of America.*

In August 1879, the year in which Edison produced the first commercially practical incandescent lamp, the Grand Union introduced the wondrous electric light to the Spa. Part of the lawn of the hotel's interior court was laid with a dance floor, the trees were festooned with Chinese lanterns, and above all—"like an opal star"—was suspended an electric lamp, "shedding a white radiance on the dancers." As the smaller drawing shows, the lamp was occasionally lowered for the inspection of tourists.

Leslie's Weekly, New York Public Library

At the same time that the Union Hotel was given a grandiose new look, a bigger and better United States Hotel replaced Elias Benedict's original guest house—destroyed by fire. On arriving at the United States during the summer of 1874, the new hotel's first season, patrons were ushered into a spacious lobby tiled with white marble.

In the rear an elm-shaded, th
acre park, enclosed by the hote
three sides, afforded guests a t
quil respite from Saratoga's b
regimen.

Along with the medicinal waters, promenades, racing and gambling, Saratoga provided its summer vacationists with a steady diet of music. Each major hotel held three con-certs a day, in the morning, afternoon and evening. Here, on the United States piazza, guests lend an ear to a morning concert.

The new United States viewed from Broadway. The continuous
length of the hotel was more than a quarter of a mile.

ing fetchingly from beneath picture hats and parasols. But in obedience to the law a provocative glance, a smile or a wink, a shapely ankle peeking from beneath a cloud of petticoats were as much as the girls were permitted to offer. The purpose of the month-long visit was simply to advertise the merchandise. When the season was over and madams and maidens returned to their houses in New York City, Boston, Philadelphia and other metropolises, they could be sure that a good many admiring gentlemen who had been provided with their addresses would not be far behind.

To the authorities' dismay, the presence of such an agreeable but inaccessible clutch of femininity further strained the patience of the Spa's unattached males and made them more difficult to deal with. The problem weighed most heavily on Saratoga's hotels. All had cast themselves on the side of the angels, and the Grand Union and the United States had constituted themselves the resort's main fortresses of propriety. Both kept their lobbies clear of girls on the prowl and refused to register couples who gave the barest hint of being unwed. Now and then, for a prized guest, the rules were relaxed. White Hat McCarty, so named for the Texas-style headgear he was addicted to, had used his knowledge of horses to speedily accumulate several million dollars and, since he just as speedily spent them, was courted everywhere at the Spa. Following the famous dandy, Berry Wall, and his manservant to the register of the United States one day, he studied the elegant entry, *Wall and valet,* looked at the nubile bit of baggage he had brought with him, and wrote, *McCarty and valise.* Both he and his companion were admitted.

In the late hours stronger measures were adopted to prevent ladies of easy virtue from plying their trade in the hotels. At eleven o'clock every entrance to the Grand Union and the United States was locked except the main one, and throughout the night this was guarded by a muscular detective while his assistants patrolled the long piazzas to stop bolder or more determined types from climbing through the windows.

By tacit agreement the cottages were free of restrictions and surveillance; they were off by themselves, independent of one another, and the price of a cottage suite (as much as $125 a day) gave assurances that the amorous pairs who dallied there would be well-behaved and inconspicuous. The latter proved to be not altogether true. Some wealthy indoor sportsmen found the arrangement so much to their liking that they stocked the larger suites with a variety of young and beautiful nieces, while younger bloods turned up with a bevy of stunning cousins. An oil millionaire was so swamped in business deals that he installed five pretty secretaries in his cottage apartment to help extricate him. Few were fooled by these fictions, but they were carried on so circumspectly they were easy to overlook.

And so, in the hotel cottages, illicit love found a home. As before, the village fathers frowned their disapproval of the sinful goings-on, but lacking a more attractive solution to the problem were content to leave well enough alone.

Chapter Four

The
exhibitionists

The end of the Civil War marked the beginning of what one observer called the "Augustan Age of American Clownery." Postwar prosperity set the stage and sudden millionaires who had struck it rich in oil, copper, silver and other bonanza soil strutted before the footlights with a shattering absence of self consciousness. Politicians, profiteers, sportsmen, social aristocrats and social climbers contributed to the gaudy pageant. It was to be expected that the star performers would be attracted to the nation's liveliest summer resort, and many were. They were more than balanced, however, by guests who were colorful or comic with no loss of dignity, and some who were quietly dramatic.

Somewhat obliquely the war itself produced one of the most noteworthy bits of buffoonery at the Springs. After Lee's surrender, famous regiments of the Grand Army of the Republic were kept busy touring the country and enjoying its grateful hospitality, and in 1869 Colonel Emmons Clark and the renowned Seventh Regiment, fifteen hundred strong, were the guests of the Spa for an August week end. The whole town had prepared for their coming and everyone turned out to see them march in, lining the streets, cheering and waving flags. Deeply appreciative of the reception, and the entertaining round of race track, Club House and lake activities that followed, Colonel Clark invited the village and its summer visitors to be his guests at a demonstration to be staged on the Saratoga battlefield. A bright young captain of Light Artillery had devised an ingenious way of wiping out a unit of enemy troops on the march, he explained, and the regiment was going to put it to the test.

It promised to be a spectacle in which history would be made, and hundreds came to watch. An imaginary road was marked out and several barrels were placed on it to represent the advancing troops. A fair distance away, two cannons were positioned in the enemy's path, each with a ball in its barrel and a hundred feet of chain attached to the ball. Fastened to every other link in the chain was a smaller ball.

At last, all was ready. Regiment and spectators stood behind the cannons, out of harm's way. At a signal, both gun crews fired. One cannon jammed, the other went off with a frightening report. Its necklace of balls and chain shot high into the air, then spun around with the snap of a whip and whirled toward the crowd with the apparent intention of flaying everyone in it. Miraculously, no one was struck as it fell to earth two hundred feet in the wrong direction.

The next day, not a bit downcast, the regiment marched out again, carrying the balls and chains on their shoulders and singing *While We Were Marching Through Georgia.*

No such threat to life and limb attended the visits of Colonel James Fisk, Jr., and New York's Ninth National Guard Regiment. Having made a fortune as a war profiteer, Fisk was above the battle and owed his colonelcy to the fact that he had financed the regiment and outfitted it and its brass-blaring, drum-thumping band in splendid regalia. It pleased him to strut ahead of the gaudy, noisy assembly along Saratoga's streets, but although they made quite a sight another parading exhibitionist marched off with the honors.

As a seven-year-old orphan, John W. Steele had attracted the eye of a Pennsylvania farmer, who had adopted him and later died leaving him an estate which was found to be steeped in oil. The young millionaire had set out to spend his inheritance as fast as his wells brought it in, and in the process won for himself an admiring sobriquet, Coal Oil Johnny.

His method of reaching the Springs was fairly original. To make the journey amusing he hired a minstrel show and installed it in a special train. Along the way he acquired an elaborately uniformed Negro band, and when the train rattled into the Saratoga depot the eye-filling entourage fell in behind their benefactor while the band played *Coal Oil Johnny Was His Name.*

At the Club House, young Johnny displayed the same cheerful abandon. After losing $10,000 to Old Smoke in a poker game, he tossed another $10,000 on the table and invited everybody within earshot to help drink it down.

Nevertheless, for unabashed glitter and extravagance, Jim Fisk was without a peer. In his youth he had been a carnival barker and in the course of this employment he came to view life itself as a circus—a notion he soon put to work by moving into the center ring of the world of finance and dazzling his rivals with virtuoso performances. Speedily enriching himself during the war as a dealer in contraband Southern cotton, Fisk found the unbridled laissez-faire period that followed altogether suited to his amoral sense of adventure. In 1868 with two others of similar taste, Jay Gould (at thirty-two just a year younger than Fisk) and Daniel Drew, he stole the Erie Railroad from Commodore Cornelius Vanderbilt, and in partnership with Gould set out to plunder it. The next year he teamed with Gould again in an attempt to corner the gold market. The scheme failed,

Saratoga's summer guests came from all over the country and were a colorful mixture of almost every kind of people. In 1869 New York's Seventh Regiment spent a weekend at the Spa and was honored with a regimental ball at the Union Hotel.

James Fisk, Jr., pictured in a cartoon from *Punchinello*, frequently arrived in uniform at the head of the New York division of the National Guard.

precipitating a panic in Wall Street (Black Friday) and paralyzing the country's economy, but Fisk and Gould made millions even so.

Much as these and other stunningly unprincipled exploits did to make Fisk anathema to people of distinction summering at the Springs, his personal ostentation offended them more. His pomaded reddish-yellow hair flaring at the temples in kiss curls, his mustache waxed to dagger-points, his perfume, his fancy suits and the huge diamonds which blazed from his shirtfront and fingers were too ridiculous to ignore, yet they were better overlooked as Fisk was too powerful to antagonize. On top of it all he was gross, vulgar and supremely gifted at calling attention to himself in every worst way.

His most flagrant transgression was his affair with Josie Mansfield, a romance he proudly displayed at the Spa. Other millionaires endeavored to keep their mistresses a secret, but Fisk, although he had a wife in Boston, had openly established Josie in a fine four-story New York City brownstone, given her a carriage and coachman, dressed her in costly gowns and jewels, and delighted in showing her off.

It had to be admitted in his favor that she would have been hard to keep under cover in any event. Helen Josephine Mansfield in her twenties had large, expressive, black-lashed eyes, a luxuriant length of black hair worn in massive coils over a delicately shaped head, a full and dashing figure and an air of soft innocence. She had aspired to be an actress with conspicuous unsuccess and was wavering between the prospect of poverty or prostitution when Fisk came to her rescue. It was an act of Samaritanism that eventually led to his downfall.

In the summer of 1869 Fisk introduced Josie to Edward Stiles Stokes, with whom he had formed a business partnership. Ned Stokes was the son of wealthy and socially prominent New Yorkers, had married well, but was ever in difficulties due to his propensity for playing, and losing, large sums at gaming houses and race tracks, both of which drew him frequently to Saratoga. To accommodate his creditors he repeatedly dipped into the partnership's funds; and after a series of visits to the brownstone, he appropriated his partner's mistress.

To almost everyone but Fisk it seemed a natural consequence of his monumental mistake in judgment. Stokes was several years younger than Fisk, awesomely handsome where Fisk was short and fat, and a fashion plate of impeccable taste. Josie surrendered herself to him gladly, and after a noisy interim of public charges and countercharges all three took their injured feelings to court.

Fisk took the scandal in stride, but his co-owner of the Erie, Jay Gould, quailed before the lurid publicity. Fully as unscrupulous as Fisk in business matters, in his private life the little black-bearded man was a paragon of virtue, devoted to home and church. At Saratoga, which he visited every summer, he sometimes climaxed a day spent in telegraphing orders to Wall Street with a request to the hotel band to play *Lead, Kindly Light—*

whether by design or simply because he liked it, no one could be sure. In December 1871, Gould forced Fisk to resign as vice-president of the Erie and on January 6, 1872, the falling titan was dealt a final blow: Ned Stokes shot him dead.

Although he was clearly guilty of murder, Stokes was let off with a light prison sentence. At that he was less fortunate than another acquitted assassin with whom he was frequently seen at Saratoga. In 1859, in Washington, D.C., Congressman Daniel E. Sickles had shot and killed his wife's lover, Philip Barton Key, son of the author of *The Star-Spangled Banner,* for "defiling" his marriage bed, and had gone scot-free. Retribution of a sort, perhaps, had been exacted at Gettysburg, when Confederate marksmanship had parted Sickles from his right leg while he was commanding the Third Corps. The loss hadn't interfered with his career, however. He had served as Minister to Spain, was now a power in New York politics, and would go on to a new term in Congress. At Saratoga he cut a jaunty if aging figure of heroism, brandishing his crutch as if it were a medal.

Dr. Dowd and Mr. Travers   The antics of visiting celebrities added another touch of piquancy to the Spa's already flavorous reputation and thus were good for business, for which Saratoga was grateful. More valid and more permanent claims to fame, however, were provided by residents and guests who gave the resort a touch of renown without personal fanfare, and of these Saratoga was quietly proud.

Dr. Charles F. Dowd arrived at the Springs in 1868 and purchased Temple Grove Seminary, which had been notably unsuccessful in the dozen years since it had been built. He at once converted it into an attractive and respected select school for young ladies (later Lucy Skidmore Scribner was to found Skidmore College on the same site) and devoted his leisure to the fulfillment of a long-cherished dream: a uniform and orderly time system in the United States.

Most American communities set their clocks at noon by the position of the sun over the town hall, a custom that kept country-wide travellers busy adjusting their watches. Dr. Dowd theorized that life in America would be a lot simpler if time was arbitrarily advanced by one hour at each meridian west of Greenwich, England. Some eight thousand computations seemed to prove his point, and he recommended that the country be divided into four time zones based on every fifteen degrees of longitude, the zones to be called Eastern, Central, Mountain and Pacific. For twelve years no one was inclined to accept his view. Then the railroads, weary of trying to disentangle confused travel schedules which had trains running on fifty-three different times, endorsed the change—and at noon on November 18, 1883, Standard Time, the uniform system Dr. Dowd had developed after classes at his Saratoga seminary, was adopted throughout the nation.

Fisk's favorite portrait of himself was this 1870 sketch in *Wild Oats*.

Although he was married, Fisk proudly exhibited his mistress, generously proportioned Josie Mansfield, at the Spa.

This solemn portrait of Fisk, showing him with his original bushy mustache (he waxed and twirled it to needlepoints after he met Josie), was published after his death in 1872. He was shot by Ned Stokes (right), who had replaced him in Josie's affections.

Jay Gould was a seasonal regular at the resort.

William R. Travers gave his name to Saratoga's famous
Travers Stakes.

Among the famous families who summered at the Springs was the Vanderbilt clan. Cornelius II and William K. Vanderbilt were the old Commodore's grandsons.

On the north piazza of the United States Hotel, a clutch of millionaires gathered around William Henry Vanderbilt (center), made million-dollar deals and t information that might later shock the market with seismic tremors.

William R. Travers also brought laurels to the Spa. Largely due to his initiative the now oldest race track in the United States was placed at Saratoga, and on its spanking new turf he introduced and gave his name to the nation's now oldest stakes race. Both earned the patronage and gratitude of the fast-growing horse society, but no less pleasing to Saratogans who knew him was the wealthy socialite, clubman and *bon vivant* himself, for Travers' wit was widely quoted and seemed all the more pointed because he stammered.

Best remembered and most repeated was his reaction on being shown a splendid array of yachts at Newport, almost all of which were owned by Wall Street brokers. "Wh-wh-where," he inquired, "are the c-c-customers' y-yachts?"

Passing by New York City's exclusive Union Club with an acquaintance, Travers was asked if all the men who sat in chairs at the great windows were actually habitués of the club. "N-n-no," he replied, "s-some are s-s-sons of h-habitués."

Again in Manhattan he ran into an old friend from Baltimore and engaged him in conversation. The other expressed his concern at Travers' difficulty in getting his words out. "You seem to stutter more in New York than you did in Baltimore," he said sympathetically. "B-b-bigger p-place," said Travers.

On Wall Street, a companion called his attention to a disagreeable odor. "P-p-perhaps," Travers told him, "they've taken the l-lid off the Chamber of C-c-commerce."

In Saratoga one summer, strolling along Broadway with Berry Wall, he met a lady with whom he was acquainted coming from Congress Spring, famous for its cathartic qualities.

"Lovely water," she said. "I've just had four glasses."

Travers hastily lifted his hat. "T-then, M-m-madame," he stuttered, "p-p-pray do not let us d-detain you."

"What is your yearly income, Mr. Twombly?"

Of the distinguished families that frequented the Springs during the postwar years none was more colorful or more intriguing than the Vanderbilts. The founder of the clan, proud and profane Cornelius Vanderbilt I, had long been a faithful visitor and favored the races and whist tables with the same fierce will to win that had made him the richest man in America. The old Commodore, a title to which he had laid claim after using a Staten Island ferryboat to spawn a fleet of steamships, had sired twelve children by his first marriage. Nevertheless, in 1867, when he was a snowy-haired but erect seventy-three, he brought a Mobile, Alabama, belle to Saratoga as his bride—proof, though none was needed, that he had also retained his eye for youth and beauty.

190 &

In the summer of 1877 a Western Union clerk, Hamilton McK. Twombly, confronted William Henry Vanderbilt at the Spa and asked for his permission to marry his daughter, Florence. The nuptials took place in November in New York City's fashionable St. Bartholomew's Church. "Miss Vanderbilt's toilet was simply exquisite," a society reporter wrote, "a veritable poem of sheening satin, rustling brocade, fairy lace, and, oh, such orange blossoms!" The Twomblys are shown leaving the altar after the ceremony—"the fair young bride leaning proudly upon the arm of her jubilant lord"—followed by the bride's parents.

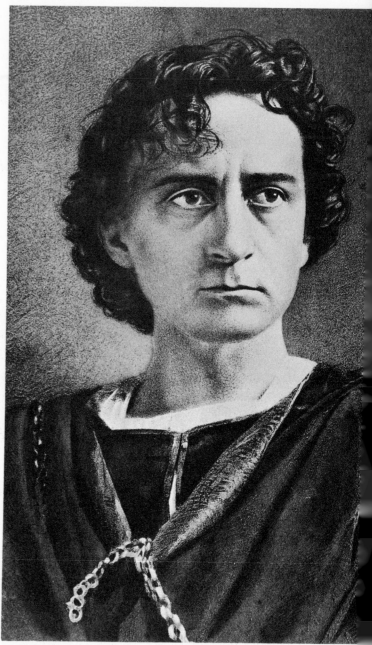

BRADLEY & RULOFSON.   SAN FRANCISCO.

Edwin Booth frequently went to Saratoga to rest after a tour as Hamlet. The photo at left was, he wrote the photographer, the best portrait of him he had ever seen.

Ill and in debt, Ulysses S. Grant went to Mount McGregor in the summer of 1885 to finish writing his *Memoirs,* which he hoped would at least partly restore his fame and fortune. Sightseers from nearby Saratoga trooped out for a glimpse of the old war hero. This drawing was made from a photograph taken a few weeks before Grant died.

Eight years later young William Kissam Vanderbilt, following his grandfather's example, married another Mobile nymph, Alva Smith, daughter of a cotton planter, and set out to honeymoon at the Spa. A special train was turned over to the loving couple and given the right of way over all other trains travelling from New York City to Saratoga on the Vanderbilt-controlled New York Central Railroad.

Neither the original Vanderbilts nor their progenies had shown any desire to climb to the top of the social ladder, but Alva changed that. She became a lavish hostess and in later years contrived to bring a title into the family by arranging a marriage between her lovely daughter, Consuelo, and the ninth Duke of Marlborough.

Not all of the Vanderbilts were willing to follow Alva's lead. Indeed, one of Willie's sisters, Florence, accepted a proposal of marriage from a twenty-eight-year-old Western Union clerk, Hamilton McKown Twombly. Thus armed, the young man nervously approached William Henry Vanderbilt on the redoubtable north "millionaires'" piazza of Saratoga's United States Hotel and asked for his parental consent.

"What is your yearly income, Mr. Twombly?" Vanderbilt inquired.

"Eighteen hundred dollars, sir."

"And do you think you can maintain my daughter as she is used to living on that?"

"I don't know, sir," Twombly said. "But I can keep her as well as you kept her mother when you married her."

This seemed to require an answer that only the mother could give. Vanderbilt sent the young suitor to speak to his wife; if she didn't object to the match, he wouldn't.

She didn't, and after an elaborate wedding Mr. and Mrs. Twombly settled down to simple living. It didn't stay that way long. Very soon Twombly was elected a vice-president of Western Union at a salary of $15,000 a year and some years later, on her father's death, Florence inherited an elegant Fifth Avenue house in New York City and $10,000,000. Just before the turn of the century the Twomblys joined Florence's brothers and sisters on a mansion-building spree—choosing Convent, New Jersey, as the site of a hundred-room house of rosy brick and bristling chimneys overlooking great lawns. In tribute to their happy union they called their estate Florham, a coupling of the foreparts of their first names.

Pursuers of the muses   Art and letters were also well represented at Saratoga in the period after the war. Writers, painters, actors, composers found the resort at once entertaining, relaxing and replenishing. Among the most illustrious pursuers of the muses were two whom the war had touched in a painfully similar way.

Slight, darkly handsome Edwin Booth was at the crest of his fame as the most magnificent Hamlet of his time when word reached him in Boston that his younger brother, John Wilkes Booth, had assassinated President Lincoln. The resulting fury forced him into retirement, but in January 1866, pressed by debts and the need to retrieve his fame, he dared to appear on-stage again, and won an ovation that at once restored his rank and removed him from the shadow of his brother's crime.

In the summer of 1879 it again seemed that his career was finished. A dry, furry black spot, as large as a silver dollar, appeared on Booth's tongue, and it seemed to him that his tongue swelled until it was too big for his mouth. Booth was in a panic. Convinced that he had cancer, he went from physician to physician, announcing each visit with, "I'm the man with a black tongue!" At last Dr. Ghislani Durant, a New York City cancer specialist, diagnosed the spot as a rare type of fungus and scraped the tongue clean.

With lifted spirits Booth went to Saratoga to recuperate. A few weeks later he stared open-mouthed at himself in his mirror and sent the doctor a telegram:

BLACK, BLACK, BLACK, BOOTH.

Dr. Durant journeyed to the Springs at once. Microscopic particles of mold, untouched by his knife, had multiplied and revived the spot until it was as frightening as before. He stayed with Booth and day after day delicately scraped the tongue until he was satisfied the fungus was gone. At the end of six months Booth knew that he was healed. Mere payment of the fee seemed an insufficient token of his gratitude; he sent Dr. Durant, in addition, a silver loving cup from Tiffany's engraved with a quotation from *Macbeth*: "The mere despair of surgery he cures."

Like Booth, Ulysses S. Grant saw his bright fame tarnished by the misdeeds of others. Almost literally carried into the White House on the shoulders of millions of admirers, the conqueror of the Confederacy departed eight years later stained and diminished by an administration so shamelessly corrupt that it was a national disgrace. The private life into which Grant tried to escape was also unkind. The business partner to whom he entrusted his entire capital proved to be a crook, their joint enterprise a fraud. In the collapse that followed, Grant was left destitute. Soon afterward he learned that he had cancer of the throat.

Given little more than a year to live, Grant entered into a race with death to redeem his name and recapture the nation's esteem. Through months of anguishing pain he wrote his recollections of the war to save the Union, and when time grew short he accepted the invitation of Joseph W. Drexel to spend the summer of 1885 in the wealthy Philadelphian's house on top of Mount McGregor, near Saratoga Springs. Both hoped that the mountain air would make it easier for Grant to finish his task.

Grant's publisher, Mark Twain, visited him often, and just as frequently went to the Springs to enjoy a friendly game of billiards. Saratoga

Mark Twain visited Grant often during his last days, and made several trips to the Spa to play billiards.

Lillie Langtry, the Jersey Lily, caused a sensation when she ventured forth in shoes with flaming red heels.

Charley Mitchell, an English prizefighter, turned up at the Springs during a pugilistic tour. He is shown beating the American Sheriff in 1883—one of the first prizefights in which boxing gloves rather than bare knuckles were used.

The season of 1888 was enlivened with a memorable sartorial performance by socialite Berry Wall, shown at left in a photo taken in 1910. A well-known actor, Robert Hilliard, was Wall's rival for the title, "King Of The Dudes"—symbolized at right by the drawing of a dandy a clothier of the period used to decorate his trade cards.

In the post-Civil War years Saratoga-bound vacationists journeyed comfortably to the Spa via steamboat or train or a combination of the two. These three views illustrate the improvement in Hudson River and railway travel since steamers such as the *Clermont* and the primitive, wood-burning trains.

sightseers made daily excursions to Mount McGregor with the hope of glimpsing the gallant figure on his front porch.

Late in July, Grant died. But the race was won; he had completed his voluminous manuscript a few days before. Acclaimed as one of the great narratives of military history, his *Personal Memoirs* widely revived his prestige as a war hero and provided some $450,000 for his impoverished family.

"I rather enjoy it myself."

The droll stories of Saratoga's playful summer citizens had not been allowed to die in the American press; foreign periodicals had published them also, and beguiled by the goings-on Continental cut-ups made their way to the Spa.

Perhaps the most accomplished was an English sportsman, Squire Abingdon Baird. His wardrobe was colorful and extensive, and included a $10,000 supply of walking sticks, each selected to harmonize with one of his suits, and an assortment of gems and boutonnieres also chosen to blend. The latter were artificial; he had no patience with real flowers because they wilted and lost their scent.

Squire Baird owned a racing stable in England and was a shrewd backer of prizefighters and theatrical talent. One of his enthusiasms was Lillie Langtry, the darling of London society whom bankruptcy had forced onto the stage. Gossip had linked her intimately with the Prince of Wales, and this, together with her patrician beauty, made her an instant favorite with both theatergoers and the merely curious who tagged after her whenever she appeared on the streets. In America her triumph was no less complete. At Saratoga, which she visited regularly, she once caused a sensation by turning out for the evening in shoes with lacquered red high heels.

Another of Squire Baird's admirations was the clever English boxer, Charley Mitchell. Despite his unimpressive weight, Mitchell had fought John L. Sullivan to a bare-knuckle, three-hour draw on the Chantilly estate of France's Baron Rothschild, and the Squire was confident that he would be unbeatable on a tour of the United States. It didn't work out that way, but the Squire's esteem was unshaken; he travelled with Mitchell, bet heavily on him, paid most of his expenses and cheered him with costly good times.

Such devotion was bound to win attention and Squire Baird was greatly pleased with the publicity. One day at the bar of the Saratoga race track he had a few words with Mitchell and slapped his face. To the surprise of those looking on, Mitchell made no reply. The provocation was repeated in other crowded places at the Spa; still Mitchell refused to strike back. At last, when the papers were full of the one-sided bouts and Mitchell's reputation as a pugilist appeared to be almost beyond repair, he explained: "The Squire likes it, and since he pays me a hundred dollars for every blow he lands, I rather enjoy it myself."

A Prince Albert with white tie

As the age of clownery flowered toward the Gay Nineties, wherein it would reach full bloom, an eager offshoot unfurled itself at Saratoga with such audacity and suspense that it won plaudits everywhere.

Evander Berry Wall moved in the best social circles,* a handsome and elegant young man in his mid-twenties with a winning disposition he shared impartially with both sexes; however, in the words of an admirer, he was "never happier than when he was the center of a group of good fellows, leading them on to some amusing sport." Wall commanded attention even on the rare occasions when he was alone, for the splendor of his dress was usually unsurpassed wherever he chose to go. Admittedly, he sometimes went to extremes, but to the more advanced connoisseurs of fashion even these were in excellent taste. He had once flown in the face of convention (white tie and tails) by turning up at the ballroom of the Grand Union in a tailless dress coat, designed by his London tailor, and had been so rudely cold-shouldered that he had departed in a huff to a rival New York resort, Tuxedo Park, which became so enamored of the innovation that it named the jacket after itself.

The single fly in Wall's ointment was Robert Hilliard, a matinee idol with whom he had waged sartorial battle over a period of years. The rivalry was so engaging that newspapers reported every skirmish and announced that the eventual winner would be crowned "King Of The Dudes."

In the summer of 1887 Wall had won a slight advantage, showing himself at the Saratoga race track with his walking stick gayly beribboned with the racing colors of two stable-owning friends. During the following winter, however, Hilliard had evened the score by striding through blizzard-swept New York City in a stunning pair of hip-length, patent-leather boots he had been sporting on stage in his role of a Western gambler.

In the summer of 1888, when he was again at the Springs, Wall decided that the time had come for an all-out assault. On an evening in August he announced that the next day, between breakfast and dinner, he would appear in forty complete changes of costume. He had no sooner retired than thousands of dollars were bet on the question of whether he could do it, and early the next morning a crowd gathered to see the issue decided.

* On his eighteenth birthday, Wall had inherited well over two million dollars from his father and grandfather, spent it all by the time he was twenty-nine; a third inheritance, from his mother, was put in trust for him and carried him through his remaining years in a comfortable state of solvency.

Pullman cars provided luxuries comparable to those of a well-appointed home. In the 1870's railway travellers were extended the hospitality of a parlor and a smoking salon.

Meals were delivered and consumed in style, while outside the scenery whizzed by at some 20 miles an hour.

On Sunday passengers could conduct their own religious service, with organ music and hymn singing.

Leslie's Weekly, New York

The arrival of each train at Saratoga was heralded by a bell clanging in the depot cupola. Equipages of every description hurried toward the station and porters lined up under the hotel signs to take possession of the luggage. Natives and visitors crowded the platform to see or greet the newcomers. It was a scene of cheerful bedlam.

Just before breakfast Wall emerged from his suite at the Grand Union suitably arranged in black and white. He ate leisurely, took his leave and reappeared in white linen. After a chat with friends, a stroll on the piazza, he retired again and came forth in new attire. So it went through the day: a quick change, dazzlingly different from anything he had worn before, an exchange of gossip, a stroll or a drink, another retreat to his suite, where his valet had laid out each piece of apparel in fireman fashion, and a fresh sortie.

As the hours passed the crowd and the size of the bets steadily increased, and in mid-afternoon the band tuned up for dinner-time with the outcome still in doubt. Then, precisely as the dinner gong rang, the musicians struck up *Hail, The Conquering Hero Comes;* John L. Sullivan led the crowd in three hearty cheers and started to collect the winnings. Smiling, Berry Wall stood on the piazza in his fortieth costume of the day: a Prince Albert with white tie, boiled shirt and poke collar. a narrow piping of white piqué on his vest. From that moment on no one disputed that he was the crown prince of fashion.

No wonder the crowd almost applauds! Season after season the Steeles, Fisks, Bairds and Walls were the star performers at the Springs, but for unflagging entertainment their audience relied on the ever-changing yet comfortably familiar pageant of the streets. To enjoy it one had only to sit on the front porch of one of the fine hotels, particularly on the great piazza of the Grand Union or the United States. The sidewalks and promenades were a continuously eye-filling fashion show, for at Saratoga everyone "dressed up" throughout the day. The women especially were something to see, for "it was a time when each dress was made to order as an individual masterpiece with hat and parasol to match; when dresses had pleats and ruffles and lace and ribbons and swelling puffed sleeves, and hats were miniature flower gardens or aviaries."

Along Broadway's triple width of dirt road, shaded by giant elms, rolled more horse-drawn vehicles than most onlookers had thought existed. Years after she witnessed the spectacle as a young girl, a visitor recalled the wonder of it:

> Surreys with a fringe around the top were there in myriad, single and double; slender buckboards whirled past drawn by long-tailed Morgans; basket phaetons with high-stepping, bob-tailed hackneys; heavy Victorias, haughtily displaying their glittering silver monogrammed harness, two men in livery on their box and the ladies behind, with lacy parasols, sitting in richly upholstered state; high dogcarts with a booted groom, maintaining a sometimes

precarious balance with folded arms on the back seat (he usually sat backwards). And weaving through the throng were impatient sulkies, their drivers with their feet stretched out on the poles, sitting on the tails of their pacers or trotters . . . Then suddenly would come the faraway tally-ho of a horn, and presently bearing down on lesser vehicles a four-in-hand would be brought up with a dramatic dash to the steps of a hotel. While grooms leaped to the heads of the foam-flecked leaders, beautiful women with veils swathed round their enormous hats would be lifted down from the exalted seats beside or behind the Whip with his covert coat and boutonniere, whose inevitable lap-rug, tightly tucked about him, must never, never come below his knees.

There was never a lack of wealthy and famous Whips. Even a perfunctory lookout was sure to be rewarded with a glimpse of William Henry Vanderbilt driving Adelina and Maud S., said by some experts to be the fastest pair of thoroughbreds in the world, or Elias Jackson Baldwin, who handled his coach and four with the skill of a Western stage driver. Lucky Baldwin had earned his nickname and $30,000,000 in California's gold fields and gambling halls; he owned the Santa Anita Ranch and the Baldwin Hotel in San Francisco, whose lobby was paved with gold pieces. Saratogans who had seen the lobby insisted that Baldwin's carriage was fancier still. He refused to allow any man but himself to ride in it and only the prettiest women who applied. When the spirit moved him he selected only blondes, or only brunettes, as his passengers, and whirled them off to the race track to watch his horses run and see him win or lose anywhere from $5,000 to $50,000 on a single nose.

One could also marvel at the aplomb with which Giulia Morosini weaved through the traffic in her high, single-seated gig, three thoroughbreds in tandem responding to the slightest flick of her white doeskin reins, or take pleasure in the little ritual she and her father, the celebrated banker G. P. Morosini, enacted each afternoon. A reporter for a metropolitan newspaper described it in detail:

> Miss Morosini is undoubtedly the best horsewoman in Saratoga. So attractive is she in beauty, style and manner, as well as in her horsemanship, that every afternoon a little crowd of ladies and gentlemen gathers about the north piazza of the United States Hotel to see Miss Morosini start off on her ride. Promptly at 4:45 the groom appears, riding a handsome but rather heavy bay, while Miss Morosini's choice of her six fine horses that have been sent here follows behind in charge of another groom. In a moment Mr. Morosini, whose shock of curly gray hair and gray imperial and moustache and whose military bearing would attract attention anywhere, appears, radiant with smiles, leading his lithe and supple daughter by the hand. She is clad in a tight-fitting,

The most rewarding entertainment at the Spa was staged by the summer guests them-selves. Broadway was a never-ending variety show. "Not the Prater of Vienna nor the Unter der Linden of Berlin, not even the Champs Elysées of Paris, offer a more dazzling display of fashion, beauty and wealth," a visitor wrote after witnessing an after-dinner promenade on Saratoga's Broadway, such as this one in front of the Grand Union Hotel in 1875.

Fashionable shops also animated
the Broadway scene.

WINDSOR HOTEL
✳DINNER✳
WEDNESDAY, AUGUST 4, 1880.

Soups

Ox-tail with vegetables   Italian paste au Parmesan

Hors d'Œuvres

Cervelles de veau, Villeroi

or French olives   Sliced tomatoes   French sardines

Fish

Striped bass à la hollandaise   Broiled bluefish, ravigote sauce
Mashed and baked potatoes   Sliced cucumbers

Boiled

of English mutton   Vermont turkey
Ox-tongue   Maryland ham, Madeira sauce

Relevé

Rump of beef à la Nivernaise

Entrées

phia squab, jardinière
Calf's tongue, sauce piquante
Stewed breast of lamb, Irish style
Fried soft-shell crabs
Macaroni, Piedmontaise

CARDINAL PUNCH

Roast

Ribs of prime beef   Green goose, apple sauce
Saddle of lamb, mint sauce   Bucks' County chicken

Cold Dishes

ef   Chicken   Beef tongue   Spring lamb   Ham
Breast of corned beef   Spring duck

Salads

ken mayonnaise   Tomato   Lobster mayonnaise
Cucumber   Lettuce   Beet

Vegetables

tatoes   Beets   Mashed potatoes   Fried egg plant   String beans   Cream spinach
corn   Green peas   Succotash   Stewed tomatoes   Boiled rice   Summer squash

Pastry

dding, crème de nougat   Whortleberry pie   Assorted cake
Peach meringue tart   Biscuits à la reine   Port wine jelly

Ice Cream and Confectionery

Lemon ice cream   Pastilles à la rose

Dessert

English cheese   Roquefort cheese   Edam cheese
Raisins   Assorted nuts   Peaches
FRENCH COFFEE

HOURS FOR MEALS:

akfast,   From 7 to 11 o'clock.   Supper,   From 7 to 9 o'clock.
ner,   "   2 to 4   "   Sunday Breakfast,   "   8 to 11 "
A Separate Table is Provided for Children and Private Servants.
akfast,   7 to 9. | Dinner,   -   12 to 1:30. | Supper,   6 to 7:30.
All meals, lunches or fruits sent to rooms will be charged extra.

Full Price Charged for Children Occupying Seats at the Public Table.

OGA SPRINGS.   CHARLES H. SHELLEY,
Manager.

DEMPSEY & CARROLL,
ART STATIONERS, UNION SQUARE, N. Y.

Dinner was an event all by itself, as this Windsor
Hotel menu suggests.

The morning ritual at the springs.

Famous Whips drove thoroughbreds whose names were almost as well-known as their own. Here, William Henry Vanderbilt guides his celebrated team, Small Hopes and Lady Mac.

Lucky Baldwin was so proud of his coach and four that he permitted only lovely ladies to ride with him.

modest English riding costume of the latest London style of solid dark blue. Her finely-cut features, aquiline nose and sparkling eyes are partly concealed by a thin veil. In her hand she carries a gold-headed riding whip. At her approach the noble animal bows his head and swings it toward her with a pleasant nod of recognition, and comes nearer the walk as if to invite her to a seat. With a gentle, easy motion she springs into the saddle with grace and dignity, and in a moment the horse is off at a gentle canter, as if proud of its precious burden. It is a beautiful sight. The young lady petite and pretty, balanced with such skill and ease upon her perch; the horse with arched neck and prancing feet, moving swiftly around—a perfect picture of beauty in motion. No wonder Mr. Morosini stands till the vision fades, drinking in the pleasant sight! No wonder the little crowd almost applauds with pleasure!

Best of all, from the piazzas one could watch the stately, unbroken procession of high-stepping horses and superb carriages as every afternoon they set out along Broadway for the fashionable drive to Lake Saratoga. They came in all styles and sizes, but none were so grand as the tally-hos with their four matched thoroughbreds in trappings embellished with shiny monogrammed plates of silver or gold. Two footmen perched behind, sitting impassively in high black boots, tight white knee breeches, long red coats with a double row of brass buttons down the front, and low black sugar-loaf hats. The owner sat proudly in the driver's seat, handling the reins. And inside and on top of the coach rode a dozen or more elegantly dressed men, with toppers matching their suits, and women with sun parasols they seldom stopped twirling. As the procession curved away on the boulevard to the lake, the musical notes of the footmen's long brass horns floated back over the village.

The four-mile drive along one side of the tree-lined boulevard and back along the other, with time out for bathing or boating or a lakeside stroll and one of the famous fish suppers, was a hallmark of quality to which Saratoga society clung year in and year out despite efforts to dislodge it. Only the attractions of Woodlawn could shake this fealty.

Woodlawn was the million-dollar estate of Judge Henry Hilton, fifteen hundred acres of leafy forests and landscaped gardens through which wandered twenty-five miles of gravel roads. *Hiawatha,* Augustus Saint-Gaudens' first major sculpture, rested reflectively on a pedestal in front of the Hilton mansion, and stretching away from the great house were quarters for twenty-eight servants, stables for sixty horses, a carriage barn and a dairy, poultry farm, sheep farm and vegetable farm from which the Judge extracted an undiminishing supply of home-grown food for his table. Amusements, too, were close at hand. A club house provided cards, billiards and other games, and there was a ballroom for dancing. An athletic field stood ready for sports, and from the grandstand guests could watch and wager while their horses raced over Judge Hilton's private track.

Inevitably, the guests were a select circle and often included America's first families, but non-notables also were permitted to enjoy the grounds if Judge Hilton approved of them. Two uniformed guards stood at the gate to the estate and visitors who produced admission cards given to them by the Judge were allowed to enter and drive over the gravel paths or stroll along the walks. Two hundred or so sightseers were admitted at a time, but it is doubtful that any of them were Jews. Appointed by Alexander T. Stewart as the executor of his estate, Judge Hilton had taken charge of the Grand Union Hotel after the merchant's death in 1876 and promptly revised the rules to prohibit Jews. It was hardly an extraordinary move; anti-Semitism had been and was being practiced at all leading resorts from Bar Harbor to Palm Beach; notices were displayed on hotel reservation desks reading, *Jewish patronage not solicited;* and at Saratoga a distinguished gentleman named Moses Thompson had no sooner written the second *s* in *Moses* than the registration book was snatched from him by a horrified clerk. Nevertheless, the village was dismayed by the Judge's act, and in New York City a boycott instituted against the firm of Hilton, Hughes & Company, which had taken over Stewart's department store after his death, compelled it to go out of business. Trouble also multiplied at the Grand Union, and the Judge let it revert to the Stewart estate.

In later years the attitude toward Jews of Saratoga's hotels became less frosty and in some instances almost friendly. Joseph Smith, the ubiquitous head usher at the United States, noted in his diary in 1894: "Among the Jewish guests this year there are some excellent families who have been coming to the States as regularly as the coming of the seasons. They have become not only very prominent but very profitable patrons at the Spa."

The
superior
horse
To many Saratogans the most memorable spectacle of the quarter century following the Civil War was the result of a rivalry not between show-offs or showplaces, but between two great-hearted race horses.

In his first start, on the Saratoga track, Harry Bassett had fallen to his knees at the drop of the flag and almost unseated his jockey. It was his only defeat. Within the next two years he had run up an impressive string of victories and it appeared to racing enthusiasts in the North that the compactly built, light chestnut colt was the fastest horse in the country.

In the South they disagreed. The Kentucky bluegrass had yielded a horse of similar superior qualities, a giant of a horse seventeen hands high aptly named Longfellow, and there was no question in the minds of his admirers that he was the first racer in America.

"In the late afternoon," *Leslie's Weekly* said in a report on summer life at Saratoga in 1879, "it is 'correct form' to be en route to the lake. The road in some places is literally blocked with vehicles of all sorts, shapes, sizes and descriptions, from the stately drag, tooled by four 'bits o' blood,' to the dumpy basket-phaeton attached to a pony not much bigger than a Mount St. Bernard mastiff. To stand on the top of the hill and gaze into the dip in the road is a sight worthy the seeing, while it conveys a wholesome idea of the wealth, magnificence and luxury of the sojourners at fair Saratoga. As far as the eye can reach, carriages roll onward, while equestrians in the horsiest of pantaloons, and *equestriennes* in the sauciest of hats, enjoy the fierce fascination of the gallop or the bland beatitude of the amble. The horseflesh is 'all there,' and the display of satin coats, dainty limbs, tossing heads, and the glittering paraphernalia attached to the realm of the stable is worthy of Newmarket at its best, or even of the road to Royal Ascot. . . . Everybody meets everybody else on the drive. Everybody feels bound to take it, as invalids take the Congress water."

Excursionists on Lake Saratoga were treated to a glimpse of Interlaken, Frank Leslie's summer estate.

INTERLAKEN" FOR SALE.

THE COUNTRY HOME OF
HE LATE FRANK LESLIE, ESQ.,

sisting of 92 acres, situated on LAKE SARATOGA, and nding back to Lake Lonely.

The house contains twelve rooms, gas and water.

The stable, finished in fine woods, has six box-stalls.

Finely appointed billiard-room, and three handsomely fur-ed sleeping-rooms over coach-house.

Gardener's cottage.

Conservatories profusely stocked with rare plants.

The furniture, steam-yacht, sail and row boats, French bus, etc., will be sold with the place.

Apply to

HOMER MORGAN, 2 Pine Street; or,

V. K. STEVENSON, 1 Pine St., and 35 E. 17th St.

After the publisher's death, in January 1880, Interlaken was put up for sale. This advertisement describing the estate appeared in the spring issues of *Leslie's Weekly*.

Another favorite destination of he daily carriage procession was Woodlawn.

Woodlawn was the home of Judge Henry Hilton, a magnificent 1500-acre park threaded with gravel roads. Guests at the Hilton mansion were attended by 28 servants, and in the winter, together with privileged outsiders, amused themselves by coasting down the toboggan slide.

Lou Fain

The season of 1872 was distinguished by the meeting of Harry Bassett and Longfellow in a race for the Saratoga Cup. Thomas Scott painted this likeness of Harry Bassett (top), and rival Longfellow (bottom) is shown in a portrait by Edward Troye.

Currier and Ives' interpretation of the classic event.

On July 2, 1872, forty thousand people assembled in Monmouth Park, New Jersey, to see Harry Bassett and Longfellow, a year older than his rival, compare their stamina and speed over a two-and-a-half-mile course. Money was literally heaped on the two horses. Confidence in Harry Bassett swelled to such a peak that shortly before the race he was almost 2 to 1 in the betting. John Morrissey placed more than $25,000 on him.

It was hardly a contest. Longfellow won easily; so easily that it appeared to almost everyone except the Southern gentlemen who carried off Northern capital that there had been dishonesty afoot. Harry Bassett's owner, Colonel David McDaniel, indignantly denied the rumors of wrong-doing. The colt simply was out of condition, he said; it would be a different story when the two horses met again at Saratoga.

In mid-July another extraordinary crowd gathered at the track at the Springs for the two-and-a-quarter-mile showdown, and this time the betting odds were reversed. No other turf reporter captured the meeting as well as Charles E. Trevathan. In his *The American Thoroughbred* he wrote:

On that brilliant Saratoga afternoon when Longfellow appeared in front of the stand with all his lofty grandeur of appearance and marks of high estate, he was loudly cheered. Harry Bassett was well received by his friends, but the multitude favored the big one from old Kentucky.

They cantered to the head of the stretch together, turned, and broke away head and head at the first jump. There was a third horse in the race, but he cut no figure. At the very start it is almost certain that Longfellow struck the quarter of his near forefoot and twisted the plate.

They came on at a strong pace, Harry Bassett slightly in the lead, and at the stand the latter was a short length ahead. Longfellow ran under a very hard pull. He soon got to Bassett's girths and then was taken back again. It seemed that he could have collared Harry Bassett at any time. The first mile back to the head of the stretch was run in 1:45½. Coming down the homestretch the second time, the pace was increased to the stand, where Longfellow was at Bassett's head. On the turn, running on the inside, Bassett led a little again. But once more Longfellow hauled up on him and was going strongly and gamely. At this time he must have been much incommoded by the plate, which had doubled itself and bedded into the sole of his foot.

They had now run a mile and a half, and the pace for the last half mile had been very great. It had been run in better than fifty seconds. Soon after passing the quarter pole, Longfellow faltered in his stride, and his rider had to call on him. It was the first call which he had heard in that season. He answered with the finest resolution.

But something had gone wrong. Longfellow faltered, gave a lurch in his stride, and then spread his forelegs so wide that you

might have rolled a barrel between them. The boy pulled him together and called upon him the second time. With a noble effort
he got up to Bassett's girths again, as the latter was doing all he
knew.

Longfellow, wobbling in his stride, still fighting, still struggling, still answering the call of his boy, forced Harry Bassett out
to the very last ounce to beat him a length.

The shouts of the great multitude rent the afternoon air.
But the acclamation for Harry Bassett was quickly and gallantly
changed to expressions of sorrow for Longfellow when they saw
the Kentucky horse trying to pull up. When the boy endeavored to
stop the big horse, Longfellow's pain was so terrible that twice he
came near falling on his head. With difficulty he finally came to a
standstill, and then, as he limped back to the judges' stand, his
progress was marked by only three hoofprints in the dust of the
course. The fourth foot he did not put down at all.

After the race the great horse stood in his box, holding the
foot upon its mangled edge, and as each visitor came in he would
turn his large eyes upon him and then drop them to his foot,
as if asking sympathy for his misfortune.

Once more the meeting of the two racers had been inconclusive; it
still had to be shown which truly was the superior horse. But there was no
further rivalry. Longfellow never raced again.

PART THREE

"God, What A Lovely Time It Was To Live!"

Chapter One

⤜⤛

A gentleman named Canfield

In the closing years of the nineteenth century all America bathed in rosy optimism. As far as the eye could see a splendid destiny lay ahead, and the nation confidently and vigorously pursued its bright promise of a richer and fuller life.

The affluent society, already in possession of more money and leisure than it knew what to do with, accented the carefree mood with such exuberance that the period was to go down in history as the Gay Nineties. Saratoga Springs became more popular than ever, its gayety and games and fountains of energy fitting in perfectly with the spirit of the times.* To these pleasures in 1894 a new arrival at the Spa, Richard Albert Canfield, added several enticements of his own; and Saratoga went on a spree that would extend over seventeen years, the best years of its long and eventful life.

Richard Canfield was a gambler, as well known in New York City's gaming circles as Saratoga's former leading citizen, John Morrissey, had been before him. There the resemblance ceased. Old Smoke had tooled his way to the top with his fists; Canfield used his wits. And where Morrissey had been denied his fondest wish, to be accepted as a gentleman, Canfield, though he shared the social burden of their profession, was regarded as a friend and equal by the rich, famous and respected.

Born in 1855 in the great whaling port of New Bedford, Massachusetts, the fifth of six children, young Canfield remained discouragingly aloof to both the advantages of an education and the necessity of helping his father—a man of an independent but improvident turn of mind—obtain a living for the family. When his father somewhat prematurely died, however, the boy was persuaded to attend grammar school and pleased his mother by becoming a diligent pupil. After he graduated he was employed in the shipping department of a prominent Boston store, but the insuffi-

---

* At the United States Hotel, head usher Joseph Smith wrote in his diary: "The season of 1890 is especially replete with wealthy and conspicuous visitors. All the millionaires of the land seem to be in Saratoga . . . and there are thousands of men here with their families who are spending hundreds of dollars a day."

⤛§ 223

ciency of his salary, two dollars a week, together with the dull future he envisioned in merchandising soon induced him to quit his job and seek greener pastures in Providence, Rhode Island. He was fifteen.

In Providence, Richard Canfield decided that the most attractive antithesis to a meager income and an unexciting career was gambling. He became a gambler. In three years, he and another youth were partners in a ten-cent poker game which flourished daily in a barely furnished room until the police caught wind of it and threatened to close it. Canfield moved on to other places in Providence, and to nearby Pawtucket and Boston. In 1876 he sailed to Europe with his considerable winnings and spent both the money and the summer in sightseeing. When he returned he was twenty-one, without a dollar, and determined to establish himself as the proprietor of a fashionable gaming house.

Quite clearly he would need help, Canfield reasoned, and the first step was to meet the kind of people who could assist him in building an elegant clientele for his casino of the future. He persuaded his mother's cousin, who was the manager of the Union Square, one of New York City's most desirable hotels, to put him on as night clerk. There, his courtesy, charm and efficiency made him a favorite of the celebrities and socialites who formed the late-hour traffic. Most of the men gambled, and when they discovered that the young desk clerk also enjoyed testing his luck they took him with them. As Canfield expected, their wagers were extravagant and he was unable to match them, but his adroit and skillful play impressed his companions and improved their acquaintanceship.

After two years he used his connections to become night clerk of the Monmouth House, a summer retreat at Spring Lake, New Jersey. There too he became favorably acquainted with distinguished guests and made such an impression on the owner that in his second season he was appointed manager. The job was demanding, but Canfield met its challenges with such a variety of talents that he was urged to seek a career as a hotel magnate, banker, lawyer or actor, depending on the profession of the well-wisher. None of the suggestions had any effect. During the winters, when the hotel was closed, Canfield profitably operated a poker game in Pawtucket, Rhode Island, and in 1882 he met and married a pretty Pawtucket girl, Genevieve Martin. He was twenty-seven and impatient to become a full-time, big-time gambler.

He went to Providence and became a partner in a faro house. Business was brisk, and when the police raided the establishment one Saturday evening it appeared to be merely a token of law enforcement. To the owners' dismay they were prosecuted and sentenced to six months in prison.

During his early acquaintance with the rich and famous Canfield had been disconcerted by his lack of formal knowledge, and while he had covered his inadequacy he perceived that his meager education was an obstacle in the path of his ambition. In the slack hours of his night-clerk duty he had read and studied assiduously, and enjoyed it. He resolved to use

The Gay Nineties were Saratoga's golden years. A sojourn at the Spa was more prestigious, and more fun, than ever before. One who helped to make it so was Richard Canfield, the Prince of Gamblers, who bought and refurbished Morrissey's Club House and renamed it the Casino.

SANCTUM
TALKS.

Saratoga's growing reputation as a gamblnig resort brought Anthony Comstock to the Spa to crusade against its evils. A professional do-gooder, he is shown here as lampooned by *Life* in its popular "Sanctum Talks" series. "We couldn't do without you, Anthony," *Life* assured Comstock when he asked for its opinion of his anti-vice sorties. "When we want to see how big an ass someone else is, all we have to do is place him alongside you."

his six months in prison toward further self-improvement. From the prison library he procured books on literature, history, religion, philosophy, art and other subjects, and when his term was up he not only felt prepared to hold his own in social discussion but was enthusiastic about knowledge for its own sake.

As soon as he was released Canfield left Providence and opened a poker room on the lower east side of New York City. Within a year his profits were $300 a week, but Canfield was in a hurry now and it wasn't anywhere near enough. In 1888, with another gambler, David Duff, he opened a gaming club close to Delmonico's, the Hoffman House, and other celebrated restaurants and hotels, with separate rooms for faro, roulette and poker. Here the associations he had cultivated at the fashionable Union Square and Monmouth House paid off; distinguished acquaintances patronized the club and brought their friends. Play was so vigorous that it soon became necessary to keep $50,000 in the safe to cover the club's losses in the event of a bad night. The rush of prosperity was more than Duff could handle. He began to turn up drunk and make a nuisance of himself, and Canfield bought him out.

In a few years Canfield was a millionaire and one of the most popular gaming hosts in the city. Still it wasn't enough. For several summers he had been visiting Saratoga Springs and looking things over at the Club House. After Morrissey's death it had fallen to Albert Spencer and Charles Reed, a pair of New York City gamblers.

Reed was an socially ambitious as Morrissey, with a similar lack of credentials. He talked loudly, dressed flashily and had once killed a man during a difference of opinion. Nevertheless, he installed himself in a $50,000 mansion, attended church each Sunday, gave generously to Saratoga's charities, and otherwise invited the camaraderie of the Spa's elect. After some years it became discouragingly clear to Reed that he was socially unacceptable. He sold his interest in the Club House to Spencer and returned to New York City.

Spencer was a different stripe. Quiet and unobtrusive, he was uncommonly well educated for a gambler and had made a profitable hobby of collecting and selling fine paintings. Canfield too was especially fond of art and this, and their profession, drew them together.

His study of the Saratoga Club House had convinced Canfield that under proper management it could become the most lucrative gambling establishment in America. He called Spencer's attention to the missed opportunities and proposed that they work as partners to take advantage of them. Spencer, who had all the money he needed and was well along in years, had thought more and more of moving to Paris, where he would be close to many of the great artists. He countered with a proposal of his own: for $250,000 he would sell the Club House outright. Canfield accepted with alacrity. In the winter of 1893 he paid Spencer the purchase price and at once set about making his vision come true.

His plan for improvement was simple: to give his patrons the very best in food, drink and comfort at the most expensive prices. It would then follow, he was confident, that to be seen at the Casino—his new name for the Club House—would be a feather in the cap, a mark of distinction only the wealthy could afford. And the satisfying glow produced by choice edibles and vintage wines would not only lead free-spenders to the gaming tables but console them over their losses.

Canfield stocked the Casino store-rooms with delicacies and arranged for fresh meats and vegetables to arrive each day. He filled the wine cellar with costly beverages and replaced the dining room's linen, silver and china with selections from New York City's most luxurious shops. With a cool eye for poise, neatness and tact, he picked fifty new waiters, each of whom could expect to pocket $50 a day in tips, and hired a highly-paid headwaiter to supervise them. Most important of all, he induced a famous French chef, Jean Columbin, to preside over the kitchen. It was a hard bargain—$5,000 for each July-August season and Columbin's expenses throughout the rest of the year while he travelled in Europe seeking ideas for new concoctions—but Canfield hadn't a single doubt that it was worth every penny.

When the completely refurbished and freshly staffed Casino opened for the summer of 1894 it was an instant success. Columbin's hands worked magic and there were few complaints when Canfield scaled the prices of his cuisine higher than Sherry's and Delmonico's in New York City. Indeed, for special favors enthusiastic gourmets were willing to pay more. Eager to see what Columbin could do with a favorite dish not on the day's menu, they had only to notify the kitchen early in the morning to find it in front of them at night. The chef had no patience with guests who elected to choose the fish they wished served to them, however. In the course of his improvements Canfield had arranged for a fish pool to be placed near the Casino, and patrons ordering fish were invited to go to the pool and point out the trout, bass or whatever that most appealed to them. The fish selected were scooped out with a net and dispatched to the kit-chen, where there was every reason to believe they would be cooked in style. Canfield had thought it an intriguing idea and the customers liked it too, but Columbin regarded it as nonsense. His assistants tossed the fish into a pipe connecting the kitchen with the pool and washed them back to their daily abode, and from the icebox Columbin chose substitutes he deemed better suited to his talents. When the fish reached the table everyone was content; its taste was superb.

To further project the Casino's stylish new image Canfield had let it be known that he expected his guests to wear evening clothes. They did so gladly, weighting their finery with such costly jewels that he was obliged to hire private detectives to mingle with them and protect them against thieves. In the gaming rooms the tails and tuxedos presented a more formid-able problem. Canfield disliked carrying a sizable amount of cash in his dress suit because it ruined the tailoring, and if, as he suspected, his gambling patrons felt the same way it would severely limit their play. He solved the dilemma by extending a liberal amount of credit, a risk no other American gambler had been willing to take. His guests returned the compliment with open-handed betting and requests for higher stakes. To accommodate them Canfield raised the limits far beyond Morrissey's prudent ceilings. In the public gaming room he valued white chips at $1, red at $5, blue at $10, yellow at $100 and brown at $1,000. In the private rooms upstairs he allowed the heavy plungers still wider latitude, valuing the white chips at $100 and in the same way raising the worth of each succeeding color to $100,000 for the brown.

To his Saratoga confreres (there were more than ten gambling houses at the Springs that summer), it appeared that Canfield was courting disaster. They were convinced of it when he installed in his office safe a million dollars in currency, half of it in thousand-dollar bills and the rest in five-hundreds, one-hundreds and fifties, with which to pay his losses. Canfield was unperturbed. In his view the money was almost as secure as if it were in a bank. The safe had three heavy steel doors and five combinations and this, together with the odds favoring the house, seemed to him to provide ample protection. There was always the possibility of a calamitous night, of course, and if it happened he was prepared. But mainly the money was there because he knew it made a good impression to reward the winners with cash. Generous credit and ready cash not only would keep his present gaming patrons coming but attract others, he felt.

At the end of his first season Canfield saw that his judgment had been entirely correct. The dining room, despite its high prices, had deprived him of $70,000, but as a lure to the gaming rooms it had succeeded admirably. In just two months he had won back almost all of the $250,000 he had paid for the Club House.

The winds of change Saratoga enjoyed its most profitable summer in 1894 and could look forward to greater prosperity in seasons to come, but not all Saratogans were happy about it. Gambling, the magnet which drew most visitors to the Springs, had placed an almost indelible stamp on the village and to the discomfited minority, few in numbers but rich in resources, it was a disgrace and a detriment to the community's progress.

The original mistake, they felt, had been in allowing John Morrissey to introduce the Club House; it had encouraged other gamblers to the point that in 1873 a dozen gaming houses were operating openly. By 1886 things had gotten so far out of hand that an outsider, Anthony Comstock, secretary of the New York Society for the Suppression of Vice, had come to the Spa to crusade against its evils. Comstock, a bulky, bearded avenger armored in a silk hat and frock coat, already had battled Satan with signal success, but his most tumultuous clash of arms lay in the future. In 1913, while strolling past the window of a New York art dealer, he observed a painting in which a demure but undraped young woman was tiptoeing into the uncomfortably cool waters of a lake. The work, by Paul Chabas, was called *Matinée de Septembre* (September Morn), but to Comstock's outraged eye there was "too little morning and too much maid"; he marched into the shop and ordered the painting removed. In the uproar that followed the picture became famous. Newspapers and calendars carried it on their front pages and copies were framed in innumerable homes.

Comstock's sortie against Saratoga had produced similar results. Twenty gambling houses had closed their doors during the few days he was in town and reopened them directly after he left, and the publicity attending his visit had attracted more people to the gaming tables than were drawn to them before.

Three years later a wealthy New York banker and broker, Spencer Trask, had tilted against the gamblers. In common with other patricians Trask owned a large estate in the vicinity of Saratoga and was concerned about the village's reputation. More civic-minded than most he had, as a financial supporter of Thomas Alva Edison's early experiments, induced that inventive genius to exhibit his spectacular new incandescent lamp from the tower of the Grand Union Hotel.

The Saratoga *Union,* which Trask controlled, was the spearhead of his attack. Editorials cried out against the tents of wickedness and a map of the village was printed which showed the location of each gambling house. The effect was not at all what Trask had hoped for; all but a few of his readers condemned him as a threat to their prosperity and newsdealers refused to carry the paper.

Even the church had given him little encouragement. Some clergymen saw no difference between gambling at faro, roulette or poker and gambling on stocks at the branch office Spencer Trask and Company maintained in the Grand Union, or at rival brokerages in the community, where men sat all day speculating on prices and playing the market. They suggested that he start cleaning up the village by closing up his own games of chance.

Trask had reached into New York City for help. Private detectives had slipped into Saratoga and gathered sufficient evidence against gambling proprietors for him to have several arrested. A few hours later they were free on bail and back in business. In the fall the county grand jury had refused to indict them. Trask had spent some $50,000 on his crusade and its only accomplishment was a stiffening in the village's resistance to reform.

In 1892 the majority of Saratogans had again shown that they preferred things as they were by electing Caleb Mitchell president of the village. Mitchell, popularly known as Cale, had long been one of the Spa's chief boosters and believed, as did his constituents, that a mixture of health

From the Swell Tally-Ho.

The Betting Ring—A Rush on the Favorite.

Touting.

The Inevitable Blind Man.

Last Instructions.

Won, Hands Down.

Mud!

Familiar Figures.

Peanuts and Lemonade.

Looking On.

Polo Ponies.

A Pitch in the Steeplechase Race.

and pleasure was essential to maintain Saratoga's prosperity. As his contribution to health he operated a store famed for its fine imported groceries and wines, and balanced it with a well-run gambling establishment on Broadway for the convenience of pleasure-seekers.

To reformists Mitchell's victory was the final disgrace: the village president himself was a gambler and operated openly on the village's main street. They had demanded that he give up his gaming activities or at the very least remove them to a secluded place. When both requests failed, they had turned to Albany for remedial action.

In Senator Edgar Truman Brackett of the New York State legislature they had found an excellent spokesman for their cause. He was young, shrewd, ambitious, a comer in state politics; indeed, it had been hinted that he would make a fine governor. Senator Brackett had introduced a bill which amended the charter of Saratoga Springs so that in the future the village president would be chosen by the village trustees, rather than by the vote of the electorate. Seeing no harm in the bill the legislature had made it a law, and Cale Mitchell had appealed to the courts to disallow it.

The chill winds of change threatening the Spa had not deterred Richard Canfield from acquiring the Club House, but he had taken pains to comfort the critics in every way he could. From the day the establishment first opened its doors women and village residents had been barred from the gaming rooms and they had been closed to everyone on Sunday, and Canfield had continued to enforce these rules in his new-style Casino. As the previous owners of the gaming house had too, he gave generously to churches and charities, and his personal behavior had been above reproach. It was well-known that once a month he visited his wife, son and daughter in Providence, where they lived, preferring to keep his family life and his professional life separate, and the pillars of the community found much in this and his other qualities to admire. It was also true that he enjoyed an occasional affair; but these were conducted circumspectly, and except for a whisper now and then they were a secret between Canfield and his lady loves. If the winds did blow up a storm it seemed to many Saratogans that the Casino at least would escape.

Canfield was not so sure. Spencer and Reed had countered every threat to close the Club House with a threat to close the race track, which they also controlled, and always theirs had been the last word. Canfield didn't have this advantage. Spencer had sold the race track three years before he sold the Club House, and the purchaser, Gottfried Walbaum, was operating it in such a way as to pour fuel on the fires of antagonism.

Walbaum had come to the Springs with virtually nothing to recommend him. He was boastful and profane, a gambler, bookmaker and, it was said, had once run a brothel; it was also claimed that at the Guttenberg race track in New Jersey, which he had owned, horses had been stimulated with electric shocks to make them run faster. Under his management the Saratoga track had none of the elegance Canfield brought to the Club

232 &

House. It was a haven for touts and thieves, and the races were so flagrantly dishonest that the better stables refused to participate. To cap it all, Walbaum had provided a room in which women and children could bet on the horses, the only race track betting room of its kind in the country.

In the summer of 1894, Canfield's first season at Saratoga, the criticism mounted. Late in August, Joseph Pulitzer, publisher of the New York *World,* sent his most enterprising reporter to the Spa to expose its evils. A determined young woman named Elizabeth Cochrane, she recently had achieved the status of a national heroine under her pseudonym, Nellie Bly, by circling the globe in seventy-two days, six hours, ten minutes and eleven seconds, thus eclipsing Phineas Fogg's famous record-breaking journey *Around the World in Eighty Days.*

Nellie Bly was appalled by what she saw at the Springs and told her legion of readers so in a Sunday article banked with indignant headlines:

OUR WICKEDEST SUMMER RESORT

Nellie Bly Pictures the Wild Vortex of Gambling and Betting
by Men, Women and Children at Saratoga

Money-Mad By Day and By Night

The Shameful Story of Vice and Crime, Dissipation and Profligacy
at This Once Most Respectable Watering-Place

Little Children Who Play the Horses

Reputable and Disreputable Women, Solid Merchants, Bankers,
Sports, Touts, Criminals and Race-Track Riff-Raff
Crazed by the Mania for Gold

"Cale" Mitchell, Village President and Boss Gambler

His Astonishing Admissions of Saratoga's Reckless Lawlessness
—Church Member and Giver to Charity—Rise of the Racing
Czar Walbaum, and Guttenberg Ideas for Night Scenes
in the Gaming Sport-Rooms and Hotels

A supplementary story was entitled *The Monte Carlo of America,* and began:

> This town has gone mad with the mania of gambling. From the Carlsbad of America, Saratoga has become its Monte Carlo —a Monte Carlo with the reckless law-breaking of Leadville combined with the vulgarity of the Bowery.
> Gambling is in the atmosphere. Formerly men of wealth and social position, statesmen, philosophers, students and artists

In 1894 the famous globe-circling reporter, Nellie Bly, "exposed" Saratoga's wickedness in the New York *World*.

gathered here to drink the waters that nature forces through a hundred fissures and enjoy the crisp, invigorating air and the picturesque scenery which have united in making Saratoga America's most famous summer resort. They came to ride, to drive, to dress and to secure that freedom from business and domestic care that gives perfect rest and brings back bodily health and vigor.

Now the great summer population of Saratoga is largely composed of those gathered here to gamble or to live off those who do gamble. From one of the most reputable and most exclusive of American watering places, it has been transformed into the wickedest and the wildest.

The following spring, the law amending Saratoga's charter having been upheld, the reformists took matters into their own hands. Caleb Mitchell was displaced as village president and the new chief executive, Charles H. Sturges, closed every gaming house in the community.

It resulted in a frustrating and unfriendly summer. The race track operated as usual but the horses were undistinguished and the crowds grew smaller as the season progressed. Indifferent to the charms the *World* writer had described, many visitors drifted away from the Spa altogether.

In the spring of 1896 the reformists retreated to a more tenable position. A new president was appointed and the Casino and five other gaming establishments were given permission to reopen; however, Mitchell and all other proprietors situated on Broadway, Saratoga's main street, were ordered to remain closed. No one had any solution to the problem of the race track, and Walbaum was allowed to go his own way until a syndicate of wealthy sportsmen headed by William C. Whitney bought him out and set about restoring the track's prestige.

The way was clear at last for the era of opulence at the Springs.

Chapter Two

The many-splendored summers of Saratoga's golden age were attended by an average of fifty thousand guests and one recurring complaint: at the close of each season visitors firmly declared that there would never be another to compare with it.

In spite of this melancholy consensus a dazzling procession of Saratoga summers marched from the old century into the new, and almost all who witnessed them could wholeheartedly agree with the reluctant valedictorian who wrote of one such season at the Springs:

> Another beautiful summer has gone and autumn, wrapped in her misty robes and haloed with a crimson and golden glory, comes over the distant hilltops . . . The time has come to say goodbye to Saratoga. The gay season is over, and only bright memories of all the brilliant scenes which have just passed come to take their place. But go where you will, in Europe or America, there is no other Saratoga, no other place which offers so much to the summer guest, whether he is in search of health, rest or pleasure; for Saratoga is all things to all men. It is a miniature world in itself; and here you may be grave or gay, wise or foolish, giddy or devout, as the mood seizes you. And the man or woman who cannot be charmed by Saratoga must indeed be hard to please, and would fail to be delighted anywhere on earth.

Possibly not the brightest, but certainly the most glittering memories summer visitors carried away with them early in September centered on the prodigal passage of Diamond Jim Brady and Lillian Russell through each season at the Springs.

In his childhood James Buchanan Brady had been cast on his own resources, and while these hadn't managed to provide him with polite manners and a formal education, in all other respects they had done well by him indeed. At forty he possessed twelve million dollars and could look forward to an additional million each year. He had achieved his fortune by supplementing an extraordinary talent for selling railroad equipment with a gift for personal aggrandizement which had captured the public imagination and made him a national figure. Uncouth and almost illiterate, he loomed in the popular eye as monumental evidence of the munificence that lay within reach of even the least privileged citizen who showed the proper gumption. It intrigued wealthy railroad men to do business with him, and since many of these were seasonal regulars at Saratoga, Brady enjoyed both pleasure and profit during his sojourns at the Spa. When the Master Car Builders held their convention there in the summer of 1896, Brady arrived with a silver-plated railroad undertruck and twenty-seven Japanese houseboys whom he installed in three rented cottages together with the choicest food, drinks and cigars. It was a rewarding enterprise all around—for the host, his guests, and at least one houseboy, who pocketed so many hundreds of fifty-cent Havanas that he opened a cigar store after he returned to New York.

Whether seen on the streets, the verandas, at Canfield's, the lake or the race track, Diamond Jim was something to write home about, and doubtless most Saratoga visitors did. His nickname, though accurate, was a feeble description of his presence. He owned thirty sets of jewels consisting of more than twenty thousand diamonds of varying size and shape, and six thousand other precious stones. Each day of the month a different set of gems was distributed over his person, flashing from collar buttons, shirt studs, neck-tie pin and neck-tie clasp, scarf pin, cuff links, belt buckle, watch-chain and watch, eyeglass case, pencil, pocketbook clasp and so on (even his underwear buttons were bejewelled). Most stunning of all was his "Transportation Set," which included a shirt stud ornamented with a bicycle made of 119 diamonds and an eyeglass case emblazoned with a 210-diamond-studded locomotive. In the complete array there were 2,548 diamonds, and he wore them all at once.

More remarkable still was the view he offered at meal-time. His stomach, which was held to be six times normal size and curved in a majestic sweep from his several chins to his sturdy thighs, seemed capable of absorbing whatever was put on the table. An entire dinner menu from soup (green turtle) to nuts (almonds) presented no challenge, although in between there was a staggering variety of provender: for example, oysters, boiled salmon in lobster sauce, sweetbreads, fillets of beef, supreme of chicken, terrapin, Saratoga Chips, partridge on toast, Roquefort cheese, ices, fruits, champagne, Roman punch and Benedictine. True, he had no appetite for the beverages. He disliked wines, liqueurs and whiskeys, preferring instead freshly-squeezed orange juice; but of this he could, and often did, drink four gallons during a sitting. Single portions of food were seldom enough. At a typical repast attentive observers might see four dozen oysters, a dozen hard-shell crabs, a half dozen lobsters, a huge steak

Diamond Jim Brady reflected the era of opulence at the Springs. He is shown outside the race track with Jesse Lewisohn (right), the sporting banker. The little man at left suggests the awe in which Brady was held.

Glamorous Lillian Russell was Brady's favorite companion at Saratoga. This 1887 portrait depicts the bountiful curves and charm that made her the idol of men and the envy of women.

By 1906, Miss Russell had given up the fight to keep her waistline. She is pictured here with Jesse Lewisohn on the lawn outside the Saratoga race track.

Louise Montague was one of the famous lady's rivals at the Spa.

A view of Broadway from the United States Hotel.

The rear piazza of the United States.

The hotel's interior court and music pavilion.

Cottage Row.

Two 1903 menus of the United States Hotel. At left the luncheon menu of August 18, at right the dinner bill of fare of August 19.

Luncheon

Cream of Barley, Carlsbad

Hot or Cold Consommé in Cup   Beef Tea, Toasted Sippet

Onions   Chow Chow   Olives

Fried Smelts, Tomato Sauce

Cucumbers   Potatoes, Persillade

Salisbury Steak

Lobster en Casserole, Newburg

Scrambled Eggs with Fresh Tomatoes

Ribs of Prime Beef   Leg of Mutton, Brétonne

Mashed Potatoes   Baked or Boiled Potatoes

Stewed Corn   Peas   Boiled Rice

COLD—Smoked Beef   Ham   Lyon Sausage

Smoked Beef Tongue   Pressed Corned Beef   Pickled Lamb's Tongue

Sardines   Roast Beef   Turkey

Head Cheese   Pickled Pig's Feet   Beef à la Môde

Boned Goose with Aspic   Beef Filet, Larded   Pickled Salmon, Tartare

Bologna Sausage   Veal Fricandeau

SALADS—Cold Slaw   Caprice   Beet

Green Peppers   Potato   Lettuce and Tomato

Cup Custard à la Vanilla

Blueberry Pie   Hot Ginger Bread

Cream Puffs   Sponge Cake   Pound Cake

Assorted Cake .   Small Gelocée   Butter Cake

Cream Cheese Wafer Crackers with Guava Jelly

Griddle Cakes with Maple Syrup

PINEAPPLE SHERBET

Preserved Apricots   Preserved Cherries   Preserved Peaches

Orange Marmalade   Raspberry Jam   Quince Jam

Stewed Prunes   Canton Ginger   Sliced Pineapple

CHEESE—American   Swiss   Neufchatel   Cottage   Edam

Milk Crackers   Wafer Crackers

Tea   Coffee   Cocoa   Milk   Buttermilk

Saratoga, Tuesday, August 18, 1903.

Vegetables Fresh Daily from United States Hotel Farm

United States Hotel
DINNER.

Gumbo Filet Bresilienne

Hot or Cold Consommé in Cup   Noodle au Bouillon

Olives   Radishes   Caviar   Onions

Anchovies à l'Italienne

Striped Bass, Genoise

Filet of Sole, Margueri

Potatoes, Hollandaise   Cucumbers

Fresh Tongue, Sauce Piquanté

York Ham with Spinach

Veal Fricandeau, Turtle Club

Lamb Sauté, Chasseure d'Afrique

Frogs' Legs, Cardinal

Bartlette Pears, Portugaise

Roast Spring Chicken au Jus

Ribs of Prime Beef   Saddle of Mutton, Currant Jelly

Mashed Potatoes   Boiled Potatoes

Green Corn   Onions, Béchamel   String Beans

Celery, Marrow Sauce   Russian Turnips

ROMAN PUNCH

SALADS—Watercress   Chicken   Escarole

Chicory   Lettuce and Tomato   Romaine

Tutti Frutti Pudding, Kummel Sauce

Apple Pie   Custard Pie

Assorted Cake   Coffee Eclairs   Lady Fingers   Pound Cake

Cocoanut Drops   Chocolate Africaines

Genoise Glacé   Rhine Wine Jelly

VANILLA ICE CREAM   MARBLE ICE CREAM

Oranges   Peaches   Plums   Bananas   Watermelon   Figs

Pears   Layer Raisins   Assorted Nuts

CHEESE—American   Pineapple   Cream   Roquefort   Cottage

Edam

Albert Crackers   Banquet Wafers   Water Crackers

COFFEE

Saratoga, Wednesday, August 19, 1903.

Vegetables Fresh Daily from United States Hotel Farm

The Grand Union Hotel at this time.

A morning concert on the piazza of the Grand Union.

he hotel's interior court.

and an assortment of French pastry disappear inside Brady's princely two hundred and fifty pounds of flesh.*

As grand a spectacle as he was, Diamond Jim was obliged to share his audience with, and indeed lost a great part of it to, the exquisite lady who usually accompanied him. Lillian Russell was the apple of every sporting male eye and the envy of practically all women. More than a dozen years had passed since she had first captivated New Yorkers at Tony Pastor's Music Hall as a radiant eighteen-year-old, originally named Helen Louise Leonard, whose golden hair and creamy complexion seemed natural products of the Iowa dairyland from which she came. Her girlish figure had ripened into bountiful curves and she constantly fought to keep her waist-line, but in the plush and plentiful Nineties she appeared more delectable than ever. Men liked an armful and women put on weight in attempts to resemble her. In the realm of beauty, however, she was rivalled only by raven-haired, statuesque Maxine Elliott. It was popular to express one's choice by purchasing cigarettes whose boxes contained the favored lady's picture.

Lesser claimants to the crown found occasional solace in personal triumphs over the queenly pair. At Saratoga one summer Miss Russell was challenged by a rising young charmer, Louise Montague, in a field in which she considered herself nonpareil: picking winners at the race track. As the competition grew keen stable owners, jockeys, trainers and bookies allied themselves with one beauty or the other and supplied them with a succession of tips. They came into the late August homestretch with Miss Russell the victor by a nose, and she gave a party to celebrate. Miss Montague, who earlier had suggested that her rival owed her reputation as a handicapper to blind luck in picking winners with a hatpin poked through the racing programs, arrived bearing a gift from Tiffany's. Miss Russell unwrapped it as everyone watched. She took out an expensive three-tined fish fork. "Now you can pick them to finish first, second and third all at once," Miss Montague said.

Whatever hurt this may have caused her as a horse-player, as a figure of glamour Lillian Russell was untroubled at the Springs. Whether she rode about town encased like a jewel in her smart little black victoria drawn by its two matching black thoroughbreds, or pedalled over the boulevards astride the gold-plated bicycle Brady had given her (with her initials formed in diamonds and emeralds in the handlebar), or strolled along Broadway and the renowned piazzas with her Japanese spaniel and its $1,800 collar, or sat at a table in Canfield's while Jean Columbin, with his own

---

* In his memoirs, Berry Wall wrote: "Diamond Jim Brady never touched alcohol and never smoked, but he did know food and always knew where to get it. And he knew the ladies, too! And what ladies! None of us who knew him will ever forget them. They were the pick of the Floradora Sextette and later the *Follies*. Blonde or brunette, they were the loveliest charmers on Broadway. Like his excessive jewelry, they were part of Jim Brady's game, part of his business, part of the endless advertising that he managed so cleverly, and, of course, they helped entertain his friends. The idea that he was on intimate and tender terms with any of them, let alone all of them, is much exaggerated. He was much too fat for that."

hands, served her the sweet corn and crêpes suzette she adored, she was the reigning cynosure of admiration.

To many onlookers she seemed a tantalizing enigma. Was she Diamond Jim's mistress—or was she not? The best-informed opinion said they were just good friends, that her lover was another with whom she was often seen, the sporting banker, Jesse Lewisohn. The speculation took on spice when Lewisohn, told by his doctor that he would have to choose between Miss Russell and his health, chose his health and went to Brady's farm to recuperate. There he fell in love with Brady's mistress, Edna McCauley, and married her.

Drawn closer, perhaps, by this mutual adversity Diamond Jim and Lillian Russell continued to seek each other's company. Well after the turn of the century they could be seen rolling along the avenues in one of the new electric broughams; built with special comforts Brady had ordered, it glistened at night with a hundred interior lights which bathed the famous couple in a milky glow.

Somewhere a voice said, "Kiss me"

Guests and residents who enjoyed an after-supper stroll along Broadway in the cool Saratoga evenings were pleasantly assaulted by soft and spirited melodies from the nearby ballrooms and interior courts of the hotels. Popular concert music mingled harmoniously with the rhythms of the latest dance steps, and more often than not a band struck up a lively recital from the bandstand of Congress Spring Park for romantic couples and casual visitors who paced the curving walks or sat under the trees.

Indeed, the nights were literally filled with music. The hotels competed with one another in bidding for the services of popular conductors and singers. John Philip Sousa led his band through a season's program of marches, many of which he had composed himself. Caruso came and Schumann-Heink; and Chauncey Olcott, the Buffalo-born Irish tenor, lifted his sweetly nostalgic brogue in *My Wild Irish Rose* and other reminiscences of the proud old sod he never saw until after he was famous. All were paid huge fees, but none was so handsomely recompensed as Victor Herbert— or took so little of his salary away from the Spa at the end of the season. "He had an Irishman's enthusiasm for betting coupled with the ill luck that has kept Ireland poor," Herbert's publisher, Edward B. Marks, said in explanation.

Summer after summer the outcome was the same, but Herbert dismissed his heavy losses with a light Irish heart. He was content to make music and sit with his friends. Twice a day, morning and evening, he went to the bandstand beneath the stately elms in the garden of the Grand Union and waved the fifty-four piece orchestra through the opulent Victor Her-

Adolph Yvon's painting, *The Genius of America,* in the ballroom.

Victor Herbert conducted two concerts a day at the Grand Union and wrote the score for *Mlle Modiste* during one summer's stay at the hotel.

Congress Hall. Completed in 1868, it replaced the original Congress Hall, destroyed by fire in 1866.

The Congress ballroom was not inside the hotel but in a building across Spring Street, and was connected to the hotel by a bridge.

bert melodies the entire country seemed to know by heart yet never tired of hearing. When he was done, and the fashionably dressed audience began drifting away in the shadowy silence, he repaired to the Grand Union café and presided at the head of a table crowded with theatrical producers, actors, agents, horsemen and others—a glass of Pilsner never far from his hand, for his thirst was unquenchable.

During one season at the Springs, Herbert wrote the score for *Mlle Modiste* and found the inspiration for its most popular song in the course of an after-concert stroll with the Grand Union's house detective, Tom Winn, who later recalled:

> It was a cool moonlit evening, one of those evenings generally advertised as being especially made for love. Mr. Herbert had finished his program and the crowd was dispersing. We walked in the garden, as we often did, since Mr. Herbert liked a few minutes of quiet before rejoining his friends. The lights were being dimmed. Off in the shadows somewhere we heard a soft voice say, "Kiss me." A silence, then, "Kiss me again." Mr. Herbert gripped my arm. "By God, Tom," he said. "By God." He was unusually quiet and busy for several days and I thought no more about it.

The following year *Mlle Modiste* opened in New York and *Kiss Me Again* was on almost everyone's lips. Winn was pleased to find in his mail two passes to the show together with a note from the composer which hoped that since he was an in-law to the song he would enjoy hearing Fritzi Scheff sing it.

Herbert's most generous gesture, however, came at the end of each summer when he handed over his baton to the small son of the Grand Union's proprietor, W. Edgar Woolley, and allowed him to briefly lead the orchestra. Neither then nor in early September, when he customarily rode in a flower-bedecked pony carriage in Saratoga's popular Floral Fetes, did the boy reveal that he would one day emerge as the satanically-bearded, terrible-tempered actor, Monty Woolley, and achieve instant stardom with a merciless portrait of Alexander Woollcott in the Kaufman-Hart comedy, *The Man Who Came To Dinner.*

Nettled, Nellie Bly let fly   Theater people had long been partial to Saratoga as a convivial place to catch up with old friends and new gossip and get themselves in shape for fall engagements. Some found the resort's captive audience impossible to resist; DeWolf Hopper and John Drew bravely essayed Shakespeare on a grassy stage in the Grand Union's garden. But most actors, actresses and entrepreneurs were content to be themselves, a mass performance which virtually converted all of the Spa into a summer playhouse.

Although he had yet to present his first *Follies,* a tall, slim, dark young man named Florenz Ziegfeld was clearly destined for fame and fortune. He wore pink shirts, wing collars and, at the gaming tables, a cool disdain for insolvency, which had flirted with him all through his career.

In 1896 he displayed the long expected Ziegfeld touch. From the Paris music halls he brought to New York lovely, naughty-eyed Anna Held, cast her in a musical comedy which made the most of her vivacity, and carefully made it known that her delicate complexion and exquisite figure were due in no small measure to her daily bath in a tub full of milk. Next, he married her.

In the successful years which followed, Saratoga saw them often: Ziegfeld in pursuit of lady luck, Miss Held's admirers in pursuit of Miss Held. It came as no surprise that at a supper party, when speculation arose as to how many consecutive kisses could be exchanged before the lips of the kissers became numb, Miss Held was chosen by a sporting male guest to put the question to the test. He would, he wagered, kiss the lady two hundred times with loving embrace. After one hundred and fifty-two kisses he was unable to continue and wandered away in confused euphoria.

Nettled by such exhibitionistic behavior, Nellie Bly had let fly at actresses and their escorts ("married men publicly flaunting their attentions to shameful women") in her report on Saratoga in the New York *World.* Other commentators were inclined to dismiss the didoes as part of feminism's growing pains. In the Nineties the movement had flowered in a profusion of new freedoms for women, and the clamor for suffrage was spreading across the land. As a center of pleasure Saratoga quite naturally was somewhat ahead of the times; a lady could enjoy herself there in ways scarcely available to her at home. Said *Everybody's:* "She may do with impunity in Saratoga those things which she may not approach even in thought elsewhere, and it is perhaps because of this temporary freedom that she loves her Saratoga as she loves no other resort." Strongly resistant to such sentiments as these, the Spa's old guard rallied to the banner of Nellie Bly. They agreed that she spoke for all of them when she described how "shocking" were the broken social barriers and vanishing class distinctions at the Springs, how "disgusting" was the free intermingling of men and women, and of high society and the *hoi polloi.* She seemed the voice of wisdom when she wrote of the lesson to be learned from Saratoga: "If woman's suffrage would produce such a scene, then God prevent suffrage. I claim to be liberal in my views; I believe in liberty and the right to do as one pleases, but I don't think I should like to see such an assemblage again, even at the day of judgment."

The last word was spoken not only at Saratoga but everywhere in the country by a young woman who asserted her independence with an insouciance that endeared her to all. She was the Gibson Girl, created with pen and ink by Charles Dana Gibson from society's confident debutantes who un-

Charles H. Hutchins

Congress Hall as it appeared when it was torn down in 1913.

The Windsor Hotel as it was seen from the Clarendon.

The Kensington Hotel.

Charles H. Hutchins

Charles H. Hutchins

The Windsor parlor.

Floral fetes were a popular featu
Saratoga's summers during the
Nineties.

A children's party in the court of the Grand Union Hotel.

Lovely Anna Held was escorted to the Spa by Florenz Ziegfeld, who had discovered her in a Paris music hall.

The last years of the nineteenth century were marked by a profusion of new freedoms for women. At Saratoga, independent-minded young ladies behaved with a daring and verve that ignored the traditional rules of decorum. The Gibson Girl—Charles Dana Gibson's pen-and-ink heroine who appeared regularly in the pages of *Life*— symbolized the New Woman, and in her shirtwaist blouse with its mannish bow tie, and in her bitter-sweet farewell to a summer romance on the last day of the season, she was widely emulated at the Spa.

hesitatingly tripped along paths their mothers had feared to tread. The Gibson Girl embodied these vibrant creatures, and through Gibson's drawings their progress was eagerly attended by young women all over America and their Gibson-style shirtwaist blouse with its mannish bow tie, worn as cockily as if it were a badge, was widely emulated.

All
any gambler
wants

The arrival of the twentieth century found the Springs fat, prosperous and relatively uncomplaining. In season visitors spent a million dollars a day for food, shelter and other necessities; the total was more than enough to carry the thirteen thousand permanent inhabitants of the village through the remaining ten months of each year and keep them well supplied with comforts.

Saratoga's gaming proprietors thrived too; it was estimated that two million dollars were gambled each weekday. But fortune smiled on none so sweetly as on Richard Canfield. In 1900 he was the richest and most favorably known gambler in the United States. His reputation extended even to the casinos of Europe and Asia. By any reckoning he was, as he was often called, "the Prince of Gamblers."

Canfield had three gaming establishments now. In 1897 he had purchased the Nautilus Club at Newport and the next year, after Delmonico's had moved uptown in New York to Fifth Avenue and 44th Street, he had abandoned his original club and opened a new casino in a handsome four-story brownstone a house away from the famous restaurant. It was as much a showplace as a place for gambling. With the same aim at distinction as he had shown in refurbishing Saratoga's Club House, he had not only provided his sophisticated guests with such elegant paraphernalia as hickory roulette wheels inlaid with ivory and ivory chips but also surrounded them with fine paintings, ceramics and furnishings. As Canfield expected, his altruism was well-advertised and attracted new customers; each year he cleared over $500,000. But the art exhibit was there for his own pleasure as well as that of his patrons. He had fallen in love with paintings and almost every year went to Europe to visit the art galleries and add to his collection. Books had captured his fancy too. In his apartment on the top floor of the brownstone he had assembled one of the most notable libraries owned by an American. The cram course in self-improvement he had put himself through in prison had led to an obsession for learning which had altered his values. He still enjoyed making money but no longer regarded it as an end in itself; now he prized it for the splendid things it could obtain.

At Saratoga, Canfield was as familiar a figure to summer visitors as the publicized stars of stage, sport and the social world, and was just as frequently pointed out. Newcomers who expected to see a coarse-mouthed, uncouth fellow built along the lines of John L. Sullivan were surprised when he proved to be an erudite, unobtrusive, elegantly dressed gentleman with courtly manners. In his mid-forties, he was fighting a losing battle with fat and wore a corset to contain the most evident portion of his more than two hundred pounds. Nevertheless, he walked briskly, his head flung back, his chest out; a tall, brown-haired, gray-eyed, clean-shaven, self-made man custom-clothed in black or gray. He would wear no other color.

His habits were equally admirable. The course of his day was usually set at six o'clock, when he awoke and rang the bell for his breakfast. Generally, it was the same: scrambled eggs, water rolls and coffee (if he had been drinking hard the night before, which he often did, though always in private and rarely at Saratoga, he felt obliged on arising to fortify himself with an enormous plateful of corned beef hash). While breakfasting he studied the results of the previous evening's gaming and the stock quotations in the New York *Sun,* then bathed, shaved, dressed and strolled to the branch office of his brokers to play the market. In the afternoon he went to the races, as nearly everyone did, and on his return enjoyed his favorite part of the day. It began with dinner, at which he presided in white tie and tails, in the Casino dining room. His guests were an always entertaining, if sometimes abrasive, mixture of society bluebloods, Wall Street titans, theatrical personalities and *nouveau riche* opportunists; Whitneys and Vanderbilts and J. Pierpont Morgan rubbed shoulders and viewpoints with such as Ziegfeld and John W. Gates. After dinner Canfield briefly visited the gaming rooms, then went to his office. At midnight he retired. Alone in his apartment, he slipped into an old-fashioned nightgown and settled in bed to read, sometimes until two or three o'clock in the morning. One after another he absorbed books on art, history, religion and kindred subjects. When his interest was caught by something in particular, he bought all the books he could find on the topic and concentrated on it until his understanding was complete. His bedside companions for one entire winter were books on ancient Egyptian art.

Meanwhile, his profits mounted at the faro, roulette and poker tables. Heavy bettors such as James Keene, Marcus Daly and John Sanford parted with sizable portions of their fortunes made in Nevada silver and Montana copper mines and New York carpet mills. The free-spending young millionaire, Freddy Hostetter, lost $213,340 in three successive nights of roulette. Waiting on the veranda of the Grand Union to escort two tardy ladies to a lake-shore supper, Willie K. Vanderbilt stepped over to the Casino to amuse himself for a few minutes at the games and returned to the hotel minus $130,000.

Big losers were invited to Canfield's office to split a consoling pint of champagne. It was the only consolation their host offered. There was no comforting pat on the back, no jollying "Better luck next time, old man"—the spurious ritual deemed suitable to the occasion by the gaming profession at large. On the contrary, Canfield told each loser that his loss was to be expected, and that if he played again with the hope of recouping it the chances were that he would lose still more. It was pointless to put on a show

◄§ 255

"Bet-a-Million" Gates. At Saratoga in 1902, he launched the biggest gamble in resort gaming history.

of encouragement, Canfield felt; his guests would gamble again anyway, and honesty was the hallmark of his reputation.

In line with this reasoning, he gave a New York *Herald* reporter some blunt statistics reflecting the odds in favor of any gaming house which virtually guaranteed a profit to the proprietor:

> All any gambler wants is to have play for a long enough time and he'll get all the money any player has. In business, if you or I can lend money enough. at five per cent we think we are doing pretty well. Every time a roulette wheel is spun the percentage on a thirty-six-inch wheel is $5\frac{5}{19}$ per cent against the player. Therefore, you will say that I get an interest on my money of $5\frac{5}{19}$ per cent every time a roulette wheel is spun. If I have any patronage at all, you can imagine what interest I get on my money in any one night.

The major threat to the prosperity of the Casino came from plungers who possessed almost unlimited wealth and enjoyed risking it in exhausting hours of play. Such was John Warne Gates. A millionaire many times over, he often wagered immense sums for two or three days at a stretch, without sleep and with only brief pauses for refreshment. Gambling was his business, and the higher the stakes the better he liked it. Before he was thirty he had made a fortune selling barbed wire to cattle-rich Texas ranchers, and employed it in audacious speculations which had earned him a staggering income and a sobriquet he detested, "Bet-a-Million" Gates. In his free-wheeling career he had upset markets, precipitated panics, created mammoth trusts, tossed away his profits on the gaming tables and regained them with daring new enterprises. Tall, stout, heavily mustached, he had shocked New York, London and Paris with the vulgarity of his ways, and had so offended J. Pierpont Morgan that the latter had excluded him from the billion-dollar United States Steel Corporation, a project Gates had originated.

It mattered little to Gates whether he gambled on an investment, the speed of a horse, the turn of a card or a wheel, or the progress of two raindrops down a windowpane. If the stakes were high, he bet. After one wager at the Saratoga race track he was obliged to collect his winnings in a large market basket.

It was this ability to overcome the odds that made Gates anathema to gaming establishments. His resources were greater than theirs and he drew on his wealth unsparingly in his zeal to win. "I think no man should bet unless he's sure he's right," he had once explained. "And when he's sure he's right, he should be willing to bet every dollar he owns. That's the way I bet. For me, there's no fun in betting just a few thousand. I want to lay down enough to hurt the other fellow if he loses, and enough to hurt me if I lose."

On an afternoon in August 1902, Gates set in motion a series of events which culminated in the biggest gamble in resort gaming history. Pyramiding his bets at the race track, he threw good money after bad on a string of losers, and at the end of the day's program was out $400,000. That evening he dined at the Casino, and then began playing faro in the public gaming room at the regular limit of $500 on case cards and $1,000 on doubles. He lost $25,000, and went upstairs to the private rooms, where the limit was more generous: $2,500 and $5,000. His luck stayed put; at ten o'clock he was in the hole for $150,000.

Gates sought out Canfield and asked him to raise the limit; he would consider it a favor if he was permitted to play for twice the amount— $5,000 on cases and $10,000 on doubles. Canfield regarded him thought-fully. "Are you sure that's enough?" he said.

Gates returned to his table and began betting $5,000 or $10,000 on every turn of the cards. Before midnight his luck began to change. By two o'clock he had retrieved the $150,000 he had lost. And at dawn, when he discontinued the game, he was $150,000 ahead.

All in all he was satisfied. He had cut his losses for the day from well over a half million to $250,000.

Chapter Three

Jerome vs.
a saintly smile

On December 19, 1901, Reginald Vanderbilt, a grandson of the renowned Commodore and an undergraduate at Yale, celebrated his twenty-first birthday by tossing a dinner party for a group of congenial classmates at a posh New York City restaurant, and afterward treated them to an evening at a gaming house, where they parted with $70,000.

Small as it was, the incident touched off an explosion. For some time the church, the press and various reformists, notably the Parkhurst Society, had been agitating against gambling as an incitement to crime and corruption, and one and all trumpeted the frivolity as an example of gambling's evil influence on impressionable youth. Since Richard Canfield was the most popular gambler in New York, it was assumed that the disgraceful episode had occurred at his establishment "next to Del's," and he was harshly attacked for profiting from the Vanderbilt party's immature folly.

Canfield quickly proved that he was not involved, that the collegians had visited another gambling house, but now the reformists were in full cry. William Travers Jerome, a crusading lawyer who had been elected district attorney with their support, vowed that after he took office on New Year's Day he would rid the city of Canfield and every other gambler.

The clamor rose and Canfield decided to withdraw until it subsided. When play was completed in his gaming rooms on New Year's Eve, he announced to his guests that the house would be closed until further notice. New York's other leading gamblers followed suit, but in the spring reopened their establishments. Canfield, except for the use he made of the living quarters on the top floor, kept his famous brownstone shut. Nevertheless, in the public view he remained "the Prince of Gamblers," and Jerome was determined to obtain evidence with which to arrest and convict him and send him to prison.

On arriving at Saratoga that summer, Canfield found the atmosphere somewhat chilly. Once again there was talk of prohibiting gambling at the Springs, and when the season opened only a half dozen gaming houses were permitted to operate. The visiting public, however, was as friendly as before. In September Canfield counted close to $600,000 in profit, a hundred thousand more than he had made from the Casino the previous summer.

With the future of his Manhattan establishment in doubt, and the earnings of his Newport club discouragingly low, he wondered what he might do to improve his position at the Spa. The answer seemed to lie in an unkempt tract of land adjoining the Casino's grounds. Every summer, from the reservations at Montreal and Quebec, Indians had descended on the land, put up huts and laid out a great assortment of beadwork, moccasins, bows and arrows, and other souvenirs calculated to attract the tourists. Saratogans had long been offended by the sight and Canfield felt that it detracted from the elegance of the Casino, but the owners of the tract had remained adamant in their refusal to sell the property or eject the trespassers.

At the close of the 1902 season, Canfield redoubled his efforts to purchase the land, and succeeded. With suitable fanfare he announced that he would use the site to provide Saratoga Springs with the most magnificent gaming establishment and park in North America. He at once engaged an outstanding architect, Clarence Luce, to redesign and beautify the Casino and its now expansive spread of acres, and obtained his promise that the place would be ready for business the following summer.

Late in November a private detective in the employ of a New York reform organization gave a statement to the district attorney's office in which he said that he had recently gambled in Canfield's Manhattan house. It was the break William Travers Jerome had been hoping for; on December 1st he ordered the police to raid the place, and went along to see that it was properly carried out.

Except for Canfield and a few friends he was entertaining at dinner, the house was unoccupied; there was no sign of either gambling or gamblers. But dismantling a wall, the police came upon a store-room full of gaming paraphernalia. They confiscated it and arrested Canfield.

Jerome was disappointed. Although he had Canfield in custody, the evidence against him was much too meager to support the sweeping charges he had envisioned. He proposed a compromise: if Canfield would plead guilty to being a common gambler, he would be let off with the minimum punishment the law allowed, a twenty-five dollar fine.

Canfield rejected the offer. The term "common gambler" was not in the least applicable, he felt, indeed was insulting. He had often described his occupation as "Gentleman," and he was certain that none of his friends would disagree. More to the point, he intended to press for damages against Jerome and the police for entering his home illegally.

He turned the matter over to his lawyers and went off to London while Jerome sought to make well-known patrons of his house testify to play in the gaming rooms. All refused and one, Jesse Lewisohn, carried his wrath against the district attorney all the way to the Appellate Division of the Supreme Court.

An era ends, another begins: in the early 1900's motor cars gradually supplanted horses and carriages at the Springs. Here, an automobile chugs along Broadway past the United States Hotel.

Keeneland-Cook

Reginald Vanderbilt in a classy model of 1902. His twenty-first birthday celebration at a New York City gaming house aroused so much public criticism that Richard Canfield was forced to close his Gotham casino. The diagram shows the interior of the Canfield casino, the rooms captioned (from bottom up): Free Lunch, Reception Room, Card Room, Faro, Roulette, Private Gambling Rooms and Sleeping Apartment.

New York World, courtesy of the Press Publishing Company

James Abbott McNeill Whistler (from a dry-point drawing by Paul Helleu) painted this portrait of Canfield, which he named *His Reverence*, but died before he completed it.

Congress Spring Park continued to attract Saratoga's residents and guests after the turn of the century. Band concerts were held three times a day.

Canfield's arrival at the Claridge, where he usually stopped, initiated a procession of art dealers to his suite. His expertise, together with his willingness to pay a little more than the established prices, made him a favorite in England's art circles. The American painter, James Abbott McNeill Whistler, was especially taken with him.

The two had been introduced in 1901 by Charles Freer, the Detroit art connoisseur, and had hit it off at once. Whistler was charmed by Canfield's taste and enjoyed the paradox of a professional gambler who conversed with the erudition and authority of a college professor. Canfield revered Whistler as one of the great artists of his time. Having been exposed to a series of exhibitionists at Saratoga, he was also at ease with Whistler's egoism and eccentricities, which, along with his stinging wit, still served to remind Londoners of the swaggering days of the old artist's youth, when, to attract attention to his disturbingly original talents, he had shocked Victorian sensibilities with such whimsies as costuming his slender figure in a fawn-colored frock coat, fancy gloves, polished black slippers with pink or yellow ribbons as shoe-laces, topped off with a monocle screwed into his right eye.

Soon after Canfield arrived in England, Whistler began painting his portrait. Canfield sat for him almost every day, but the work progressed slowly. For days at a time Whistler left his palette untouched and they just talked. In May the painting was still unfinished, but Canfield could sit no longer. His remodelled Casino at the Springs was nearly complete and he was impatient to see it and arrange for a grand opening at the start of the new season.

Whistler told him to take the portrait with him, as they might never have a chance to complete it. It showed Canfield in solemn attire, hands clasped over his chest, a saintly smile on his lips and one eye half shut. Whistler was pleased with it and named it, *His Reverence*. It was his last work. Two months after Canfield sailed, he died.

*Nymphs,
satyrs,
music
with French
dressing*

Neither the absence of his enemy nor an unusually attractive spring had tempered Jerome's determination to bring Canfield to heel. The legal battle had moved into the courts, and it promised to be a long drawn-out fight. Through the newspapers, New York City's reformists had kept up a running attack which grew more heated with the gambler's return. Canfield shrugged it off. In reply to reporters' questions, he said, "I do not care a rap what other people think about me. The only person whose respect I want is that of Richard Canfield. I have made it a rule to look at myself in the mirror every morning, and I feel that if I can look in my own eyes and be satisfied with the examination, then I have no reason to regret anything I have done."

At Saratoga he was greeted more cordially. While the authorities were apprehensive that his intention to resume gaming in the village might invite unwanted attention from the state law-makers in Albany, the new Canfield Casino was a thing of beauty. Already, though it hadn't been formally opened and the season hadn't officially begun, visitors were arriving at the Springs in unprecedented numbers to have a look at the highly publicized attraction. In June, Canfield took a large party of friends and reporters on a pre-opening tour of the house and grounds, and all agreed that they were indeed something to see.

First on the itinerary was the garden. The original acres on which the Casino sat adjoined Congress Spring Park, a tranquil site of curving walks, benches, flower-beds, fountain, pond, bandstand and Congress Spring, whose name Dr. John Clarke had made famous the world over. Since the early days of High Rock, more than a hundred and fifty springs had been discovered and drilled in and about the village, each somewhat dissimilar in chemical deposits but all skilled in repairing the damage brought on by excessive work, worry, food and drink. The Congress waters, however, attracted the most visitors. People enjoyed the cool shade and comforts of the pavilion which stood over the boxed-in spring and gossiped contentedly while water-boys dipped glasses set in metal frames at the end of sticks and placed the bubbling liquids before them. In visualizing his new Casino, Canfield had pictured the two adjoining properties as one continuous park, and Clarence Luce had been at pains to carry out his wishes. The one-time camping ground of the Indians and Morrissey's elm-shaded lawn had been landscaped to resemble the courtyard of an Italian palace. Nymphs and satyrs carved from clear white marble by Florentine artists frolicked in flower-beds of many brilliant hues. At either end of a fountain two marble Tritons spewed water at one another through conch-shell trumpets. Marble benches rested beneath tall, leafy pines.

Entering the Casino, the sightseers came upon a variety of treats. One wall of the public gaming room was paneled with mirrors, with statuettes of renowned Frenchmen standing between them on marble pedestals. Glittering chandeliers dropped from the ceiling, and underfoot was a $10,000, 72 by 44 foot rug from Scotland, said to be the largest rug ever woven in one piece. Next to the gaming hall was the café, with marble-topped tables at which patrons could assuage their thirst and reflect on the vicissitudes of gambling. And a discreet distance away was a library, lined with books, and Canfield's office, in which sat the famous Canfield safe. Apart from the books, a stained-glass window which had been installed by Tiffany's was the library's major conceit.

The most rewarding sight, however, was the restaurant. A wing had been added to the Casino to provide Jean Columbin with an expanded domain. It contained huge kitchens and pastry ovens, and a vast European-style dining room suffused with light filtered through octagonal stained-glass win-

The Congress waters also remained popular. "Although Congress Spring has discharged its health-giving waters for well over a century," the park brochure said, "it has lost none of its most efficacious qualities. The Congress Spring waters still retain the delicious flavor and smooth cathartic action which have always been their characteristic recommendations." Pictured here is the entrance to the Congress Spring pavilion, its interior, and guests drinking the waters.

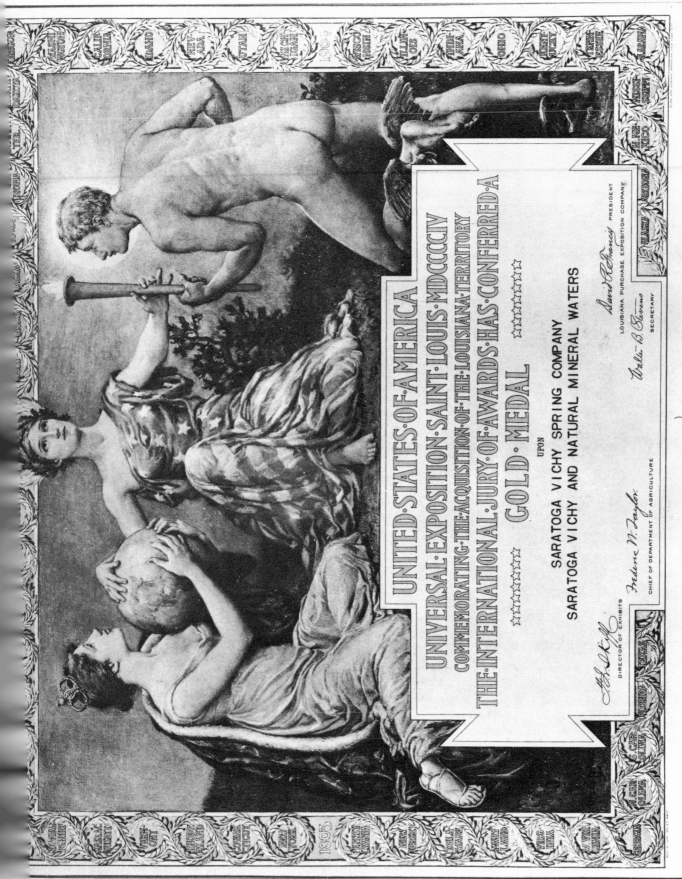

In 1904 a jury at the Louisiana Purchase Exposition at St. Louis awarded a gold medal to Saratoga's Vichy waters.

Charles H. Hutchins

dows in a vaulted ceiling. Twelve of the windows displayed the signs of the Zodiac; the others portrayed the love story of a Greek warrior and his maid. Vaulted archways at either side of the room served as entrance and exit, and semicircular extensions at both ends stood ready to accommodate guests who wished to dine in private. Hidden tiers of gas lights could be lit all at once, touched off by an electric spark from a central switch.

To the admiring tourists it seemed all that a restaurant should be; only William C. Whitney dissented. There should be an orchestra to play at dinner-time, he told Canfield, and he knew just the one: an *intime* group which had recently charmed him in Paris. He would be delighted to bring the musicians over at his own expense.

Canfield had made no provision for an orchestra for a personal reason: he loathed music with his meals. Nevertheless, he thanked Whitney for his suggestion, said that he would act on it and wouldn't think of letting his friend foot the bill. He went to Paris, returned with the group, and on opening day installed it behind a cluster of potted palms at one end of the dining room. Shortly afterward he learned that the Parisian artists Whitney so highly prized and warmly recommended had for four years played at a commonplace café on Sixth Avenue in New York City.

Canfield kept his temper, said nothing to Whitney, and allowed the musicians to play out the season. It had cost him a million dollars to remodel the Casino and grounds, $200,000 of which had been spent on the dining room and kitchens. To this he added $30,000 as the price of French dressing.

"They gambled in the Garden of Eden"

Despite the Casino's undeniable attractions—indeed, partly because of them—the village trustees, with a nervous glance at the rising tide of anti-gambling sentiment in the state, decreed that Canfield's and all other houses in the gaming community must operate behind closed doors. Canfield submitted ungraciously. It was a poor reward, he thought, for having invested the Spa with new grandeur, and it was bound to be ineffectual because it went against the grain of human nature. "They gambled in the Garden of Eden," he had once pointed out, "and they will again if there's another one." The decree restricted the gaming rooms to regular patrons and newcomers they introduced and approved, and while this considerably reduced the traffic at the Casino Canfield had little reason to complain when the season ended. As usual he lost on the restaurant, $80,000, but made over $400,000 on the games.

That winter Jerome won a major victory in his war on gambling; the New York State legislature passed a law amending the code of criminal procedure so that witnesses could be compelled to testify; he began to summon Canfield's patrons to tell what went on in the famous house "next to Del's."

Alarmed by the new developments, the Saratoga authorities notified the gaming proprietors that in the 1904 season there would be further restrictions and gambling would have to be conducted even more secretly than before. Canfield replied that under the circumstances it would be better if he kept the Casino closed. He stood by his decision against all pleas, refusing even to open the restaurant. As a final affront, he spent the summer at Newport, Saratoga's closest rival, supervising his Nautilus Club.

It was a dull season at the Spa. Although the other gaming establishments operated under the new rules, the fashionable guests missed the elegance of the Casino, Canfield's lordly presence and the epicurean wonders Columbin conjured. Canfield too had an unhappy time. The season's profit at the Nautilus Club came to eleven hundred dollars.

The day after he closed his Newport house, Reggie Vanderbilt came with a party of friends and asked for a chance to play. Canfield consented to one spin of the roulette wheel and Vanderbilt put a thousand-dollar bill on the red. The wheel spun and the red won. Canfield left the resort with a hundred dollars to show for his summer toil and a resolve never to let it happen again. A few months later, he sold the club.

In December his two-year battle with Jerome expired in an uneasy peace. An important part of the district attorney's case had rested on the statement given to him by the private detective who said he had gambled in Canfield's Manhattan house during the time it was reported to be closed, testimony which had persuaded Jerome to raid the premises. Recently, however, the detective had confessed that he had never been inside the house, and was sentenced to prison.

Jerome and Canfield met in court, and the prosecutor moved to dismiss the proceedings providing Canfield pleaded guilty to being a common gambler and paid a thousand-dollar fine. It was the same offer Jerome had made at the outset with a higher, though still reasonable, penalty. This time Canfield accepted. It had cost him $100,000 in legal fees to fight the case and he was reluctant to spend more. Too, while it still wounded him to be called a common gambler, he was convinced that a compromise was the most favorable solution.

Saratoga's trustees breathed a sigh of relief. The next summer eight gaming establishments were permitted to operate unhindered by the closed-door ruling; however, as a cautious postscript all were obliged to close at two o'clock in the morning.

It was a frustrating season even so. The state-wide agitation against gambling had encouraged the Spa's reformists to enlist the aid of Albany politicians, and together they were mounting an all-out attack on gaming in the village. From one day to the next there were rumors that the gambling houses would be raided and this, together with the restricted hours of play, kept many customers away. The following summer only the Casino and two other establishments were allowed to open, and the closed-door ruling was reimposed. All prospered until the racing season opened in August, when

The most magnificent innovation at the Spa in the early 1900's was Richard Canfield's new Casino, designed by one of the country's leading architects, Clarence Luce. These three photos show a fountain in the Italian gardens adjoining the Casino, the Casino itself (Canfield's living quarters are at left and a fountain erected by John Morrissey in 1869 stands in the center of the lawn), and the restaurant, its vaulted ceiling perforated with octagonal stained-glass windows.

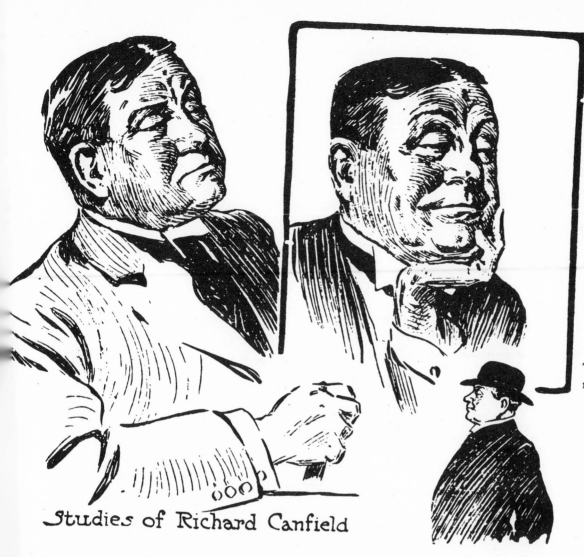

The Prince of Gamblers as a newspaper artist saw him.

Studies of Richard Canfield

In 1907, after reformists mounted an all-out attack on gambling, Canfield closed his famous Casino and put it up for sale. Saratoga's high-stakes card games were confined to private hotel rooms.

the gaming rooms were shut tight after a friendly visit from the local sheriff armed with a suggestion from the governor. During the summer of 1907 there was no play whatsoever in Canfield's public gaming room and only occasional gambling in the private rooms upstairs.

In September of that year, Canfield announced that the Casino and its landscaped acres were for sale. Few took him seriously; he had become so much a part of the Spa that villagers and visitors couldn't imagine Saratoga without him. The newspapers were full of assurances that he would return in the spring as usual.

Canfield disappointed them. At the close of the 1907 season he had estimated his wealth at $12,000,000—five million of which had been earned through gambling and the rest in Wall Street. It seemed senseless to continue exposing himself to the uncertainties and irritations of his profession when his real interest was art and he could well afford to pursue it. His position was rudely shaken when, before the year was out, he lost more than half of his fortune in a stock market panic, $1,500,000 in a single day, but he clung to it nevertheless. Only twice was he tempted to resume his old life—once when he was asked to manage a casino in Monte Carlo and again when, shortly before the revolution which overthrew him, President Porfirio Diaz invited Canfield to take charge of Mexico's National Lottery. He declined both offers.

Early in 1911 he sold his Saratoga property for $150,000 to the village of Saratoga Springs, which wished to retain it as part of a system of public parks, and in May the Casino's furnishings were disposed of at public auction. It was Canfield's last visit to the Spa.

Since his retirement he had resided in a brownstone in New York City's fashionable East Fifties, and travelled to Europe each year to view the new art collections. He was greatly pleased when he was elected to the Walpole Society, a select group of art connoisseurs, and hoped that he would be included in one of the forthcoming editions of *Who's Who in America,* but lost whatever chance he had when he slipped and tumbled down a flight of subway station steps on returning from a business trip to Brooklyn in December 1914. The fall fractured his skull and he died the next day.

The obituaries said that his death marked the end of an era, but in Saratoga it had ended with Canfield's departure from the Springs. After his withdrawal public gaming had been barred from the village, and for a while the big spenders had tried to make the best of it with high-stake poker games played in the privacy of their hotel rooms. Then, gradually, they had stopped coming to the Spa. Without the Casino the resort didn't seem to be nearly as much fun.

Chapter Four

*Whitney
and the
dowager queen*

In the gay parade which crossed the Spa's golden divide into the 1900's, none marched with a jauntier step than the Saratoga Racing Association. Led by William Collins Whitney, the wealthy sportsmen had reason to be proud. In the seasons following their purchase of the race track from Gottfried Walbaum they had restored its old-time dignity, integrity and style. The celebrated stables which had avoided the track while Walbaum was in charge had returned with a glittering array of spectacular horses and famous jockeys, and high society flocked to the races in greater numbers than ever before. Once again the old descriptions of the Saratoga course rang true: "the dowager queen of the American turf," "the proving ground of champions," "the graveyard of favorites," "the most beautiful race track in America."

William C. Whitney originally had taken up racing simply to beat his Wall Street rival, the Nevada silver king, James Keene. Now, such was his love for fine blooded horses, his stable was second to none in America and he gave it a major share of his attention. His eminence and enthusiasm for racing, along with that of other prominent men who regularly sported their colors on the turf, soon made horse-owning a hallmark of social prestige, as it was in England. The pleasures of belonging to the new horse society became evident when one of Whitney's thoroughbreds, Volodyovski, won the Derby at Epsom Downs in 1901; the elated owner sent word to his stable at Saratoga to buy champagne for his entire legion of friends at the race track. (When the wine wasn't chilled and served just right a new caterer, Harry M. Stevens, took over, and then and there launched an enterprise which was to take him, via the redoubtable Stevens serving organization, to every race track and baseball park in the country.)

Whitney's largesse during the racing season at the Spa was carried off with such attractive impetuosity that it gave still another touch of luster to the newly transfigured Saratoga track. When he entered Goldsmith in the first Saratoga Special he called in a young betting commissioner, Johnny

Walters, asked him to get a list of the guests staying at the Whitney place, and a list of the many maids, waiters, bartenders, barbers, clerks and so on who had served his party at home and in the hotels, and place a hundred dollar bet on Goldsmith's nose for each of them. The total wager came to $12,000—and when Goldsmith won at 6 to 1, Walters distributed the windfall in one hundred and twenty identical envelopes marked with Whitney's initials. That evening Whitney was the most celebrated host at the Springs.

In possible imitation of the master, the same prodigal hand, though restrained by much more modest means, was displayed by some who worked for Whitney. Tod Sloan, the Kokomo, Indiana, barber's son who rode in England for the Prince of Wales and other members of the British nobility, came to Saratoga to ride Whitney's Ballyhoo Bey. He brought with him two English valets and ten trunks, and checked in at the United States for an extended stay at $125 a day. Visiting the Casino on the night of his arrival he saw so many of his friends that he took Canfield aside, produced a roll of bills as thick as his wrist and told the proprietor that his friends were his guests and to give them anything they requested.

The blue-ribbon quality Whitney and his associates imparted to the Saratoga course infected even the bookmakers; however shrewd they might be, their word was their bond. No more respectful tribute was paid to the track than by Johnny Walters after Whitney's death in 1904. Walters, who had become a bookie with Whitney as a client, went to Whitney's lawyers and wrote out a check to his estate for $150,000 to settle a debt only he and the dead man knew about.

Sporting gentry   In the summer of 1908 membership in Saratoga's turf society was more sought after than in any previous season. The Casino gaming rooms and its elegant restaurant were closed, and the race track was the one place left at the Springs where gambling, fashion and the social graces were combined.

One of the most attractive rewards of membership was the invitation to drop in at any of the daily half dozen six A.M. track breakfasts and watch the horses gallop through the morning mists. The practice of breakfasting at the track had been introduced in the 1870's, when Southern stable owners who had routed themselves out of bed to attend the workouts had spared themselves a trip back to the village for their morning repast by eating with their Negro stablehands. It had proved to be such a pleasant diversion that Southern belles had also turned out for it, with predictable results. Tables were set up and the cuisine was enlarged and improved. Melon, berries, steak, fried chicken, corn bread, preserves and coffee were fairly typical of the morning menus. In the early 1900's, when so many of the guests came in evening clothes after a night of gaming at Canfield's, a more stylish breakfast seemed in order: frogs' legs and champagne. Whenever a gentleman failed to survive the combination the headwaiter put a screen around him.

As non-members of horse society the general run of race-goers were denied such privileges, but the track had enough attractions to satisfy everyone. And to at least a portion of the local population it remained a pleasure even out of season. Recalling his boyhood at the Springs, Frank Sullivan wrote, "The race track was a playground made to order for youngsters. It lent itself wonderfully to all sorts of games, especially those needing plenty of room. The horse barns provided unlimited hiding places, the steeplechase jumps served admirably as forts, and the harrows stored in the paddock in the off season made fine Roman chariots."

The August racing program, however, capped the year for the villagers as well as the horse-players. "In August all the householders in Saratoga Springs with spare rooms rented them to racing folk," Sullivan wrote. "They enjoyed the extra income and also the colorful characters, so unlike themselves, who became their guests. They were a novelty, part of the seasonal fun, and most Saratogans rejoiced in their in-season guests, their high-spirited visitors, and were a little lonesome when they left . . . When August ended, the races ended too. Overnight the horses, the jockeys and all the pleasant racing folk vanished. The carnival was finished, the fanfare and the tantivy of the bugles were stilled, and a quiet that was deafening dropped . . ."

Saratoga's racing season got underway the day before the opening program, when the Cavanagh Special rolled into town. This was a deluxe train of Pullman cars, diners and a day coach or two, and its passengers were almost exclusively bookmakers and their assistants. Some six hundred strong, they fell in behind their leader, John G. Cavanagh, for whom the train was named, and marched to their hotels cheered on by a band and a crowd of horse-players who had turned out to welcome them.

Originally, the Spa had been fairly indifferent to bookmakers and their method of betting. The system had been introduced at the English courses in 1840 and hadn't been adopted in the United States until thirty-one years later, but for some time afterward Saratoga's sporting men had continued to play the horses through private wagers or the auction pools John Morrissey conducted at the Club House and the race track. By the 1880's, however, bookmakers were active at tracks throughout the country, and in New York State, fancying themselves no less reputable than Wall Street brokers and their function no less worthy than that of the Stock Exchange, they advertised themselves in the newspapers as Turf Exchanges. Pursuing this line of thought the most successful New York bookies had formed the Metropolitan Turf Association, an exclusive group which quickly gained control of betting at all state race tracks. Buttons, signifying membership in the association, were sold as were seats on the Stock Exchange, and were just as difficult and almost as costly to obtain.

William C. Whitney headed the wealthy sportsmen who comprised Saratoga's early horse society.

Johnny Walters, a respected bookmaker of the period.

The gentleman jockey, Tod Sloan, came to Saratoga from England to ride Whitney's Ballyhoo Bey.

Bookmakers had taken over the betting at the race course in the 1880's, exhorting the crowd from their stalls in the betting ring. Blackboards listed the horses in each race and odds offered on each entry.

Irish John Cavanagh, the leader of the bookies.

In 1897 Irish John Cavanagh had become head of the group and set about exercising his authority with a quick tongue and a firm hand. Before long his power was absolute: he ruled on who could join the association and who could not, and settled all disputes between members. The Cavanagh Special was his seal of approval, and the hundred or so bookies permitted to ride in it with their retinues were acknowledged as the elite of the betting fraternity.

They were a colorful lot with nicknames to match their idiosyncrasies: The Boy Plunger, Big Store, The Orator; Orlando Jones was called Fashion Plate in mock deference to his Victorian attire and Tiffany Wolfgang had won his sobriquet by guaranteeing the prices he quoted to be as good as anything in the country's most famous jewelry shop.

At the Saratoga track they took command of the betting ring, an open-sided shed near the finish line. Here, they mounted the large circle of stilt-raised stalls and exhorted the crowd while their sheetwriters and pay-off men waited to do business. Above each stall a small blackboard was chalked with the name of the bookmaker and the names of the horses entered in the next race, with the ever-changing odds posted opposite each entry. The crowd was perpetually in motion, each bettor shopping from stall to stall for the most favorable odds. When he found a wager to his liking, he stepped up to a window in the stall, named his horse and put down his money to win, to place (finish either first or second), or to show (finish either first, second or third). He was then given a ticket by the sheetwriter who recorded its number on the bookmaker's "sheet." If the horse ran in the money the bettor presented his ticket at another window in the stall and collected his winnings from the pay-off man.

Simple as it was, the transaction did not always work this smoothly. When a customer irked Virginia Carroll, a bookmaker with an easily ruffled disposition, by pointing with his umbrella to the name of the horse on which he wished to bet, Carroll reached down from his stall, seized the umbrella and hurled it as far as his strength allowed. He then instructed his sheetwriter to record a wager of five umbrellas against one umbrella on the horse selected.

On the whole, however, the bookies kept a cheerful mien throughout the season, and with good reason: at the end of each racing day the soil of the betting ring and the aisles of the grandstand were littered with the torn remains of their customers' losing tickets.

Tipsters also did well for themselves during the August running at the Springs. Like the bookmakers, they arrived by rail shortly before the opening program, but not in the same style; some emerged from empty freight cars, others from undercarriages and a few from more ingenious hideouts. At the track they sold tips on the horses, as transparent a fraud as most gold-brick enterprises, with gratifying success. While the profits didn't compare with the sums the bookies carried away at the close of each season, they were unburdened by overhead. The tipsters operated with no other capital investment than a lead pencil and a persuasive tongue.

Working independently, each tip-seller used whatever technique suited his talents. One method, employing the owner's superior memory for faces, yielded him an average of a hundred dollars a day throughout the 1905 season. Before each program the tipster picked the four best horses in the race with the fewest entries, then circulated in the crowd which he divided into four groups: straw hats, soft hats, derby hats and season badges. To the straw hats, he sold the merit of the first horse; to the soft hats, the excellence of the second; to the derbies, the third; and to the badges, the fourth. More often than not, one of the chosen horses won, and the next day he returned to the winning group—the straw hats, perhaps—subdivided it into four smaller groups, with a new set of identifying symbols his memory could retain, and touted four new horses selected on the same basis as before. Since all of his straw hat clients had profited from his advice, they received him warmly, recommended him to their straw hat friends and were undismayed by the fact that his prices for "inside information" had grown considerably overnight. Again, as expected, one of his horses won. The next day the tipster returned to the winning subdivision, divided it by four and hoisted his prices once more. The process continued until either his horses or his memory faltered, when he started over again.

On the last day of the season, richer by some $2,500 than when he arrived, he was given a genuine tip on a race by a stablehand and plunged to the full extent of his wealth. He departed with fifty cents in his pocket.

Coup de grâce The reform wave which swept New York State in the early 1900's was part of a flood tide of hostile reaction to the liberties and license introduced in the Gay Nineties and carried into the new century. In almost every state of the union the public guardians warned that the nation's moral standards were in peril.

Gambling was an immediate target of the reformists' wrath, and their efforts to put a stop to it attracted widespread support. The heaviest attacks were directed at the race tracks as hosts to the most popular form of betting and one which they had permitted, indeed encouraged, to become a public display. Newspapers depicted the typical race bettor as the dupe of crooked politicians, corrupt horse owners and greedy bookmakers working together in an unholy alliance. The result of this union, the papers suggested, was that races were fixed and the race-goer's luck was seldom given a chance.

Across the land legislators were goaded into action, and in state after state betting at the races was prohibited. Only Kentucky, Maryland and New York refused to follow suit, and in New York reformists forced a change of mind by electing as governor a popular crusader against corruption, Charles Evans Hughes.

Shortly after he took office in 1907, Governor Hughes began pushing for a bill which would eliminate bookmaking at the state's race tracks. Resistance was stubborn, but he triumphed. The Agnew-Hart Bill was passed and in June 1908 became a law which made it illegal to quote odds openly, solicit business or stand in a fixed place recording bets—all of which bookies had made a practice of doing. Detectives mingled with the crowds at the tracks and those who spurned the law were hauled off to court in patrol wagons.

The effects of the legislation far out-reached its provisions. Throughout the rest of the year in which it was enacted, and the two succeeding years, attendance at the New York tracks steadily dwindled. Gambling, rather than horses, had attracted the majority of race-goers, and without the book-ies to accommodate them they preferred to stay away. The poor gate re-ceipts in turn led to heavy operating losses at the tracks, and one after another the owners were forced to close them.

At Saratoga the situation was somewhat brighter. Visitors still turned up in large numbers to relax at the Spa and enjoy its pleasures, and the race track continued to draw them as a center of fashion and fun. Those who were disposed to gamble on the horses simply met with the bookies in the privacy of their hotel rooms; since all were lodged in the same hotels, betting and collecting was easy and convenient.

Even these advantages were not enough to keep the track open, how-ever. When the 1910 running came to an end, all of the race courses in the vicinity of New York City were shut. Convinced that the sport of kings was finished in the United States, many stable owners declared that in the future they would restrict their activities to England and France; others decided to quit and offered their horses for sale.

Their defection was the *coup de grâce* to the struggle of the Saratoga Racing Association to hold out. In the spring of 1911 it announced that "the dowager queen of the American turf" would not be in a position to receive guests for an indeterminate time, and in August, the traditional month of thudding hoofs and roaring crowds, the track was silent, the gates closed.

PART FOUR

How The Times
Do Change

Chapter One

The hole
in the gloom

Spring 1911 had few of its usual charms for the famous village near the luxuriant foothills of the Adirondacks. The news that the race track was closed, coupled with the sale of the Casino and the auction of its furnishings, plunged Saratoga into unseasonal gloom. It appeared to most residents that all of the excitement had gone from the Spa, and some prophesied that its days as a popular resort were numbered.

The following two summers bolstered this prediction. Both in quantity and quality the season's guests dropped sharply, and many of the wealthy and distinguished regulars who had built homes in the village or established large estates nearby spent the summers in Europe. Almost all of Saratoga felt the pinch—tradespeople who relied on the swift upturn of business during July and August for the bulk of their profit and home-owners who met their yearly expenses by renting their houses for the season—and the great hotels, the Grand Union and the United States, were wistful ghosts of their once lavish and lively selves.

Then, from an unexpected source, came an encouraging sign: the New York State courts were finding fault with the way the Agnew-Hart Law was drawn and, for the most part, were allowing individuals accused of violating it to go free. New York's race track owners probed for a loophole in the law through which they could restore gambling to the turf, and found it. It was a sizable hole. Through it they could readmit bookmakers to the tracks to practice a method of betting that was little different from the former system. Previously, a bettor had studied the odds chalked on the various blackboards, fought his way to a bookmaker's throne and put his money down for a ticket. This was no longer permissible. But there was nothing in the law to prevent oral betting: a simple exchange in which a bettor could ask a bookie to quote him odds on a race and, if the odds were satisfactory, write the terms of the wager on a piece of paper and give it to the bookie. He would then meet the bookie the next day and collect his winnings or pay his losses.

In 1913 the race courses in the vicinity of New York City were re-opened, and the bookies moved about the grounds as they pleased. Heartened by the turn of events the leading stables returned from abroad, and powerful new rivals were formed to compete with them. At Saratoga the jubilant Racing Association threw open the gates to the track and the turf was groomed to a satiny finish for the resumption of the August running. Just about the entire village, headed by a brass band, turned out to welcome the Cavanagh Special, and greeted its cargo of bookmakers as though they were rainmakers come to revive familiar splendors at the Springs after a long drought.

Superhorse   The following August war exploded in Europe, and while America's resolve to stay out of it was sorely tested by the sinking of the *Lusitania,* the nation was soon absorbed again in the heady pursuit of prosperity. In tune with the boom, Saratoga Springs in 1915 cast aside its sentimental pretense of being a village and was incorporated as a city. Two years later America entered the war, and to the traditional seasonal colors at the Spa were added Army khaki and Navy blue. The effect was not in the least sobering; the war seemed far away and once the Yanks were fully in it would doubtless soon be over; meanwhile, the horses were running better than ever. Civilians, soldiers and sailors cheerfully abandoned themselves to the track's pleasures, the most popular of which was a spunky little gelding named Roamer.

Roamer was thoroughly at home on the Saratoga course. Andrew Miller, his owner, was secretary-treasurer of the Racing Association, and after Roamer had briskly captured three major prizes awarded by the track, the Spa had virtually adopted the horse as a native son. As a two-year-old he had won the Saratoga Special; as a three-year-old the Travers; as a four-year-old the Saratoga Cup; and in the latter two seasons he had considerably enriched his owner and all who bet on him with a combined total of twenty victories in twenty-nine starts.

The following year the gelding had lost form and won only once, but he retained the race-goers' affection, nevertheless, and in 1917 rewarded them by running in the money in all but four of seventeen events. And on August 21, 1918, he trotted to the post at Saratoga and made a place for himself in racing history.

In 1890, with the advantage of a straight course, Salvator had set a world's record for the mile of 1:35½, and for twenty-eight years it had withstood all attempts to break it. Roamer, a seven-year-old veteran of the Saratoga track, was chosen as the horse most likely to succeed in lowering the mark in a special race against time; to force the pace a two-year-old named Lightning was entered with him. Neither Lightning nor Salvator survived Roamer's headlong rush. He was clocked at 1:34⅘, a new world's

America's outstanding jockeys rode the favorites at Saratoga. This impressive line-up was photographed in the paddock of the race track in 1919 and includes, left to right: Red-Coat Murray, the famous outrider; Buddy Ensor, in a white turtle-neck sweater; S. Wida, four to the right of Ensor; Laverne Fator (with dark sash), two to the right of Wida and Earl Sande, then 20 years old, second from the extreme right.

Roamer, with Andrew Schuttinger up, set a new world's record for the mile run in the 1918 season at the Spa.

Superhorse: Man o' War as a two-year-old, from a painting by F. B. Voss.

From the collection of The National Museum of Racing, Inc., Saratoga Springs, N. Y.

Harry Payne Whitney (right) was a leader of Saratoga's turf aristocracy. Shown with him are Ral Parr and J. S. Cosden.

Keeneland-Cook

Marshall Field, Mrs. William K. Vanderbilt and Samuel
D. Riddle outside the track.

Mr. and Mrs. Will Rogers at the races.

record and one that would last until 1932 when Equipoise, running at Arlington Park, would reduce it by two-fifths of a second.

Roamer bowed a tendon while working out at the track for the Spa's 1919 season and rested on his laurels. As events proved, it was just as well. For it was the first stunning year of the superhorse, Man o' War, the two-year-old, star-blazed chestnut no other horse could beat, or so it seemed.

On August 13th, when he strode to the barrier at Saratoga for the start of the Sanford Memorial Stakes, Man o' War had won in a run-away all of the six races in which he had been entered, and among the twenty thousand spectators there was scarcely a doubt that he would win this one with the same ease. Not that anyone needed it, there was also the reassuring presence of Johnny Loftus in the saddle of the big red horse, confidently sporting the colors of Samuel D. Riddle's Glen Riddle Farm.

Still, it had been a fairly bizarre day. The official starter was ill and the placing judge who substituted for him had shown almost no ability at getting the horses off on an equal footing. In the Sanford he was at his worst. One of the seven entries, Golden Broom, owned by Riddle's niece, Mrs. Walter Jeffords, was especially skittish, and the starter spent several minutes trying to get the horses lined up, then sent them away with only the contestants near the rail ready for the break.

Man o' War, never a patient colt, was half turned and backing away as the barrier was sprung. Next to the outside in position, he was also next to last to leave the starting line. Harry Payne Whitney's Upset fared much better. Stationed close to the rail, he was away like a shot from a gun, and was three to four lengths in front of Man o' War before the odds-on-favorite left the post.

In a moment Big Red was in full chase. Gaining his speed in a few strides, he passed one horse after another in the six-furlong dash, then was pocketed as he came around the curve into the homestretch. Loftus broke him free and he set out to overtake Upset, who had captured the lead. He drew up steadily. A hundred feet from the wire he was three-quarters of a length behind the Whitney entry. At the wire he was behind by a neck. Given another twenty feet, it appeared that he would surely have nosed ahead of Upset, but this was just another item to be argued over in the post-mortem of the race. Officially, Man o' War had met his first defeat.

The loss in no way injured his reputation; on the contrary it was more solid than before. Struck by his achievement in coming from so far behind to catch a rival to whom he had conceded fifteen pounds, turf experts agreed that Big Red was not only the best horse in the race but the best in his class.

During the remainder of the year, and all through 1920, Man o' War made even this generous judgment seem faint praise. He won all of the fourteen races in which he ran; only once was he extended, and he simply lengthened his stride to win by two lengths. In twenty-one starts he had suffered one defeat, at Saratoga.

But the Spa was the scene of one of his most shining triumphs too. In 1920 he captured the mile-and-a-quarter Travers in 2:01⅘—a speed which would not be topped until 1946, when Lucky Draw would run the distance in a fifth of a second under the mark.

Two years of the great colt were just about all that the handicappers could take. They weighted him with 138 pounds before he won the Potomac Handicap in Maryland in 1920, and let it be known that if he turned up the following year as a four-year-old he would have to carry practically everything but the track on his back. It was too much to ask of even a wonder horse, Man o' War's owner thought. He retired Big Red to a less burdensome career at stud.

The new breed

In the Twenties, dawn of horse racing's sunniest era, a quite different run for the money also paid off. That long elusive prize, the horn of plenty, was finally reached by citizens across the land, was tipped over and spilled its favors in abundance.

Up to fifty thousand free-spenders descended on Saratoga each summer, insuring its fourteen thousand permanent residents a greater degree of permanence and enriching a new and more enterprising breed of gamblers who positioned themselves in and about the Springs. As always, in season at the Spa, prices went up: shelter about 100 per cent, food about 30 per cent, amusement like a sky-rocket. The two legendary hotels, the Grand Union and the United States, although worn and faded and unable to muster between them one room in ten with a private bath, and scarcely more than that with hot running water, charged from $15 to $50 a day, American plan, for a single room and $100 up for the cottage suites. Such was their once-fabled magnificence, their ballrooms and corridors and piazzas peopling the imagination with lordly and glamorous figures from the not too distant past, that few of their lodgers demurred at the exorbitant rates. Congress Hall, a fairly formidable rival of the Grand Union and the United States before the turn of the century, was no longer around to share the unprotesting influx. In 1913 the village had purchased the hotel and torn it down, and the block it had occupied had been added to the Congress Spring and Casino properties as part of the previously established public park.

High society and the merely very rich either built their own pleasure palaces in the country near the Springs—forty-room mansions they referred to as cottages—or rented them, in or about the city, for the season. For the month of August, the peak of Saratoga's summer, cottage rentals ran from about $6,000 to $7,500, and in 1929 Mrs. R. Amcott Wilson leased Broadview, her home on North Broadway, for $10,500 for the duration of the races. This was by no means typical; less prepossessing

Man o' War suffered his only defeat in the 1919 Sanford Memorial Stakes at Saratoga.
The big red horse (center) was beaten by Upset. Golden Broom is at left.

Revenge: in the 1920 Travers Stakes at the Springs, Man o' War trounced Upset.
John P. Grier is at left.

An auction of yearl-
at Saratoga in this pe

Charles H. Hutchins

Both Jack Dempsey and Gene Tunney trained just outside the Spa for their first meeting in the ring. Here Tunney (front center) is shown at the White Sulphur Spring Hotel, on the southern shore of Lake Saratoga. Next to him at left is Thomas Luther, the proprietor of the hotel.

By the Twenties, a procession of motor cars had replaced Saratoga's famed parade of carriages and coaches. This scene was photographed in 1922 in front of the United States Hotel.

Charles H. Hutchins

houses in town were rented for prices in keeping with their comforts; but the average recompense for surrendering their homes was so irresistible that many Saratogans moved out bag and baggage and spent the summers in Florida. The total income from rents in August 1929 was $550,000.

While gratified by the rush of prosperity, the Spa's senior citizens were troubled by the tempo of the times. In recent years a little bit more of the resort's grandeur and charm had disappeared with each vanishing season, and with the jarring arrival of the noisy Twenties most of the old traditions that remained took hasty flight. It was a change which was sweeping the country, but this was of little solace to a Saratoga steeped in private memories. Beneath the stately elms where the wealth and fashion of America had promenaded, and on the great piazzas where they had held court, flashy sports and gaudy movie stars strolled and lounged. On Broadway and the boulevard to the lake the elegant, eye-filling spectacle of high-stepping horses and superbly styled carriages was replaced by a cacophony of Stutz Bearcats, Cadillacs, Chandlers, Paiges, Franklins, Stearns-Knights, Pierce-Arrows, Packards and other rival motor cars in violent disagreement as to right of way. The once venerated mineral waters which had revived tired bodies and flagging spirits throughout Saratoga's history, were popularly used to alleviate the harsh bite of bootleg whiskey and gin, their medicinal values largely ignored. And at night strip-teasers and flimflam artists exhibited their attractions on the neon-lighted ways, and floats with garish cardboard cut-outs and brassy music prowled the streets to lure customers to the cinemas.

Most painful of all to the old guard's civic pride, there were more gambling houses than ever before. For some years after Canfield had departed from the Springs, roulette wheels, faro boxes and other gaming paraphernalia had been barred from the community. Then the Chicago Club, a reputable establishment which had enjoyed the trustees' grudging favor as far back as the days of Spencer and Reed, had been permitted to reopen with full regalia, and it had been only a matter of a few months before wheels and cards were again turning at several other places in the city. As usual, the authorities from time to time had endeavored to close the houses and throw the gamblers out, and occasionally, with help from Albany, they had succeeded. But the gamblers too had friends and protectors, in local political circles as well as in the state capital, and after a discreet interval the gaming was resumed.

With the end of the war the climate for gambling in and about the Spa was deemed so attractive that posh casinos with idyllic names such as Brook, Arrowhead and Piping Rock flowered in the countryside near the lake. All were operated along much the same lines as the Canfield Casino, but where Canfield's cuisine had been priced invitingly high the new luxury casinos, with one exception, priced their meals invitingly low. For as little as five dollars one could obtain dinner, including cocktails and liqueurs, and be entertained by such as Helen Morgan or Sophie Tucker and the orchestras of Ben Bernie or Vincent Lopez, with free limousine service from and to one's hotel. The common objective, of course, was to entice dinner guests to the gaming tables, and while their dining rooms plunged the lake clubs more deeply into the red than Columbin's restaurant had sunk the Casino, the greater number of patrons who tried their luck at the games, together with the odds (and a few hidden devices) employed against them, provided the owners with a virtually unassailable margin of profit.

The Brook disdained the cut-rate bait its rivals used to lure patrons to the games. Arnold Rothstein, the Brook's proprietor, was determined to cater to the best people, which by his terms meant the wealthiest. He refused to admit anyone not suitably attired in evening clothes, or not listed in the social stud-book if an exception had to be made. The cuisine compared favorably with the food served in New York City's finest dining rooms and there were no prices on the menus. In these respects the Brook revived memories of Canfield and the Casino (which had been converted into a community center and museum), a reaction not altogether pleasing to Rothstein; in purchasing Mrs. George A. Saportas' superb summer home just north of Saratoga and remodeling it at considerable expense into a combination casino, restaurant and cabaret, he had hoped to make the Spa's summer guests forget that a Prince of Gamblers had preceded him.

Rothstein had become a regular at the Springs starting in 1904, when as a young bookmaker he had sallied into town on the Cavanagh Special. Although he was the son of well-to-do parents, and his youthful years had been smoothed with every comfort and advantage they could provide, in his teens he had taken up gambling and found it so profitable that he had made it his career. In 1909, when he made his sixth trip aboard the Special, he had begun to feel his way into the more precarious but enormously rewarding world controlled by big-time gamblers, politicians and gangsters, and while it was only a first step he was coolly confident of climbing to the top. With his future assured, he decided to marry. Two years earlier he had fallen in love with a young actress, Carolyn Greene, a slim-bodied girl with reddish-brown hair and gray-blue eyes, and during his sixth season at the Spa they were wed and spent their honeymoon enjoying the resort's attractions, although seldom in each other's company. Every morning Rothstein took his wife to the race track and left her while he made book on the horses, and every evening he left her again while he gambled at the casinos. Saratoga's other charms—the convivial hotels, the lake, baths, theater and tennis courts—apparently compensated for the bridegroom's absences, for succeeding Augusts found the Rothsteins again at the Springs celebrating their wedding anniversaries in the same way they had celebrated their wedding.

When the Twenties arrived, Rothstein was well up the ladder to success. He owned the Brook and a stable of horses, was a silent partner in the Chicago Club and several other gaming establishments. He held valuable real estate and prime securities, maintained large accounts in sturdy

The New Windsor Hotel.

A typical Saratoga cottage of the day.

Skidmore College girls and Skidmore Hall.

Charles H. Hutchins

Charles H. Hutchins

Charles H. Hutchins

DRUGS

old banks and kept an expensive apartment on New York City's fashionable Fifth Avenue. He was friend and confidant of political bosses, business tycoons, social registerites, sports champions, stage and movie celebrities, and he was intimate with a succession of mistresses who found him entertaining and attentive and were amused by his preference for milk rather than whiskey. He was a graceful host and a sensitive collector of art, mainly Whistler etchings, fine furniture and rugs, particularly Oriental. Hinting that he was the mastermind of various shady enterprises, the press cloaked him with a sinister mystery that went well with his black eyes, pale skin and soft speech, and made him even more intriguing. It seemed perfectly logical when he was accused of bribing eight players of the Chicago White Sox to "throw" the 1919 World Series.

The White Sox, vastly superior to their opponents, the Cincinnati Reds, had been overwhelmingly favored by the betting odds before the two teams met in the traditional play-off, but when the first game got underway the odds were virtually even. It looked suspicious, and when the Reds won the series a Chicago grand jury investigated rumors of a fix and revealed an unsavory alliance which newspapers labeled the "Black Sox" scandal. Eight outstanding Chicago players were indicted for accepting money from a group of gamblers and consenting to do their best to lose the series.

Rothstein was subpoenaed to answer charges that he was responsible for the deal. He appeared before the grand jury with his attorney, William J. Fallon, whose courtroom orations had kept so many of his underworld clients out of prison that he was known as "the great mouthpiece," and listened patiently while he was accused of giving Abe Attell, the former world's featherweight boxing champion, $100,000 to distribute among the players. Fallon grandly protested Rothstein's innocence and Rothstein capped the attorney's eloquence with a blunt statement of his own. He had never in his life been connected with a crooked deal, he declared, and he was sick and tired of having his name dragged into every one that made the headlines. The jury received this skeptically, but since there was no proof that Rothstein was connected with the "Black Sox" conspiracy he was absolved from any complicity in it.

In the 1921 racing season at Saratoga, Rothstein pulled off one of the turf's richest coups and found himself in the news again. Harry Payne Whitney's splendid mare Prudery was scheduled to run in the Travers, but as the day of the race approached it looked as though she would have the track all to herself and win in a walk; other horse owners were so certain she couldn't be beaten they saw no point in trying.

With his usual eye for a sure thing, Rothstein entered a member of his stable, Sporting Blood, to pick up the purse for second money. He had no intention of betting; Sporting Blood was a good horse but was not in Prudery's class. A chain of disclosures late in the afternoon of the day preceding the race changed his mind, however.

From one of his stable spies he learned that Prudery was in a nervous state. Spurred by a tempting gratuity, a Whitney stablehand revealed that the mare had little appetite and had been allowed to miss several of her workouts. A veterinarian who often worked for Rothstein told him that he had examined Prudery and had judged her to be in fair enough physical condition, but irritable; it didn't appear as though she would be at the top of her form for the Travers, and Whitney and his trainer were concerned about her.

Rothstein reconsidered his colt's prospects. Few people knew it but Sporting Blood had improved tremendously since his last performance and was in rare fettle for the race. With Prudery at considerably less than her best, it appeared that Sporting Blood had a good chance to win. The occasion seemed propitious for a sizable bet.

Early the next day, August 20th, Prudery gave no sign of improvement, and reflecting the general ignorance of her condition the odds had the mare at 1 to 4 and Sporting Blood at 5 to 2. Rothstein waited. There was a possibility that Whitney might withdraw his entry from the race before post time that afternoon, but Rothstein doubted that he would do it. The Travers was a Saratoga institution, the oldest stakes race in America; to a sportsman such as Whitney it deserved the best, and he could be expected to keep Prudery in the running unless she became physically ill. A more likely occurrence was that word of Prudery's plight would get around. All bookmakers and more than a few stable owners were in the market for inside tips on the horses, and while Rothstein had handsomely rewarded the informers who had broken the secret of the Whitney mare, there was nothing to prevent them from selling the same information to others except fear of his displeasure. If the news got out, the odds against Sporting Blood would drop sharply and the huge profit Rothstein envisioned would dwindle to very little. With the race only hours away, it didn't appear that this would happen. Whether it did or did not, however, there was a bare possibility of a third development—in which the odds against Sporting Blood would not only be assured but almost certainly increased.

Shortly before noon Grey Lag, the champion money-winning three-year-old of the year, was entered in the Travers. Sam Hildreth, who entered him, was a partner of Harry Sinclair, an oil millionaire with whom he had recently purchased the Lorillards' Rancocas Farm. It was to be one of the most felicitous associations in racing; Sinclair was a spender and Hildreth an astute trainer of horses; in four years their stable would win $1,200,000 in purses, $272,000 of which would be won in 1923 by Zev alone. In addition, the partners shared an enthusiasm for gambling.

Now the Travers was a three-horse race. Grey Lag, with credentials superior even to Prudery's, moved slightly ahead in the betting; the Whitney entry was favored for second money and Sporting Blood for third.

In the Twenties a new breed of gamblers established themselves at the Spa. Arnold Rothstein was perhaps the most energetic, operating both a casino and a stable of horses.

During the 1921 racing season at Saratoga, Rothstein pulled off one of the turf's richest coups. A principal figure in the drama was Sam Hildreth.

Keenelan

Rothstein's colt, Sporting Blood, defeating Harry Payne Whitney's mare, Prudery, in the 1921 Travers Stakes. Combining secret information and shrewd maneuvering, Rothstein picked up $450,000 on the race.

Sam Rosoff: just the sight of him made Rothstein uneasy.

Rothstein acted quickly. Through his agents he placed $150,000 on Sporting Blood with handbook operators throughout the country at an average price of 3 to 1. To the handbookies, this was idiot money; Sporting Blood, which had appeared to have little chance against Prudery, would seem to stand no chance at all with Grey Lag and Prudery forcing each other's pace. Instead of wiring the money to Saratoga to be wagered with the bookmakers at the track, they held the bets. At the track there was only a sprinkling of money on Sporting Blood. The odds on him wavered between 2½ to 1 and 3½ to 1, and there was no indication that else-where $150,000 was riding confidently on the colt.

Thirty minutes before post time, the deadline for scratching an entry, Hildreth withdrew Grey Lag from the race. The rules did not require an explanation of his action to the stewards, and he gave none. Coming so soon after he had belatedly entered the horse, for reasons he also kept to himself, it mystified bookmakers and bettors alike. But given a choice of Prudery or Sporting Blood, most bettors spent little of the precious time left speculating about it. They switched their money to the Whitney mare in such numbers that the odds on her dropped to 2 to 7. The odds on Sporting Blood remained the same, and observing the lack of any real in-terest in Rothstein's colt at the track, the handbook operators held to their original unflattering estimate of the $150,000 that had been bet on him.

The race went pretty much as Rothstein anticipated. Prudery took command with ease and Sporting Blood trailed after her. At the mile post the colt was only a half length behind, however, and in the final quarter-mile dash down the homestretch Prudery's poor condition became stun-ningly apparent to even her most confident admirers. She faltered, fell off stride and wound up floundering, with Sporting Blood the winner by two lengths and Rothstein ahead by $450,000.

News of the coup provoked questions to which there were no certain answers, but the losers were bitterly certain they knew what had happened. Rothstein, they were convinced, had told Hildreth what he knew about Prudery and together they had planned the Grey Lag maneuver to thrust up the odds on Sporting Blood, with the understanding that Hildreth would receive part of the winnings if the race ended as expected. There was noth-ing illegal about it and no proof that it had actually occurred; Hildreth's un-orthodox moves with Grey Lag could be explained in various ways. But to most horse-players the coup bore the Rothstein trademark: a big stake in a sure thing.

The Brook carried the same stamp. Rothstein had put a good deal of money into the club because he regarded it as a safe investment: the per-centage in favor of the casino virtually guaranteed him a munificent profit. The little risk involved was mainly in the form of players who welshed on their losses, and this was kept to the minimum by Rothstein's "enforcers." He trusted none of his patrons farther than he had to—even those who were incontestably solvent. Early one Sunday a wealthy New York City real estate broker, who had been acquainted with Rothstein for years, gave him a check for $7,500 to pay for his poor luck at the Brook, and at nine-fifteen the next morning dropped into his Manhattan bank to discuss a business deal. The preliminary pleasantries revealed that the bank's first transaction of the day had been to clear his $7,500 check. Rothstein had dispatched it from Saratoga via a special messenger with such speed that the messenger was waiting on the steps when the bank was opened.

There was always a chance, of course, that a plunger with no respect for the odds against him and little concern for money would strike it rich at the Brook. Generally, the law of the percentage backed by time, patience and Rothstein's substantial cash reserves took possession of the plunger's bankroll, but in some cases the betting was too wild to control. Sam Rosoff was almost as much of a maverick in the gaming rooms as Bet-a-Million Gates had been, and just the sight of him made Rothstein uneasy.

A multimillionaire contractor, builder of most of New York City's subways, Rosoff was grossly obese, vulgar and profane, and arrived at the Brook in such a loud collection of clothes that Rothstein eventually discarded his rule requiring evening dress. Forcing his protesting flesh from the dining tables to the gaming tables, Rosoff wagered thousands of dollars as his impulses directed, and frequently enjoyed a run of luck. On one August evening, when he had won $400,000 and appeared to be on his way toward bigger earnings, Rothstein telephoned Charles Stoneham at his Saratoga cottage and asked for additional funds in case Rosoff cleaned out the Brook's reserves. Stoneham, a gaming proprietor himself, being part owner of casinos in Havana, Cuba, as well as sole owner of the New York Giants, took $300,000 from his wall safe and sent it to Rothstein with all possible haste. When the money arrived, Rosoff had lost his winnings and $100,000 more.

Whatever insight into the gaming profession he might have obtained as a casino owner, as a bettor Stoneham also blithely disregarded the odds. Laid up with a wrenched knee, he once telephoned the Brook from his summer home at the Spa and asked Rothstein on what color the roulette wheel had stopped in its last spin.

"Black," Rothstein said.

"On the next turn bet a thousand for me on the red," Stoneham told him.

Rothstein did and the red won. Stoneham continued to gamble by phone for more than three hours. When he hung up, he had lost $70,000.

Harry Sinclair dropped $48,000 at the Brook one evening and wrote a check for $50,000—the extra $2,000 as tips for the croupiers. Joshua Cosden, another oil titan, lost $300,000 one night, $200,000 the next night, and boasted of his skill at the games when he won $20,000 on his third successive evening of play.

Although he had neither oil wells nor other bountiful resources to dip into—in fact, had no means of support whatsoever except his intuition

Harry Sinclair: when he gambled away $48,000 one evening, he tossed in an extra $2,000 for the croupiers.

as to how cards would fall, dice would roll and where a wheel would stop—Nicholas Andrea Dandolos was in a class by himself as a six-figure bettor. Born in Crete, he had been raised and educated in Turkey and had arrived in the United States at the age of eighteen with a college degree in philosophy, a flair for poetry and an easy command of several languages. None of these assets had enabled him to win a girl in Chicago, with whom he fell in love, or a job in Canada, where he went to nurse the hurt of his defeat, and he had turned to gambling on the races at Montreal. Betting consistently, he won $1,200,000 and a nickname, Nick the Greek, bestowed on him, to his lasting discomfort, by an admiring editor of *Racing Form* after he had impoverished a good many horse-players in Canada. In 1913, his twentieth year, he had recrossed the border and launched himself on a gaming career in his adopted land.

The venture was a unique success, rewarding him with an affectionate following as well as a flow of funds. Bookies, gangsters, politicians, business-men, playboys, showgirls, debutantes and others who inhabited the various strata of gambling society relished his faultless attire (he never appeared after sundown out of evening clothes), urbane manners (even when he dined alone in his hotel suite, he wore a dinner jacket and ordered cham-pagne), original habits (at the races he read Plato and Aristotle while other horse-players studied the tip-sheets) and witty homilies (he ex-plained his avoidance of manual labor by pointing out that an ancient Greek philosopher had proved it was unnecessary. "Socrates never lifted a pick," he said, "but he levelled a thousand walls between man and man."). At the gaming tables his concentration and aloofness erected a subtle bar-rier between himself and others, but his style of betting so often produced drama and suspense that an audience trailed after him just to watch the play.

Nick the Greek's most memorable gambles, however, occurred in stud poker sessions in the privacy of hotel rooms and apartments. At Saratoga, once at the Grand Union and twice at the United States, he played $100,000 freeze-outs of single-handed stud. In Rothstein's apartment, after winning $675,000 at stud poker during ten hours of play, Nick faced his host alone in the closing hand after the other players had dropped out and lost to Rothstein perhaps the biggest pot in stud poker history: $605,000.

A mouse and his cheese   In 1922 a new reform wave rippled over Saratoga, removing office-holders who had become too friendly with gamblers and bookmakers and replacing them with authorities pledged to restore the Spa's lost virtue. At the end of the season Arnold Rothstein put the Brook up for sale and sold it the following year.

His departure from the Springs was accompanied by few regrets. A good deal of the resort's notoriety was due to his presence and his sly machinations had made him *persona non grata* at the race track. On the whole, the city was glad to see him leave. In Rothstein's view the move was a natural consequence of his growing affluence and importance. He was involved in so many enterprises that the Brook was no longer worthy of his time and attention.

The astounding range of his activities was not fully disclosed until after a Sunday evening in early November 1928, when he was shot in the Park Central Hotel in New York City, in a suite where a card game was in progress. He died refusing to name his assailant, and his private papers revealed that in doing so he had simply been faithful to the criminal code. As a master of the underworld, he could hardly have behaved otherwise. His records showed that he had financed coups in narcotics and bootleg liquor, organized industrial rackets and Wall Street bucket shops, and directed other illicit maneuvers—all so cautiously that he ran practically no risk of losing his life, liberty or bank accounts. He was money-lender and partner to gangsters, claiming both an interest on his loans and a share of the profits when an enterprise he backed succeeded. His fortune had mounted to dazzling proportions, but such was his passion for money he was never satisfied. At the peak of his career Rothstein's close associate and favorite "mouthpiece," William J. Fallon, summed him up in a terse biography: ". . . a mouse standing in a doorway, waiting for his cheese."

Chapter Two

Four
motor cars
and
a polo stable

The Twenties ended, not with a bang as the golden boom led almost everyone to expect, but with a whimper. The soaring stock market, Pied Piper of the easy life, plunged from unprecedented peaks with unprecedented violence, and in the wreckage lay the wealth and dreams of millions of Americans. Across the country the era of affluence and wonderful nonsense largely sank into a vast Depression, but in one locality at least it refused to be put down.

Visiting Saratoga Springs in August 1930, James C. Young reported in *The New York Times:* "In a year when everyone has talked of hard times, Saratoga represents a protest. Never in the memory of the oldest habitué has there been such display of splendor. For four teeming weeks, Saratoga lived again in the good old days."

For the most part the protesters and displayers were members of the country's richest club, horse society—a coalition of high socialites, café celebrities and Hollywood aristocrats who had comfortably survived the financial crash and casually defied the aftermath. The posh Turf and Field veterans set the pace. In the luxurious summer cottages such leaders of the horsy set as William Woodward, Samuel D. Riddle, John Hay Whitney, Cornelius Vanderbilt Whitney, George Loft, John Sanford (a dedicated player of favorites, frequently betting $50,000 in an attempt to win $30,000), Colonel Edward R. Bradley, Marshall Field, Thomas Hitchcock, Albert Bostwick, F. Skiddy von Stade, Herbert Bayard Swope, W. Plunket Stewart and the Lorillards, Pierre Sr. and Jr., mounted a month-long series of parties. At the race track, in their fashionable boxes—which were as much a part of their personal estate as their permanent pews in the churches they supported—and in the picturesque paddock fronting their stables they entertained with still more open disregard of the national gloom. F. Ambrose Clark, who had engendered concern among his confreres by the number and variety of his falls as a steeplechase rider, won the sympathy and applause of every Saratogan who yearned for the past when, looking every inch a nineteenth-century country squire, he drove his old-fashioned but dashing four-in-hand coach to the track to see how his light blue and yellow silks fared in the races.

"Going to Saratoga for the season is unlike going anywhere else," Young went on in describing the Spa's esprit in August 1930 for readers of the *Times,* and continued:

> If the visitor really belongs to the Saratoga circle, he will bring an entourage of fifteen to twenty servants, and probably arrive in his private railroad car. In these days of automobiles, when half a dozen friends are likely to drop in on any week-end, it is convenient to have the car in the railroad yard.
>
> If the host has not acquired a house in other seasons spent at Saratoga, he finds on arrival that some very comfortable places are available for $10,000 to $12,000 a month. Of course, they will not accommodate many outside guests, but there is room for the servants and the family. Part of the Saratoga legend being the quality of its dinners, not a few of those who entertain here impress New York's finest chefs into service. Since the 1870's and before, every host's table has been a measure of his standing. Yet, in this changing world of today, it is one of the resort's sorrows that public restaurants are supplanting the oak-paneled dining rooms where Saratoga used to dine. There are several favored restaurants where the cost, even upon great occasions, can be kept within $100 a plate.
>
> The man who lives up to the Saratoga tradition will need not less than four motor cars and a polo stable, either for himself or for his friends. The polo ponies will be in addition, of course, to any racers he may own, and require another retinue. The present season has seen an innovation in the form of an airplane kept for the week-end guests of one house. As for such details as private stock tickers, they are legion.

The antics too were a throw-back to earlier days at the Springs. Liz Whitney wore an emerald necklace with her riding habit and one morning went to the race track straight from a night club, wearing an evening dress and shepherding a small flock of dogs. Ella Widener threw an egg at a judge in a night court. Alfred Gwynne Vanderbilt, who resembled a diffident yearling rather than the extremely young but successful operator of one of the country's most formidable racing stables, took pity on a jockey who was to ride a hopeless entry in the Saratoga Cup and gave him, instead of riding orders, a sandwich, a bottle of milk and a wrist compass. Other wealthy members of horse society enlivened the August nights with dusk-to-dawn poker games in which, weary of betting money, they bet the horses they owned, topping the last hand with a joy-ride to the track for breakfast and a merry exchange of the thoroughbreds they had won and lost.

As the Depression deepened the capers and extravagance displayed at Saratoga in August were attacked by some observers as tantamount to rubbing salt in the nation's wounds, and the season elite retreated to a more prudent position. As a result, the resort experienced a mild recession. The elegant house which Mrs. R. Amcott Wilson had rented to a summer sport for $10,500 for the month of August in 1929, was rented in 1934 by Mrs. Isobel Dodge Sloan for $5,000. The prices of food and amusement also dropped well below their 1929 levels. Fewer Saratogans went to Florida in 1934 than in previous seasons, the total income from August rents falling from 1929's $550,000 to $200,000.

The losses which resulted from society's tightened purse strings were largely offset, however, by some thirty thousand lower-status fun seekers who invaded the Spa each racing season free of inhibitions and plunged to the full extent of their holiday finances, whether sufficient for the entire month of August, a week or a week end. They crowded into hotels, boarding houses, restaurants and bars, spent the hours of darkness in the gaming establishments and night clubs in town, and if a flicker of energy survived straggled off to catch the early morning workouts at the race track. There, in the cool, ambiguous light, they watched the horses run, and at ten o'clock, when the track was cleared, they went to their beds for a snatch of sleep, or to the mineral baths for a quick pick-up. Or they simply hung on for another day, filling in the time before the races began by laying bets with the bookies who were positioned all along Broadway in the plaid suits and pulled-down panamas that had become the uniform of their fraternity. Around noon the sleepers and bathers emerged, and almost as one the entire assembly bolted down breakfast or lunch and a few drinks and hastened to the track. For three hours they concentrated on horses, jockeys, tip-sheets and picking winners; then, at twilight, the last race over, they surged back to Broadway, now abloom with prostitutes, to make the rounds again.

The casinos and night clubs served them with an impersonal efficiency designed to separate them from their money as speedily as possible. They were owned and operated by a syndicate whose board of directors, it was reported, included such as Waxey Gordon, Owney Madden, Dutch Schultz and Lucky Luciano, and since time was fleeting—Saratoga being of interest to these gentlemen only during the August gold rush—play was fast to squeeze every available dollar into the syndicate's pocket. At the Chicago Club, the most prosperous of the gaming establishments, Lucky Luciano presided over the action in person, smiling one of his rare smiles when the betting was unusually brisk. It was estimated that each September the Chicago Club was richer by some $250,000. Saratoga fared still better. At a time when most of the U.S.A. was reaching for aspirin, Saratoga took in an average of $2,000,000 each August, more than other communities of its size earned in a year.

The swarm of horse-players, gamblers, gangsters, bookies, touts, pimps, prostitutes and others of the sporting gentry who alighted at the Springs each season in the Thirties awakened little enthusiasm among the natives, harbinger of good times though they were. To the old guard it appeared that, with the exception of the socialites, the quality of the August guests was the worst ever. In a columnist for the New York *American* and King Features Syndicate who unfailingly accompanied them to the Spa, however, the untidy throng had a champion who favored them with a kindly eye, an attentive ear and an understanding heart, and spoke of them so tenderly to an audience of millions that Saratoga's mutterings and *moues* were generously ignored.

Damon Runyon, defender and chronicler of sporting guys and dolls, was called "the Boswell of Broadway," which could be taken to mean both the Great White Way of Manhattan and Saratoga's Main Stem. A writer of short stories as well as newspaper columns, he drew upon his observations of New York's Rialto to invent a host of popular characters with names like Harry the Horse, Dave the Dude, Sorrowful Jones, Nicely-Nicely Johnson, Apple Annie and Madame LaGimp. At Saratoga he borrowed from real-life Broadway models such as Gloomy Gus, The Dancer, Blue Jaw Magoon, Crazy Moe, Cokey Flo, Gashouse Lil and Jenny the Factory.

The Dancer, a bookmaker, was particularly helpful in stirring Runyon's creative juices. A half century earlier he had been christened Maurice Hyams, but one evening after making up for a losing day on the horses by winning a hundred dollars and a silver-plated cup (pawned for an extra five-spot) in an amateur hoofing contest, he was nicknamed and henceforth known to all as The Dancer. He had abandoned the stage after this performance, but pursued by its siren call had enlivened his role as a bookie by indulging in whatever antics pleased his fancy and draping himself in the over-size, sloping suits and wild collars of the professional funnyman. At Saratoga crowds gathered in the early evenings in front of the Grand Union Hotel to listen to his prices on the next day's races and watch him put on a show.

A second bookie, Gloomy Gus, was another source of inspiration, and co-starred with Runyon in a comedy that resulted in one of the columnist's most popular articles. Unable to cover a bet he had placed with Gloomy Gus on a "sure thing" that also ran, Runyon took refuge in his room at the United States Hotel. He stayed in hiding for three days, entreating friends by phone and wire to lend him the necessary funds while the bookie attempted to reach him. The siege was lifted when the money arrived and the debt was paid. It was an experience that pointed up two of Runyon's favorite maxims, "Don't gamble" and "All horse-players die broke," but as a compulsive gambler who was inured to losing he emerged from it unchanged and promptly restored himself in Gloomy Gus' esteem. Years later he capitalized on the incident, however, by writing a wryly fictitious version of it for the Hearst papers.

William Woodward (left) and Colonel Edward R. Bradley were among the wealthy stable owners whose racing colors were represented in every August running at the Spa.

Saratoga race track in 1939.

Charles H. Hutchins

In the Thirties, Saratoga's horse society was a mixture of socialites and celebrities. One prominent member was Bernard Baruch.

F. Ambrose Clark.

Albert C. (left) and George H. Bostwick in their steeplechase silks.

Herbert Bayard Swope.

James J. Walker, the dapper ex-mayor of New York City.

Alfred Gwynne Vanderbilt, the great-great-grandson of the Commodore, operated one of the country's most formidable racing stables. He is shown with Now What, Raymond (Sonny) Workman up.

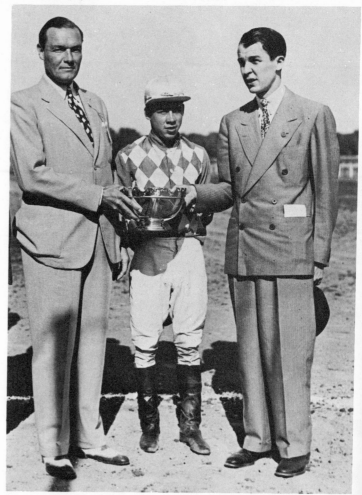

Vanderbilt (right) in the winner's circle at Saratoga with Stephen (Laddie) Sanford, after one of his horses captured the Sanford Stakes.

Sophie Tucker on the jockey's scale in 1936.

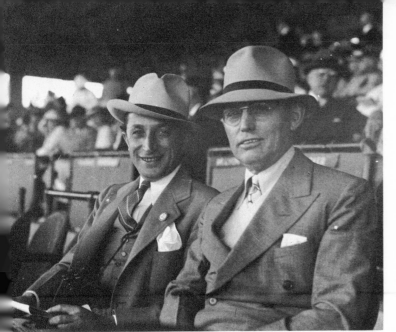

...non Runyon, the popular chronicler of sporting guys and dolls, ...w upon his observations at Saratoga in writing several of his news- ...er columns and stories. An inveterate horse-player, he is shown at ...race track (above) with David Wilentz, the prosecutor at the Lind- ...h kidnap-murder trial, and (right) with Jack Kearns, the boxing ...noter, and Patricia Gridier.

Triple Crown winner Gallant Fox, with Earl Sande up, was the favorite to win the 1930 Travers Stakes.

Gangsters who turned up at the Spa were also grist for the Runyon mill. In *A Slight Case Of Murder,* a play written in collaboration with Howard Lindsay which was produced in 1935 and later converted into a movie, Runyon described the confusion which ensued after a reformed racketeer, arriving at his Saratoga home for the racing season, found four slain gunmen resting inside the premises and disposed of the bodies by dropping them on the doorsteps of four friends.

Runyon's most enduring work with a Saratoga setting, however—in fact, the most famous piece he ever wrote— was a poem he composed after a horse with Earl Sande aboard fell on the track and rolled over on his rider, breaking the renowned jockey's legs, an arm and six ribs. Sande was Runyon's favorite jockey, and when he announced from the hospital that he would never ride again Runyon regarded it as a tragedy. As he subsequently discovered, he voiced not only his own feelings but those of practically all race-goers in a lament which began:

> Maybe there'll be another,
>   Heady an' game, an' true—
> Maybe they'll find his brother
>   At drivin' them horses through.
> Maybe—but, say, I doubt it.
>   Never his like again—
> Never a handy guy like Sande
>   Bootin' them babies in!

Sande's physicians patched him with silver plates and rendered the announcement of his retirement premature. He returned to the saddle and recaptured his winning habit with horses to such an extent that he enriched his employers by $3,000,000 before he hung up his silks. On a rainy Saturday afternoon, August 16, 1930, more than half of the thirty thousand people who assembled at the Saratoga track to watch the sixty-first running of the Travers Stakes expected him to be on the winner again, and with excellent reason. Sande's mount would be William Woodward's three-year-old champion, Gallant Fox, who had won in succession the Wood Memorial, Preakness, Kentucky Derby, Belmont Stakes (the latter three forming racing's most eagerly sought prize, the Triple Crown), Dwyer Stakes and Arlington Classic, bagging nearly $275,000 which, added to his earnings as a two-year-old, made the big, white-eyed horse the second largest money-maker in the history of the American turf. And the jockey who had piloted the Belair Stud entry to all his stakes victories was Sande.

The remainder of the audience, slightly less than half, favored Harry Payne Whitney's Whichone. Last year's king of the two-year-olds, the speedy brown colt had beaten Gallant Fox in the 1929 Futurity and had lost to him in the 1930 Belmont. In the Travers they would break the tie, and the supporters of the Whitney horse were confident that with the redoubtable Raymond (Sonny) Workman in his saddle he would revert to his 1929 form.

The betting was 1 to 2 on Gallant Fox, 6 to 5 on Whichone, all but a few in the crowd resting their money on one choice or the other. The two additional entries in the race, Willie Sharpe Kilmer's Sun Falcon and Chaffee Earl's Jim Dandy, were outsiders and were treated as such—Jim Dandy so disrespectfully that his odds rose to 100 to 1.

On his record it seemed a fair estimate of his chances. The three-year-old chestnut colt had been out of the money in sixteen of twenty starts, had spent the previous winter waging a doughty but discouraging campaign at Agua Caliente, where in only one race had he managed to finish as far front as third, and had earned just $125 all year. To dim his prospects further, Jim Dandy came from sunny California, where it rarely rained, and the Travers would be run in the stickiest mud the Saratoga track had had all season.

All of this was irrelevant in the opinion of Jim Dandy's trainer, Johnny McKee. During the previous August at the Spa the colt had run his best race to take the Grand Union Hotel Stakes from some of the smartest horses in the East, coming from behind like a bolt from the blue, and McKee predicted that he would win the oncoming Travers in the same way. He had nursed this belief through the series of disappointments at Agua Cal-iente, resting Jim Dandy after the program was over and shipping him to Saratoga in a horse car attached to the crack California Limited which the colt shared with only one other horse from his stable. Chaffee Earl, McKee's boyish looking millionaire employer, had indulged the trainer's efforts to point Jim Dandy for the Travers, but when the odds against the colt soared to 100 to 1 he lost interest in the race and stayed away from the track.

The rain had ceased when the bugle brought the horses out on the course at five-twenty that Saturday afternoon. The red-hooded Gallant Fox came first, directly behind Red Coat Murray, the outrider, on his lead pony. Whichone followed with a blue hood over his head; then came Jim Dandy—Frank Baker, a jockey as unimpressive as the colt he rode, handling the reins—and finally, Sun Falcon. They had no sooner lined up in front of the starter at the head of the stretch than he shouted "Come on!" and the race began.

Hugh Bradley, in *Such Was Saratoga,* vividly described what hap-pened next:

A flash of tape, a confused roar, two smoothly gliding machines move to the front. The duel is even as they dart past the clubhouse turn. There Sonny Workman bends closer to Whichone's ears.

Whichone goes to the front, but Gallant Fox is not to be run off his feet as the Whitney stable hopes. Earl Sande croons songs of the Western plains to his mounts, and music has its

Whichone, with Raymond (Sonny) Workman aboard, was also highly favored.

Jim Dandy, with Frank Baker in the saddle, was so widely ignored in the betting that his odds rose to 100 to 1.

The winner? Jim Dandy, in the greatest of upsets. He is shown romping home with neither Gallant Fox nor Whichone in camera range.

Jim Dandy's trainer, Johnny McKee, congratulates Frank Baker after the victory.

In the Thirties the Spa's elephantine hotels, the United States and the Grand Union, were little more than ghosts of Saratoga's glamorous past. In 1946 the United States (above) was razed.

The hotel's fabled magnificence was preserved, however, in *Saratoga Trunk,* a film starring Gary Cooper and Ingrid Bergman based on Edna Ferber's novel of the same name. Following are scenes from the film.

The Saratoga depot.

charms today. At the furlong pole the Fox draws even again; at the quarter he gets his neck ahead.

It is the high point of the race, or so they think. Now that the Fox has taken command, he never will be headed, they scream from the stands.

Yes? Then you have forgotten Sonny Workman and the brown colt which was king of the two-year-olds. Clods of mud catapult under frantic hooves as they fly to the far turn. Whichone moves up, is a scant head in the lead.

OOoooOOH!

You have forgotten something else. There has been a silence, then a strange babbling undertone, now this high pierced shriek of the crowd surprised.

Inside, next to the rail where the mud has not yet been churned into glue, a horse is slipping through, sailing past the leaders.

His chestnut coat is spattered, for a moment you do not know him even though only four started. But old Johnny McKee has known all along. Yet the white creeps under the florid mask of his face, and thick fingers clench.

On they come. Sande croons to his mount. Workman's shoulders heave as he tries to hurl the brown colt home. Baker, obscure jockey in mud-spattered silks, sits quietly. He does not have to move; matters are out of his hands. Destiny is riding the chestnut today.

Surely, though, he is only a false alarm, breathe the thirty thousand. Surely he cannot outrun the greatest colts of the year. Wait a second, he will shoot his bolt and then drop back to where he belongs.

It is a long second, and then even the doubters know. Daylight lengthens between the upstart and those supposed to humble him. Sande still sings to Gallant Fox and pleads, but it is no use. Whichone slows, seems to be in distress. Jim Dandy is six lengths in front, merely galloping.

He still is there at the wire while his jockey looks back and grins over Destiny's shoulder, wonders what has become of the champions.

In the sport and on the track which know the name so well, a dark horse has triumphed. It has been the greatest upset in American turf history, greater than the day when Upset outdistanced Man o' War, when Sysonby, at 1 to 40, finished in a dead heat in the Metropolitan, when Fashion beat Boston, sire of the mighty Lexington.

Johnny McKee's gray hair bristles in triumph; the red is back in his face when he comes to the judges' stand. He pats Jim Dandy behind the ears, whispers to him as they listen to the roar of the crowd.

Johnny McKee excepted, Damon Runyon spoke for every astounded witness in his story in the New York *American*. "You only dream the thing that happened here this afternoon," he wrote. " 'Out of the clouds,' as the horsemen say, dropped a 100 to 1 shot to beat the two greatest race horses on the American continent."

Fifteen months would pass before Jim Dandy would win again, but on a rainy Saturday at Saratoga he established himself in racing's hall of fame.

Ghosts   In the century preceding World War II, Saratoga had been host to an imposing succession of ghosts—departed splendors and dead traditions which lingered on in the city's memories and mementos of the past. The war years cast a few more fading guests into limbo.

In 1934 the Agnew-Hart Law, which for twenty-six years had prohibited bookmakers at New York State race courses from openly soliciting bets on the horses, was repealed, and led by Irish John Cavanagh a hundred or so bookies had returned to the betting ring at the Saratoga track, mounted the stalls and reigned with their old-time majesty. It was a brief victory, however. The horses didn't run at the Spa in the three seasons of 1943-1945, the railway vans which had transported them across the country from one course to another having been used to carry war supplies instead, and when the hostilities ended and racing was resumed bookies were no longer in style. Installed in place of them were pari-mutuel machines—impersonal computers minus funny names and flamboyant attire and indignant umbrellas, such as the one Virginia Carroll had thrown, and totally incapable of galloping the full length of the homestretch exhorting a horse to win, as The Dancer had been seen to do. One more colorful element vanished from the Springs.

During the war years, too, the stubbornly loyal coterie of socialites who had endeavored to carry on in the tradition of their parents and grandparents, to whom Saratoga had been a sanctuary not only in the racing season but all summer long, closed or sold their mansions and spent the summers elsewhere, leaving it to the horsy set to uphold the Spa's social prestige.

The decision to suspend racing at Saratoga for the duration of the war was a mortal blow to one of the city's ancient, elephantine hotels, the United States, and was nearly fatal to the Grand Union. During the late Twenties and Thirties, as their social standing had declined and their elegant ballrooms and other richly appointed accommodations had fallen into disuse, both hotels had been forced to shorten the periods in which they would accept guests: first from five months to three; then to two; and finally to the twenty-eight days of the August racing program. Each year the

A suite at the United States.

A bedroom in the hotel.

A view of a gaming room.

In 1952 the Grand Union followed the United States to the grave. Before the hotel was demolished, its furnishings and fixtures were stacked and marked for auction.

Furniture ready to be sold.

The grand ballroom, stripped of all but a few of its fixtures.

The Crystal Room with its famous crystal chandeliers.

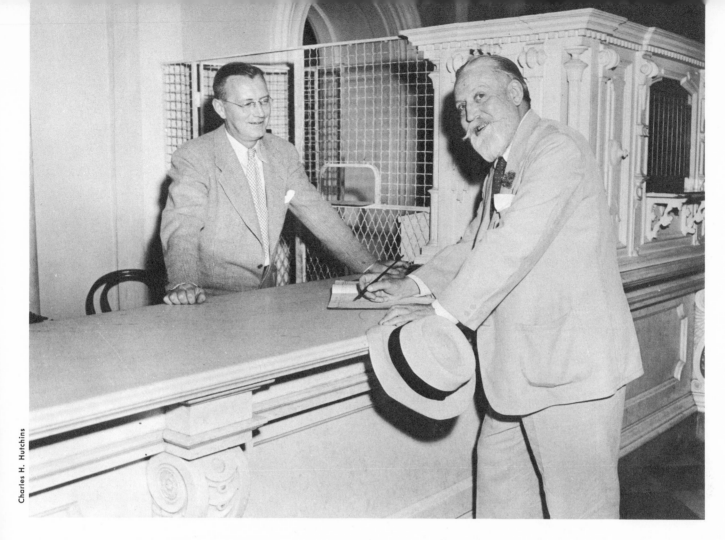

Charles H. Hutchins

Monty Woolley, the Yale professor-turned-actor, in a farewell visit to his boyhood home. His father had been the proprietor of the Grand Union during the hotel's legendary turn-of-the-century years.

Charles H. Hutchins

last two-dollar bettor, who exemplified the change in the clientele, had scarcely departed than the caretaking crews began storing the furniture away and shuttering the windows.

Deprived of the racing crowd's patronage by the closing of the track, the United States was unable to continue, and in 1943 the million-dollar showplace fell to the city in a claim for back taxes. The Grand Union teetered on the edge of bankruptcy and was rescued by a group of business-men who kept it going.

The following August the United States' furnishings and fittings were put up for auction. Fanciers of the art and upholstery of the age of ex-travagance came from all over the country to view and buy the treasures inside the old brick pile, trailing the auctioneers from room to room and bidding for crystal chandeliers, elaborately carved walnut wardrobes, marble-topped bureaus and a multitude of other mildewed but still proud pieces standing in the airless suites or stacked in the halls. Gawkers and gapers thronged the wide piazzas and promenades. They swapped jokes about the hotel's antiquities and resurrected the knee-slapper a former ten-ant of the United States, the night club comedian, Joe E. Lewis, had de-livered over the phone to the desk clerk one morning at dawn when a railroad engine let off steam almost under his window: "What time does this room leave for Chicago?" In his column in the New York *American,* Damon Runyon, who also had reason to remember a stay at the United States, poked his own kind of fun:

> When I read a dispatch about the auctioning off of the furnishings of the old United States Hotel in Saratoga Springs under tax seizure by the city, I wondered if said furnishings are deemed to include the rope fire escapes in the rooms.
>
> The United States was built 119 years ago* and either the architect forgot about putting regular fire escapes on the build-ing or they were unknown in those days. In any event, every room was equipped with a rope attached to a wall hook, the length of the rope being gauged according to the floor on which the room was located. Each rope was supposed to reach from the room to within a short drop to the ground.
>
> When I think of these ropes I always think of a friend of mine by the name of Frankie Buzzsaw. He was a horseplayer and one season at Saratoga he found himself in over his head with the books. It was back in the days when you made your bets with human beings who would take your markers and trust you until the next day,** the kind souls, and not with heartless machines that require your laying it on the line right then and there.
>
> My friend Frankie was all out of winners for two weeks hard-running and what he owed was enough to make a graven

---

* In calculating the hotel's age, Runyon went back to the original United States, which burned down; the hotel he described was opened in 1874, thus was seventy years old.
** Refers to the practice of oral betting.

image bust out crying. He owed just one gee alone a staggering sum and this gee was inclined to make something of it. In fact, he told Frankie Buzzsaw one evening that if payment was not forthcoming the following high noon he would break Frankie's legs.

Well, sitting in his room in the United States that night in black despair and also in a chair that could stand fixing if it was anything like the chairs I knew there, Frankie's eye lighted on the rope and he decided to end all. He decided to do a Jack Ketch on himself. In short, he decided to commit suicide rather than await the morrow and have the tough bookie scrag him.

So Frankie made a nice necktie for himself out of the loose end of the rope, opened the window, muttered here goes nothing and took the plunge. He fell a couple of stories before the rope went taut and then what happened, but the strands parted and let Frankie keep on falling because this was only about fifteen years ago when the rope was over a century old and you know few ropes that aged can stand such a strain.

Thus Frankie fell right on top of a fellow in the street below, and who was the fellow but the bookie who was going to break Frankie's legs and naturally when they got untangled and he saw who had squashed him the bookie chased Frankie plumb to Mechanicsville. And the tough thing about it was that the bookie was on his way to tell Frankie not to worry about his markers, that he could have even more credit.

I say that was a tough thing, but it was not the toughest, because the following day was the day Jim Dandy beat Gallant Fox and Whichone in the Travers at 100 to 1 and Frankie Buzzsaw had been waiting for Jim Dandy as the best thing of the meeting. I never could understand why he did not go ahead with his suicide idea in some other form when he got the result but the last I heard, Frankie is still alive and quite hearty only he hates ropes.

In 1946 the United States Hotel was demolished, and with it the pretty three-acre park the U-shaped structure had enclosed. A bulldozer uprooted the arching elms which shaded the walks and the bandstand. The fallen trees, even more than the debris of the hotel itself, cast a pall over much of Saratoga, for the resort's elms had been an unwavering source of pride and pleasure since 1827, when the Spa's landholders had worked as one to beautify the community by planting elms and maples wherever they would gratify the eye.

Neither the hotel nor its tree-shaded park were irretrievably lost, however. A few years before the war Edna Ferber and George S. Kaufman, who together had written such popular plays as *The Royal Family, Stage Door* and *Dinner At Eight,* had visited Saratoga one wintry week-end to weigh it as a subject for further collaboration. Kaufman had at once been

Looking backward: a wagon delivering Saratoga Vichy water passes the Grand Union.

Along with the mineral springs, the Saratoga race course upheld the resort's remaining traditions. These two paintings are on view at the National Museum of Racing. Top: a scene at the stables of the Oklahoma training track. Bottom: Nashua, with Sunny Jim Fitzsimmons (seated), who trained him, and Eddie Arcaro, who rode him.

seized with a chill while resting in his drafty hotel room and had fled south to his New York City apartment, abandoning all thoughts of the Spa. Left to her own devices Miss Ferber had decided to convert the play idea into a novel, which she did, and which became *Saratoga Trunk*. The novel, in turn, became a movie of the same name, starring Gary Cooper and Ingrid Bergman, and in relating a tale of Saratoga in the years when it was America's favorite playground the film indelibly preserved the United States Hotel in all its fabled magnificence.

The most drastic change in the Spa's way of life was the least regretted. In a program of widely publicized hearings held in New York City in the spring of 1951, United States Senator Estes Kefauver, head of a national crime inquiry, demonstrated that gambling was the basis of organized crime, and launched an investigation of Saratoga Springs, where a syndicate of racketeers controlled the casinos. New York's Governor, Thomas E. Dewey, called for a special grand jury to look into the matter too. Saratoga's casinos were closed and remained closed, thus ending a virtually continuous run of public gaming since John Morrissey had turned up at the Spa with his faro boxes and roulette wheels in 1861.

The following year, 1952, at noon of the last day of the August racing season, the Grand Union Hotel locked its doors and joined Saratoga's growing collection of ghosts. In mid-September a thousand antique seekers prowled through the tiled lobby, up and down the walnut-balustraded stairs and along the dark corridors at the heels of the auctioneers, pressing so thickly into the rooms that the smaller objects bid for had to be held aloft by an arm plunged above the crowd. China, chairs, beds, sofas, mirrors, marble-topped bureaus, carpeting were quickly and casually disposed of; special items—such as the stately chandeliers, the elaborate sconces, the somber mahogany bar against which had pressed the bellies of famous and infamous guests—engaged the viewers in spirited competition. *The Genius of America*, the wall-to-wall, floor-to-ceiling painting for which Alexander T. Stewart had paid $110,000 and hung in the Grand Union ballroom was left where it was, its value over the years having climbed to a stiff half million dollars.* Over all, where once the genteel laughter of ladies in crinoline had floated from behind lacy fans and the hearty banter of Victorian gentlemen enjoying cigars and whiskey had echoed from the bar, rose the harsh staccato of the auctioneers and the crisp, businesslike responses of the lady bidders.

The grand hotel and its elm-shaded court were razed, and in their place rose a modern shopping center. Of its many old-time attractions, Saratoga was left with just two: the waters and the horses.

* Eventually, the painting was presented as a gift to the New York State Department of Education.

Chapter Three

Second
to none

Since the day Gideon Putnam had pondered the advantages of the mineral springs and inspired his neighbors to transform the watery patch of wilderness into a popular spa, Saratoga had cherished the health-giving fountains as the one source of income of which it could be sure; a natural, permanent attraction immune to the vicissitudes of time and the vagaries of fate. The late 1880's, however, produced a change that all but ignored the resort's dependency on the waters and remained impervious to both the alarm and indignation of the villagers and the complaints of health-seeking guests.

A process had been devised to extract carbonic-acid gas from the mineral springs and use it to carbonate manufactured beverages, and with an eye to swift and substantial profits the owners of the springs permitted bottlers to pump out the waters as freely as they pleased. Over the years new wells were drilled and more and more of the medicinal liquids were drained off. The flow increased to 150,000,000 gallons a year, the cathartic and therapeutic values squandered for the sake of the gas. Saratoga looked on with growing trepidation. Ultimately the springs would be exhausted and the community's popularity as a watering place would quickly fade.

As it had before, when gambling had got out of hand, the village appealed to Albany to preserve the waters and protect Saratoga's status as a spa. Once again Senator Edgar Truman Brackett stepped forward to champion the resort's interests. Backed by Spencer Trask, George Foster Peabody and other prestigious pillars of the community, he persuaded the New York State legislature to pass a bill creating a State Reservation at Saratoga, and in May 1909, when it was signed by Governor Charles Evans Hughes, the measure became a law. As a result, the state purchased the principal springs (122 from a total number of 163), along with thirteen hundred acres of wooded terrain surrounding them, and let them idle until the water table rose high enough to spurt geysers. The period of waiting for the waters to return to their familiar levels lasted for almost eight years.

Visiting the springs soon after the state acquired them, Dr. Simon Baruch found them in such a sorry fix that in order to take a carbonated bath in the waters Saratoga proudly proclaimed as the only naturally carbonated mineral waters in the United States east of the Rocky Mountains, he had to fill a tub from bottles of costly Seltzer water which had been charged from the Spa's renowned liquids.

In 1912 Dr. Baruch began to evaluate the medicinal qualities of the springs and work out a system whereby the waters would contribute to the public welfare. It was a labor of love. Dr. Baruch had long advocated the treatment of disease by means of water. A seventy-two-year-old Jew born in Germany, he had won his M. D. at a medical college in Virginia and served as a surgeon in the Confederate Army. Then, excited by the hydrotherapeutic cures of Vienna's Dr. Wilhelm Winternitz, he had pioneered hydrotherapy in his adopted land, written two textbooks on the subject, and in New York City and Chicago established the first free municipal bath-houses in the United States. At Saratoga he took particular pains to devise a system of baths as cardiac therapy, for he was convinced that the richly endowed mineral waters would cure or ease certain afflictions of the heart.

By and large, the village asked no more than that it be restored to its old standing as America's favorite spa, but in Simon Baruch's view this was not enough. Pointing to Europe's opulent health resorts, especially to Baden-Baden, Weisbaden, Bad Homburg and the other many-splendored spas of his native Germany, he urged the state to create a watering place that would make Saratoga second to none; a spa in the European sense of the word, in which accommodations, recreation and entertainment would be such that patients would be made to forget that they were ill.

He was encouraged in this by the Saratoga waters' predominantly Jewish clientele. For many years Jews had been the most numerous and constant visitors to the Saratoga springs,* many of them having become accustomed to mineral bathing in Germany and Austria. The prospect of an American spa operated in the European manner appealed to them.

Dr. Baruch died in 1921, the spa he envisioned still no more than a dream, but in 1930, under the direction of one of his sons, it began to take form and substance. Bernard Baruch had earned a fortune in Wall Street with awesome ease (at thirty-two, he owned $100,000 in cash for each year of his life). At sixty he was a celebrated national figure—a snowy-headed, broad-shouldered six-footer with still something of the grace of the fine athlete he had been in his youth. As friend and adviser to a succession of presidents, he was well-acquainted with the world's outstanding men, but all paled, in his opinion, when measured against his father.

Simon Baruch's enthusiasm for the Saratoga waters had kindled an equal enthusiasm in his son, and he shared his father's conviction that a modern spa built on the site of the springs would cure or relieve some heart

* By way of partial explanation, a popular magazine suggested that thanks to a few thousand years of Christianity it might be that Jews were somewhat inclined to hypochondria.

ailments, arthritis and other complaints. To explain his zealous attempts to get the project underway, he said: "I am interested in physical medicine because my father was. I am interested in rehabilitation because I believe in it. I am interested in arthritis because I have it."

In 1929 the Governor of New York, Franklin Delano Roosevelt, appointed a commission to draft a plan for developing the Spa and put Baruch in charge of it. The following year the state legislature appropriated $2,000,000 to finance the recommended program and the long-delayed construction began. When the money ran out the Reconstruction Finance Corporation lent the state $3,200,000 to keep the work going. Later investments raised the cost to $8,500,000. But when the new watering place just south of Saratoga Springs * was formally opened to the public in the summer of 1935, there was no question but that every penny had been well spent. Not only was it the one establishment of its kind in the western hemisphere, but its facilities and comforts surpassed those of the German spas it emulated.

The area in which the mineral springs burst from the ground after long years of filtering through subsurface layers of rocks had been converted into a great park with gently rolling lawns and glades through which curved Geyser Brook. Huge shade trees bordered the promenades and carefully graded walks, elms, birches, particularly pines with their scent perfuming the air, and eleven miles of bridle paths threaded through the groves.

No less comforting to the eye than their surroundings, three health pavilions stood ready to serve. Named after three presidents—Washington, Lincoln, and Roosevelt who in 1933 had moved from the governor's mansion into the White House—they were a majestically arched and colonnaded yet soothing old world mixture of the Georgian and Williamsburg colonial architectural styles. In the main mall a sunken esplanade containing a pool mirrored the Hall of Springs on one side and the administration building and research laboratory on the other. Most appropriately, the laboratory, in which further researches into the sundry uses of the Saratoga waters would be pursued, had been named after Simon Baruch.

Unequivocal as it was, an inscription over an arcade to the Hall of Springs—*In this favored spot spring waters of life that heal the maladies of man and cheer his heart*— scarcely prepared the Spa's guests for the multiple pleasures that awaited them inside the vast brick and limestone showplace. Three great silver and crystal chandeliers hung from the arched ceilings, an orchestra played on a balcony and in the center hall three circular yellow marble fountains spouted Geyser, Coesa and Hathorn waters: the first a digestive aid: the second a mild laxative; and the third a vigorous cathartic. Depending on their needs, visitors filled glasses at the

---

* In 1911 the community itself had contributed to the program of conservation and improvement by purchasing Congress Park, the site of Congress Spring, and the adjoining gardens and Casino abandoned by Richard Canfield, thus securing (permanently, it was hoped) a green-shaded, marble-studded refuge which was at once a treat to the eye and a sentimental journey into the past.

fountains and sat in the lounges or strolled through the arcades sipping and passing the time until the waters worked—which for those who had chosen the Hathorn was usually within fifteen minutes.

A new hotel named Gideon Putnam, after the original founder of the watering place, had been built within easy walking distance of the mineral baths, and a new bottling plant was equipped to distribute three times the quantity of Geyser, Coesa and Hathorn waters as had been previously bottled and sold by the state. Rounding out the attractions was a recreation center, with handball and tennis courts, a swimming pool and a therapeutic golf course which, for the sake of heart patients who tired easily, contained neither hill nor dale but was flat all over.

Gratified by the state's handiwork, Saratoga looked ahead to a new era of prosperity. It was confidently estimated that twenty-five thousand health seekers would take the "cure" at the Spa each year and spend some $5,000,000 in the city, thus ending the annual drought in which money showered on the community only during the August racing season.

To the natives' dismay, it didn't quite work out that way. In the succeeding years the state owned-and-operated Spa continued to grow, but Saratoga's share of the customers' wealth became progressively smaller. Both developments could be traced to the same cause: the swelling stream of whizzing cars on the superspeed highways curving through and around the city.

In days gone by dedicated health seekers had spent a leisurely three months at the Spa, lodging themselves in the resort's hotels and savoring its amusements after the daily ritual at the baths. But the internal combustion engine had produced a new breed of vacationists. Regarding their motor cars as a combination of Aladdin's Lamp and the Magic Carpet, they were too impatiently on the go to tolerate staying in any one place for any length of time; particularly in a resort such as Saratoga which, when the horses weren't running, had so few diversions to offer.

Conversely, the state profited by the change. The ever-faster pace drew visitors increasingly to the Saratoga waters to subdue aches and pains induced by tension and anxiety, the hallmarks of the new mode of living. The health pavilions and the Gideon Putnam Hotel prospered from patients who checked in for a quick "cure."

The word was carefully placed in quotation marks by Spa officials to disabuse guests of the notion that the state was running a hospital or sanitarium. The Spa was purely a health resort, they pointed out, and "cure" meant treatment, not eradication of a medical condition. Although the staff was most capable, its members did not practice medicine. A brochure explained further: "The Spa serves as a 'right arm' for your doctor— is *not* a substitute for him. The Spa regime—the skill and knowledge of Spa technicians—will supplement your prescription. We suggest that you seek the advice and direction of a physician, concerning both external and internal use of the waters—and then put yourself in the hands of the Spa's

338 &

Saratoga's Broadway today. The Adelphi Hotel is one of the few lodging houses left from the past.

The new look: a modern motel, the Holiday Inn, offers an air-cooled Saratoga Room restaurant and Turf Lounge.

Canfield's Casino now serves as a museum, its restaurant as a social hall. It is seen here from Congress Spring Park. The twin vases in the foreground are the work of the distinguished Danish sculptor, Albert Bertel Thorvaldsen, who named them *Day* and *Night,* and were installed on the Congress grounds in 1824 by Dr. John Clarke.

Many of the old mansions and cottages still stand along the quiet, tree-shaded streets east and west of Broadway.

attendants. Their knowledge and experience, along with the carefully developed Spa regimen (rules for living), will make the most of the treatment prescribed for you."

The majority of physicians were by no means as enthusiastic as the Spa's personnel about the curative effects of the Saratoga springs, as some would-be patients discovered. Skeptics believed that any benefits derived from treatments at the Spa were psychological, the result of tranquil living while at the resort rather than the quality of the waters.

Ignoring such non-believers, the Spa's brochure addressed itself to health seekers in prose hard to resist. "One bubbling, buoyant bath," the pamphlet promised, "and you'll *know* what the Spa waters offer you. Whether you're suffering from one of the many ailments the waters may help—or just 'fagged out' from today's hectic, hurried pace—you'll be relaxed and refreshed beyond anything you've ever experienced. Literally millions of busy, bristling bubbles blanket your body, tinting your skin with a pink glow—and finding their way under your skin and into your system. There's absolutely no other physical sensation like it. You may not know the medical and scientific explanation for the action of the waters, but you're sure to experience a genuine relaxation . . . to 'feel like a million dollars.' "

To readers who might insist on some explanation, however, a later paragraph explained: "The principal minerals of value in these waters are the abundant alkalines and salines . . . There are no 'sulphur waters' at the Saratoga Spa—sodium, calcium, potassium and magnesium abound. The waters are all naturally supersaturated with carbon dioxide gas . . . carbonated at high pressures in some unknown underground laboratory by the greatest chemist of them all—Nature."

Whether moved by the brochure or Saratoga's fame as a watering place, a wide variety of sufferers put themselves in the Spa's care. A list of ailments exhibited by patients whose physicians had sent them to the health resort in a single year proved to be a pretty fair gauge of the ailments most frequently treated year in and year out. Thirty-one per cent of the guests arrived with heart trouble, eighteen per cent with stomach and intestinal disorders, and eight per cent with nervous conditions—some of which, at least, could be attributed to the high tension of the times. Twenty-four per cent turned up with rheumatic complaints, four per cent with glandular disturbances, two per cent with skin diseases, three per cent with a miscellany of irritations, and ten per cent just because they were, in the words of the brochure, "fagged out."

The Spa's pavilions, staffed and equipped to care for three thousand patients a day, provided mineral water baths, massage, heat and light therapy and similar services in private and semi-private rooms. A new health club employed a well-stocked gymnasium, Turkish and Russian baths, salt rubs and other procedures to tune up the livelier guests.

The daily consumption of the waters through drinking, bathing and bottling (several million bottles of Geyser, Coesa and Hathorn were distributed throughout the country and Canada each year) was prodigious, yet the demand was met with only a scattering of the springs in operation. A few others were allowed to spout merely for display. But the great majority were shut off to conserve their health-giving properties until needed.

Of the three famous springs that had put new zing into ailing guests in earlier times, only one was still active. Old Red, while it had never been accorded the status of the other two, had attracted a loyal following for more than a hundred and eighty years, and showed no signs of stopping. But the legendary waters of High Rock and Congress springs were exhausted.

The
forward look   In recent years the officials in charge of the Saratoga Springs Reservation have put less emphasis on the virtues of the waters and expanded and promoted the advantages of the park. "Your trip to the Spa is not all 'treatment,' " the brochure reminds expected guests, "and you'll undoubtedly wish to bring along members of your family who have no need for the 'cure.' They'll have fun—the recreational facilities at the Spa are designed to make every minute of *everyone's* stay at the Spa thoroughly enjoyable."

Today, the result of a recent expenditure by the state of four million dollars, the Spa State Park abounds with up-to-the-minute accessories of popular outdoor life, and there are considerably fewer health seekers to be seen than tanned and vigorous sports devotees engrossed in their favorite game.

From early April through November two golf courses invite play: a championship eighteen-hole course and a compact nine-hole, par twenty-nine course for the convenience of heart patients and other guests with insufficient stamina to make their way over the regulation green. A new golf house includes the comforts of a restaurant and a cocktail lounge. From June to Labor Day four swimming pools are prepared to accommodate eight thousand bathers daily, the principal one an olympic-size pool, the others, separate and smaller, a pool for divers, a wading pool with an adjoining playground for children, and a pool close to the golf house for the convenience of golfers. Large areas, paved and grass, surround the pools and encourage sun bathing and just plain loafing. Tennis, archery, croquet, shuffleboard, quoits and other such diversions are available, and for visitors who choose to walk, sit or gossip there are foot trails, benches and seven picnic areas replete with tables, fireplaces, drinking fountains, play fields,

The Gideon Putnam is modern Saratoga's most impressive hotel. Named for the founder of the Spa, its pillared entrance reflects one of the most conspicuous features of the resort's traditional architecture. At top is a front view of the Gideon Putnam; at bottom, the hotel from the rear.

The Saratoga springs today are the property of New York State, which established a State Reservation at the Spa and modernized its facilities. Left , the Simon Baruch Laboratory and the administration hall.

The Roosevelt Health Pavilion.

refreshment concessions, comfort stations and shelters to permit the fun to continue in spite of rain.*

As an extra fillip, for nine weeks of the summer season the Spa Music Theater supplies revivals of popular Broadway and off-Broadway musicals performed by a resident company of actors.

The added attractions have increased attendance at the State Reservation sixfold. The Gideon Putnam Hotel, enlarged and refurbished, has raised its "in season" rates. And the prospect of greater enrichment is splendidly in view.

Convinced that the historic resort was in danger of being inundated with sports lovers and horseplayers, a group of patricians early in 1961 proposed that an element of culture be imparted to the Spa. A Performing Arts Center was suggested, and patrons of the arts responded with enthusiasm and donations to match. To the Governor of New York, Nelson A. Rockefeller, the idea seemed at once natural and indispensable; a fitting climax to the state's program of recreation at the Saratoga Reservation. Architects were invited to submit designs for a cultural center and the cost was fixed at $2,400,000—$960,000 of which would be supplied by the state to prepare the site, provide parking lots and construct roads connecting the area with the highways close by. The funds for the arts center itself would be raised through public-spirited contributions.

On June 30, 1964, while a thousand Saratogans cheered, Governor Rockefeller climbed into the seat of a tractor and plowed up a yard of turf adjoining the Hall of Springs to break ground for the center. Representing its future tenants at the ceremony were Eugene Ormandy, director of the Philadelphia Orchestra, and Lincoln Kirstein, general director of the New York City Ballet. The two organizations had agreed to make the Performing Arts Center their permanent summer home, and the design of the auditorium had been drawn with them in mind: an open-sided, roofed amphitheater with seats for 5,100 spectators and room for 7,000 more on surrounding sloping lawns. It was announced that the ballet would occupy the stage each July and the orchestra each August, the program to start in 1966 with twenty-one performances by the ballet and fourteen by the orchestra. In addition, in August there would be weekly chamber music concerts in the Canfield Casino.

Six months later it became clear that the estimated expense of the project had been embarrassingly low. Worse, private donations amounted to a disappointing $700,000. Again, Nelson Rockefeller tendered a helping hand. The Rockefeller Brothers Fund and three of the Rockefeller brothers individually, Nelson, Laurance and John D., 3rd, pledged a total of $1,100,000 to the Performing Arts Center, leaving some $850,000 still to be raised.

In the summer of 1965 the aristocrats of horse society rode to the

---

* Still other sports and amusements are offered at nearby Lake Saratoga: fishing, sailing, motor boating, water skiing, swimming in the lake and in a new $70,000 Z-shaped pool complex in Kaydeross Park, horseback riding, band concerts in summer; ice skating, skiing, dog sled and ice harness racing in winter.

rescue. Gathered at Saratoga for the traditional August running of their racing colors, Alfred Gwynne Vanderbilt, John Hay Whitney, publisher of the New York *Herald Tribune* and co-owner with his sister—Mrs. Charles Shipman Payson, proprietor of the New York Mets—of the Greentree Stable; Mrs. Gene Markey, owner of Calumet Farm; Mrs. Elizabeth Graham, whose Maine Chance Stable was almost as firmly established as her Elizabeth Arden cosmetics; various Phippses and other leaders of the racing set tossed a benefit ball in the Hall of Springs at which five hundred blue-blooded guests fox-trotted, twisted, frugged and watusied around the three marble mineral water fountains, ate a post-midnight snack on paper plates and paid for the pleasure with a handsome contribution to the Performing Arts Center. A subsequent gesture put the center on still more solvent ground. A half dozen stable owners invited breeders to bid for the mating services of their stallions, the fees to be turned over to the new citadel of culture at the Spa. Some of the horses offered were so highly esteemed that prior to this burst of generosity they had been made available only to mares in their owners' stalls.

Later, Cornelius Vanderbilt Whitney added $50,000 to a previous munificent gift he had made, and when a construction workers' strike hoisted the price of the project to $4,000,000 the Rockefellers were heard from again; Laurance and Mrs. John D., Jr., tossed an extra $300,000 into the pot. Other sizable benefactions followed. And in the summer of 1966, with suitable fanfare, the Performing Arts Center opened on schedule.

Heartened by the refreshingly different attraction resting on its southern doorstep (the combination of symphony and ballet is expected to add thousands of art-goers to the thousands of vacationists who throng the Spa each summer), Saratoga Springs is bubbling with new vigor. More than a score of motels and a spanking-new convention hotel invite the patronage of motorists who by thruway and expressway may arrive at the resort in three hours from Manhattan or Long Island, four hours from Boston or Montreal, five hours from Buffalo or Baltimore.

At the north edge of the city another new development also promises better times. Skidmore College (founded at the Springs in 1903 by Lucy Skidmore Scribner, wife of publisher John Blair Scribner, as a young women's industrial club) is at long last moving from the Victorian mansions and stables which have largely served its students and faculty as classrooms, laboratories and lodgings to a $36,000,000 twelve-hundred-acre campus under construction in Woodlawn Park. With so much more space (the city campus was confined to forty acres), Skidmore's student body is expected to grow and infuse the city's economy with more substantial portions of parental allowances than before.

Surrounded by a famous spa, a popular recreation park and lake, an attractive cultural center and an expanding college, not to mention a half dozen manufacturing plants, and with a well-attended trotting track (opened in 1941) as well as the legendary race course in its midst, Saratoga clearly is no longer a city which, for eleven months of the year, has

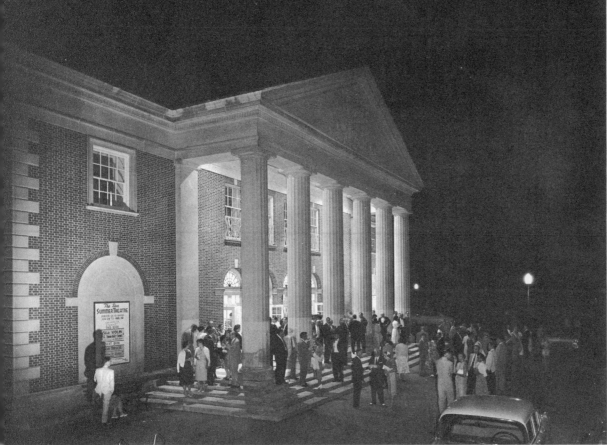

At the Spa Music Theater visitors are entertained with revivals of Broadway musicals.

George S. Bolster

Two of Saratoga's most devoted benefactors were Spencer and Katrina Trask, shown with their daughter, Christina, and son, Spencer, Jr. Yaddo, the Spa's renowned haven for writers, artists and composers, was a favorite project to which the Trasks gave their enthusiasm, energy and wealth.

Originally, Yaddo was the Trask estate—an elaborate show-place typical of architectural extravagance in the Gay Nineties. These photos show the mansion and the rose garden.

Many of Yaddo's gifted guests went on to both fame and fortune. In 1946, in the tower room of the mansion, 21-year-old Truman Capote worked on his first novel *Other Voices, Other Rooms*.

arly risers may enjoy n excellent breakfast the race track and atch the horses being rimed for the after-oon program.

Bob Mayette

A scene at the stables after a morning's effort.

Bob Mayette

he ritual surrounding the August races is all that's left of Saratoga's ceremonial re, horses and exercise boys engage in an early morning workout.

no visible means of support. Once again the sweet smell of success permeates the air and most of the community's nearly seventeen thousand inhabitants have permanently retired the old saw of former years: that Saratoga was a great place in which to live but a terrible place in which to make a living.

Yaddo   The eastern periphery of Saratoga Springs is graced by still another cultural haven, as superbly antique as the Performing Arts Center is strikingly modern. Unlike the newcomer, however, Yaddo, except for its gardens, which are open to everyone, is not for patrons but for practitioners of the arts.

A private estate of five hundred acres, Yaddo occupies the site on which Jacobus Barhyte built his dream house soon after the conclusion of the War of the Revolution. After his death the wooded bluff, little lake and forest groves over which he had placidly presided with his ever-present clay pipe had been sold and divided among various owners. Then, in 1881, the wealthy New York banker and broker, Spencer Trask, had purchased the entire property as a setting for a summer home he planned to build near the Springs.

Previous summers had been spent with the Trasks, Spencer, Katrina and their little girl, Christina, quartered in The Shadow, a popular inn on the grounds whose serene appointments had inspired Katrina to write several poems and whose name the child Christina cheerfully and constantly mispronounced "yaddo." All things considered, it appeared to the Trasks that Yaddo was an apt name for their new summer place, and Yaddo it was christened.

In 1891 a fire destroyed their Queen Anne villa, and in 1893 they replaced it with an imposingly elegant Victorian Gothic mansion whose fifty-five rooms soon housed a succession of guests famous throughout the country. Statesmen and scientists, tycoons and socialites angled for invitations to their parties, and authors, painters and composers were included by the cultured hosts as a matter of course. Non-celebrities also enjoyed the Trasks' hospitality. On Christmas morning the servants, gardeners and stablemen and their families, an assembly that frequently numbered two hundred and fifty persons, gathered in the great hall of the mansion to sing carols and receive the key to the locked room where their presents were hidden. And the year round boys and girls of Saratoga Springs came to sample the seasonal treats of the estate: chestnuts in October, skating in January, wild strawberries in late June and swimming in July and August.

Eventually, a series of adversities also visited the Trasks. Their first-born child, Alan, had drowned in a lake some years before. Suddenly Christina and her new brother, Spencer, Jr., died within twenty-four hours of each other of a malignant fever, and the baby, Katrina, died of diphtheria.

The loss of all four of her children made an invalid of Katrina Trask. She and her husband began to lose interest in Yaddo. With no one left in the family to whom to bequeath it, the estate held fewer attractions for them, and since, in the long run, the house and grounds would fall to strangers, it seemed the best thing to surrender the place at once.

Strolling through their woods on a summer afternoon in 1899, the Trasks were struck by a much better, indeed, an ideal, solution. Something about Yaddo seemed to encourage the creative urge; during months-long stays, a number of their guests had written stories, essays, poems, plays and musical compositions. Why couldn't the estate be maintained as a haven for authors and artists?

With new enthusiasm, Spencer and Katrina Trask made a will bequeathing to Yaddo their entire wealth after their deaths and set about investing the estate with an atmosphere still more conducive to creative endeavor. Thousands of trees were planted to replenish groves the previous owners had cut down. A rose garden was introduced and the sweeping lawn sloping from the mansion was intercepted with white marble statues and a white marble fountain, bird baths, Italian jardinieres filled with flowers and reproductions of ancient Italian benches. Artificial lakes were added, with ducks. Many more improvements were envisioned, but in 1907 a financial panic wiped away much of the Trask fortune. On the last day of 1909, before he could recoup their losses, Spencer Trask was killed when a train collided with the one in which he was travelling from Saratoga to New York City.

Left to herself, in poor health and supported by dwindling funds, his widow considered abandoning their project, then resolved to carry it on more modestly. New changes were made in the estate to assure its future tenants peace and privacy for artistic gestation; and when her living expenses grew to be more than she could handle Katrina Trask closed the costly mansion and moved into a farmhouse, the better to preserve the endowment which would provide the niceties of living for the guests-to-be.

In 1921 she surrendered to the pleas of a persistent suitor, George Foster Peabody, and married him. A lifelong friend of the family, he had been Spencer Trask's banking partner and before that, when she was Katrina Nichols, had been Trask's rival for her hand, the loss of which he had never fully accepted.* Peabody was sixty-nine, his bride a year younger. The union was brief. During the following January she died.

* A multimillionaire philanthropist for whom the annual George Foster Peabody Awards for "distinguished achievement by television and radio" were named, Peabody was invited by Trask to become his banking partner six years after he and the desirable Miss Nichols had wed. Still devoted to her, Peabody thought that before accepting he should make his position clear. "Spencer," he said, "I am in love with your wife." Trask replied with equal frankness. "I don't blame you, Foster. I am in love with her myself." As noted, the partnership was formed and the friendship survived.

A few months later the Corporation of Yaddo, which had been formed to receive the estate, appointed an executive director, Mrs. Elizabeth Ames, to carry out the terms of the Trask will. After a three-year interval, invitations were extended to authors, composers, painters and sculptors to enjoy a summer of creative work at Yaddo free of charge, and in June 1926, the first group of gifted guests arrived.

An assortment of ten, they shared a mutual distrust of one another, a common skepticism and a mounting apprehension of what might be in store for them. The latter was instilled by the sight of the extravagantly spired and turreted mansion and its vast rooms carpeted with costly Persian rugs, lined with books and paintings, and filled with every kind of bric-a-brac from throne chairs to Swedish sleighs. As events proved, none of their forebodings were justified. Mrs. Ames rose to the occasion with the charm of a social hostess and the tactful but firm supervision of a house mother. Before long, writers and artists discovered that they were a harmonious mixture within intellectual hailing distance of each other. And despite outside rumors that it was a free-love colony, Yaddo, as a creative community, wound up its first season an acknowledged success.

In subsequent years the Corporation of Yaddo continued to improve and enlarge the estate's facilities and with Mrs. Ames worked out a system and schedule that are still in force. To assure Yaddo of top-quality guests, each spring advisory committees in the various arts weigh the merits of applicants' published, performed or exhibited work, then select two groups of writers and artists with outstanding talent for summer residence. The first group is given the run of the place through May and June, the second through July and August and frequently part of September. Since heating the mansion would require a ton of coal a day, the great gray-stone pile is closed in the winter, but two small houses, equipped with furnaces, are available for the usual half dozen or so guests who become too wrapped up in their projects to tear themselves away.

All guests live in the mansion and some work there too, while others work in studios scattered through the grounds. (Visiting during working hours, nine to four, is not permitted, and is condoned after working hours only if one has been invited.) Breakfast, eight to nine, is cheery but monosyllabic, lest a developing conversation delay authors, artists and composers in their appointments with the muses. Lunch is packed in individual tin boxes to be eaten in the vicinity of one's typewriter, easel, piano, or in the solitude of the pine or oak groves. But dinner, at six-thirty in the mansion's grand dining room, is whatever the guests choose to make it while fortifying themselves with Yaddo's justly famed food. Later, warmed by coffee in the main parlor, or by the view of the Hudson River Valley from the huge window of the baronial hall, Yaddo's tenants are encouraged to discuss life and art, but discouraged from reading their manuscripts or playing their compositions for each other. And somewhere around ten o'clock they are expected to retire and replenish their energy for another day of creation.

Since Yaddo views each summer as a period for uninterrupted work, there are no formal social activities. Guests somewhat unstrung by the monastic seclusion into which they are plunged find relief on the estate's tennis court and croquet lawn, by fishing in the little lakes and hiking over the miles of winding woodland paths. Occasionally, they may drive to the beaches at Lake Saratoga for a swim, or drop in on Saratoga itself. But although in August the horses are running at the race track adjoining the grounds, it is tacitly understood that its attractions are "off limits" to Yaddo's consecrated, non-paying guests.

Undisputable evidence that Yaddo's regimen has been helpful rests in the solid reputations many of its guests have achieved. Over a stretch of forty years Yaddo has housed and nourished what amounts today to something of a *Who's Who* in America's creative arts.

In the late Twenties and Thirties, Mrs. Ames extended the estate's hospitality to such novelists and short story writers as Louis Adamic, John Cheever, James T. Farrell (who wrote part of *Studs Lonigan* there), Daniel Fuchs, Wallace Stegner and Henry Roth (who, after his novel *Call It Sleep* was weakly received, renounced writing, married a composer he had met at Yaddo and became a metal grinder, only to see *Call It Sleep* become a paperback best-seller in 1965); also to such critics and essayists as Malcolm Cowley, Waldo Frank, Sidney Hook, Louis Kronenberger, Max Lerner, Lionel Trilling; poets Louise Bogan, Babette Deutsch, Kenneth Fearing, Dudley Fitts, Weldon Keyes, Delmore Schwartz, Genevieve Taggard; composers Marc Blitzstein, Aaron Copland, David Diamond and Roy Harris; and several presently prestigious painters and sculptors plus a photographer, Henri Cartier-Bresson.

In the Forties a precocious writer of short stories, Truman Capote, worked on his first novel in the gold-and-white tower room that had been Katrina Trask's favorite retreat and conversed with Marguerite Young, a poet who was to spend the next eighteen years writing an epic of 1,198 pages (longer than *Ulysses* and half as long as Proust's many-volumed *Remembrance Of Things Past*) published in 1965 as *Miss MacIntosh, My Darling*. Other writers in residence during the Forties included Carson McCullers (whose novel, *The Member of the Wedding*, is dedicated to Mrs. Ames), Flannery O'Connor, Katherine Anne Porter (who employed her stay to work on *Ship Of Fools*), Jean Stafford and Eudora Welty; critics Philip Rahv, Alfred Kazin and Granville Hicks; and poets Langston Hughes and Robert Lowell.

Through the Fifties, Yaddo was host to still another glittering assembly of talent: novelists James Baldwin, Saul Bellow, Herbert Gold, William Goyen, Bernard Malamud, Wright Morris, Dawn Powell, Harvey Swados, Jessamyn West; critics and commentators Hannah Arendt, Van Wyck Brooks, Leon Edel, Leslie Fiedler and Dorothy Parker; poets Howard Nemerov and William Carlos Williams; composer Leonard Bernstein; artists George Biddle, Adolf Dehn and Antonio Frasconi. And presently

The parade from the paddock to the starting gate.

The run for the money. In 1965 a new section of grandstand (shown at right) was added to the old grandstand without jarring its venerable design.

A steeplechase race.

Philip Roth, Hortense Calisher, Anne Fremantle, George P. Elliott and Robert Gorham Davis are submitting to Yaddo's stimulating discipline.

The preponderance of eminent authors who owe part of their apprenticeship to Yaddo has stamped it as a literary colony, but it has rendered even greater service to music. Every two or three years it has sponsored a music festival devoted completely to modern work, and in September 1952, when the estate celebrated its first quarter of a century of service to the arts, music critic Robert Evett paid his respects with an article in *The New Republic*:

> The history of American music has, for some 25 years, been intimately concerned with that of Yaddo . . . Before Yaddo was opened, American music was usually a genteel imitation of outmoded European work. Its services were made available at the time when Roy Harris, Aaron Copland, Walter Piston and the other composers of their generation were returning to the United States with the talent and the imagination necessary for bringing our music to maturity and calling it to the attention of the rest of the world. Most of these men spent time working at Yaddo, and all of those who subsequently developed great prestige were performed at the Yaddo festivals. In the nine music periods to date, Yaddo has performed the work of over 130 composers. Some of these have died, some have lapsed into obscurity (or, indeed, never left it), but a good quarter of the composers have attained considerable celebrity; in most cases, their reputations were established after their first Yaddo performances. The Yaddo committees have shown an uncanny knack for recognizing talent earlier than the rest of the world, and can claim at least partial credit for the launching of several brilliant careers.

Yaddo's founders, Katrina and Spencer Trask, buried in the rose garden on the estate's highest hill, could hardly have a more flattering epitaph.

A congenial elegance   On August 3, 1863, a filly named Lizzie W. had streaked over John Morrissey's original Saratoga track to become the first thoroughbred ever to cross the finish line at the Spa. In the summer of 1963 Saratoga set out to recapture the grand and glorious past with a centennial celebration of the historic event.

The hoopla got underway in April with a competition for barbershop quartets and picked up momentum with a Victorian-flavored regatta on Lake Saratoga, band concerts in Congress Park and a parade of once elegant carriages and coaches that had graced Broadway when to be seen on Broadway in the fashionable pageant-on-wheels was a badge of social distinction. Local males sported side whiskers and beards, and the traditional arrival of horse society and its retinue of trainers, jockeys, grooms, exercise boys, stablehands and fleet-footed thoroughbreds was heralded with bunting and banners arching over Saratoga's main streets and decorated with the racing colors of more than one hundred and twenty horse owners and stables. To cap the celebration, the resort's August elite journeyed (some in equipages their socialite forebears had used) to Richard Canfield's famed Casino and dined and danced by candlelight at a gala centennial ball.

A good deal of the gayety of Saratoga's centennial summer grew out of surprise and relief that the ancient race course, the oldest in the country, was still on hand to observe its hundredth birthday. Not for years had racing at the Spa been the big business it used to be. Indeed, for several seasons the old-fashioned oval had not earned enough money to cover the full amount of its purses. In 1955 the New York Racing Association, which was obliged to make up the deficit, had acquired the track from its stockholders, and ever since, rumbles from Albany had stirred gloomy expectation that the August meeting would go the way of Saratoga's other beloved but expensive anachronisms.

That there was ample cause for Albany's irritation not even the track's most ardent defenders could deny. Thoroughbred racing had become the most popular spectator sport in New York State and each year contributed more and more in tax revenue to the state treasury.* The big yield came from "Big A," Long Island's Aqueduct. Since Saratoga's race course could accommodate only thirty thousand spectators against eighty thousand at Aqueduct, and Aqueduct's daily pari-mutuel receipts were almost three times the size of Saratoga's, it was plain to see (as tax-hungry legislators kept pointing out) that the state's kitty would be fattened considerably if racing were discontinued at the Spa and its August program turned over to "Big A."

But while the mathematics of the state's argument were unassailable, they ignored the old-world charm the Saratoga track alone possessed, a congenial elegance that had endeared it to generations of horsemen. With some pointing of their own (to a state law guaranteeing Saratoga twenty-four days of racing each year), the aristocrats of horse society appealed for benevolence to the state's chief executive, a fellow patrician who had previously arranged himself on the side of the angels seeking to preserve Saratoga's traditions, Nelson Rockefeller.

The result was a compromise that made the legislature a little less disgruntled and mightily pleased Saratoga and its August guests. Three and a half million dollars were poured into the track to provide extra enticements for horse-players and their taxable purchases and give the grandstand a zippier look, the first major changes in well over half a century. But each improvement was accomplished with such solicitude for the track's venerable charm that when it displayed its new curves and contours for the first

* In 1965 the state derived almost $70,000,000 from thoroughbred racing.

Sunny Jim Fitzsimmons, the grand old man of the turf. From 1893 until his death early in 1966, he seldom missed a racing season at Saratoga.

Bob Mayette

Although Saratoga's gaming casinos were closed long ago, high-stakes gambling still goes on at the Spa. Wealthy stable owners gather at the Fasig-Tipton auction ring and place five and six-figure bets on untested yearlings. Left, Mr. and Mrs. Alfred Gwynne Vanderbilt confer at a Fasig-Tipton sale.

George D. Widener ponders the worth of a colt in the ring.

Mr. and Mrs. Cornelius Vanderbilt Whitney at a yearling auction.

time in the season of 1965 even octogenarian devotees who had feared the worst were forced to agree with the Racing Association's reassuring ads: "It's still the same charming, beautiful Saratoga—but now there's more of it."

Extending eastward, over the areas once occupied by the field stand and the betting ring, idle and unused ever since the bookmakers had bowed to computers, a new five-hundred foot section of grandstand providing 4,500 additional seats had been joined to the old grandstand so deftly that it was hard to tell where the old woodwork left off and the new portion began. The roofline of the added section faithfully imitated its predecessor, even to the Victorian peaks and gables William C. Whitney had requested when he had enlarged the grandstand in 1902. Other improvements included a cafeteria on the grandstand veranda, overlooking the cool green paddock, two sets of escalators and additional pari-mutuel windows. Even these modern accouterments had been made to blend with the track's jaunty, nineteenth-century dress by a generous dose of the candy-striped red and white decor that had long been a familiar sight to Saratoga's race-goers.

Clearly, there were better reasons than ever for going to the races at Saratoga, and for the one hundred second running at the Spa, when the old track's new look was trotted out, patrons arrived in sufficient numbers to thaw, ever so slightly, the New York legislature's frosted heart. For the present, at least, Saratoga and its legion of horse lovers could relax; the grand old race course was not only still alive but was as frisky as a yearling.

The traditions of August   Today, the pleasant ritual surrounding the August running is all that's left of Saratoga's ceremonial past. It commences, as it always has, with the magical transformation of the community itself. Almost overnight the quiet city becomes a bustling metropolis as racing enthusiasts invade it by land, air and water—the latter a route largely favored by the resort's wealthy summer colonists who sail their yachts up the Hudson River to Schuyler-ville, where their chauffeured limousines await to transport them along the last short leg of the journey. As always, too, Saratoga's prices take flight. Motel rates ascend fifty per cent, restaurant fees twenty-five per cent. The Gideon Putnam Hotel, which supplies both room and board on the American plan, escalates from its July rates of up to $30 a day for single occupancy, $48 for double and $85 for a suite to a flat $55 for single, $68 for double and "none available" for suites through August. Hundreds of Saratogans leave home on a month-long vacation of their own, renting their houses to August guests for anywhere from $500 to $1,500.

The socialites reopen their multiple-room cottages and estates and settle down for the traditional round of horse watching and wagering, cocktail and supper parties, and whatever surprises the season might produce. Mrs. Charles Payson returns to the clapboard house that previously belonged to her mother; her brother, Jock Whitney, reclaims the summer home and acres he named Oeeweekin, a phrase borrowed from the Mohawk, meaning "Journey's End"; and together they share the small, chalk-marked winner's circle at the track whenever an entry from Greentree, the bluegrass empire they jointly inherited, noses ahead of its rivals. The Cornelius Vanderbilt Whitneys reassert their proprietorship of Cady Hill; the Stephen (Laddie) Sanfords move back into Ideal View; the Albert C. Bostwicks again occupy the home of the late Mrs. Isobel Dodge Sloan, whose Brookmeade Stables had made her one of the country's leading horsewomen. The Howell Jacksons renew their acquaintance with Red Shoes, the cottage they named after one of their fillies who triumphed at Saratoga; the F. Skiddy von Stades preside once more over the ninety-year-old place that has housed his family for five generations (a Hudson River steamboat that once brought Saratoga-bound vacationists from New York City was named *Francis Skiddy*). Rear Admiral and Mrs. Gene Markey (he a one-time movie producer and husband of actresses Joan Bennett, Hedy Lamarr and Myrna Loy, she the mistress of Calumet Farm—famous for Triple Crown and Kentucky Derby winners: Whirlaway, Pensive, Citation, Ponder, Hill Gail, Iron Liege, Tim Tam) reinstall themselves on their great estate, Westway; and the list goes on.

Still other leaders of the horsy set rent for the season. Among them are the Alfred Gwynne Vanderbilts and the several Phippses, whose tribe is led to the Spa each year by the shy *grande dame,* Mrs. Henry Carnegie Phipps, who has watched her yellow and purple Wheatley Stable silks running at Saratoga for nearly forty years. Never a summer passes without a quorum of racing's royalty staked out at the resort: Whitneys, Vanderbilts, Chenerys, Wideners, Guggenheims, Phippses, Morrises, Galbreaths, Sanfords, Bradys, Bostwicks and other standard-bearers of the sport.

But the pastoral pleasures of Saratoga's August meeting are available to everyone, not just the rich. And if one is an early riser the rewards are especially satisfying, for in the dawn's early light the age-old formalities in which the horse is king begin. Through the morning mists enveloping the stables and training ovals surrounding the race track come familiar sights and sounds and smells dedicated to the afternoon program. Slabwood stove fires burn against the pale chill and grooms and exercise boys fortify themselves with the smoky warmth as they listen to instructions from the trainers. Soon the pampered subjects of their ministrations appear, sniffing the acrid mixture of smoke and damp leafy pines and stepping nervously with the most expensive legs in the land. After a few minutes horses and riders head slowly under the trees toward one of the training tracks— Oklahoma or Horse Haven, the narrow runway built by John Morrissey and subsequently abandoned as inadequate—or toward the race track itself. Gradually the early stillness is rent with thudding hoofs and sudden, explosive gusts of breath as the horses fly around the white-fenced ovals to the encouraging grunts of the exercise boys bent low in the saddles. Then, the workout completed, they return to the stables, where each glistening thoroughbred is sponged and rubbed and blanketed and fed and left to rest for the challenge of the afternoon's events.

Visitors who choose the main track for observation while the horses are being primed may at the same time enjoy another custom in the traditional August ritual: breakfast on the club house porch. Seated in comfort at a table characteristically draped in candy-striped red and white, one might also gather a profitable fund of information from the conversation of owners, trainers, breeders, turf writers and horse-players breakfasting at neighboring tables while one appraises the form of the colts and fillies flashing by a short distance away.

At ten o'clock the premises are cleared and the race course is primped for the races, but if one's astrological signs are especially benign a visit to the stables may result in a few pleasant recollections of the old days with a gentleman who has been a fixture at Saratoga's horse ceremonies for so long that he is a tradition all by himself. As exercise boy, jockey, owner, breeder and trainer, Max Hirsch has been coming to the Spa since 1890. For the past thirty-five years he has been training the thoroughbreds purchased by the King Ranch, and at Saratoga habitually rises at five o'clock, hops into his Cadillac and whirls around the grounds on a tour that enables him to supervise the form and feeding of some two dozen horses. When he is not in motion, Max Hirsch likes to reminisce about the Saratoga that was: "Champagne and frogs' legs for breakfast. Big bettors in the club house and bookmakers ready to handle their action. Fun—all that was fun." *

Early in the afternoon the first of the program's contestants are escorted, saddled and blinkered, across the elm-shaded paddock and into the white-fenced walking ring, where the jockeys await them. And shortly before two o'clock, post time for the first race, red-coated outriders lead the multicolored and readily combustible collection of horses and riders toward the starting gate as spectators crowd in for a close look at their favorites.

From the grandstand one sees the procession file into the arena, stiffly moving or suddenly shying dabs of color on a canvas already gleaming with hues. Petunias and geraniums brighten the porches, the track is a ribbon of sandy red and the infield a sea of grassy green from which clusters of trees and shrubbery fountain. Blue and white pennants wave beside the steeple-chase jumps (the arena harbors three tracks now, dirt, hurdle and turf— the latter a one-mile grass course added in 1961) and swans and Muscovy

---

* The grand old man of Saratoga racing, James E. (Sunny Jim) Fitzsimmons, died in March 1966, at the age of ninety-one. As jockey, owner and trainer, he had graced the Spa's turf for three-quarters of a century. In later years, his spine twisted by arthritis, Mr. Fitz spent the early mornings of the August racing season in a chair at the Oklahoma walking ring, watching the horses cool off after their workout, and the afternoons on a green bench in the paddock, watching the horses parade to the post. Both the chair and the bench will miss him. So too will a veritable army of friends and acquaintances. He was the most beloved figure in horse racing, a gracious, gentle nobleman in the realm still called the Sport of Kings.

ducks glide over the water of the lake adjoining the tote board. Another, but by no means final, dash of vivacity is flaunted by a canoe that also idles in the lake. Each year it is repainted with the colors of the stable whose entry captures the Travers, the oldest stakes race in the country.*

Soon the procession is at the starting gate, and with the crowd's suspended movement and almost audible hush before the horses spring from their cubicles the traditional ritual accelerates to a climax. What follows is, of course, perversely unpredictable, Saratoga having become famous on one hand as the proving ground of juveniles with championship ambitions and on the other as the graveyard of established winners who thought they had it made. But the quality of both horses and jockeys is the best, and on at least one sunny afternoon during the four-week season race-goers are apt to experience a thrill that will have them talking to one another for days; just possibly, they might also see racing history made. It happened (history, that is) as recently as the seasons of 1962 and 1965.

In 1962 the fourth largest crowd ever to assemble at the Saratoga track stood on its feet almost from start to finish as a dark bay named Jaipur and a light bay named Ridan ran head and head for the entire mile and a quarter in the ninety-third Travers. Willie Shoemaker rode Jaipur and Manuel Ycaza rode Ridan, and Jaipur won by a nose in 2:01⅗, a clocking that equaled the track record and bettered, by a fifth of a second, the stakes record set in 1920 by Man o' War. Thousands of dollars were wagered directly after the finish by spectators who couldn't agree on the winner, and diehards continued to disagree even after the official film showed Jaipur ahead by a nostril. The race itself, however, afforded no room for dissent: without a doubt, it was the greatest Travers of all.

In 1965 Kelso, a stakes-wise, eight-year-old gelding who had been acclaimed "Horse of the Year" for five years in a row (doubtlessly more important to his owner, Mrs. Richard C. du Pont, he was also the richest money winner—not far from $2,000,000—in thoroughbred history), went to the post to pick up the $35,360 first prize in the thirty-eighth running of the Whitney. Named for William C. Whitney, the race had been cap-tured eight times by various members of his clan starting in 1930 with Harry Payne Whitney, and in 1965 hopes were entertained by the Greentree Whitneys that their entry, Malicious, would return the trophy to the fam-ily. To almost everyone's surprise, it appeared until the last split-second of the mile-and-a-furlong dash that indeed he would. Four years younger and sixteen pounds lighter than his celebrated rival, who carried the top weight, Malicious was first out of the gate and set a furious pace. Kelso was slow to get going and swung wide entering the homestretch. But then he blazed past the pack, came even with Malicious and poked his nose in front as they arrived eyeball-to-eyeball at the winning post. It was the most dramatic

* And the second oldest stakes race on the American continent. First run in 1864, the Travers was preceded by the Queens Plate in Ontario, Canada, first run in 1860.

victory the great horse had ever produced, and the pandemonium that acknowledged it was comparable to the frenzied acclamations that shook the old race course on its memorable occasions of the past.

Where the action is Today's Saratoga is no kin to yesterday's "wild vortex of gambling and betting" decried by Nellie Bly. There are no casinos where money once flowed from dusk to daylight, and cautious two-dollar bettors monopolize the mutuel windows at the race track. Too, there are no more legendary tales of heavy plungers such as "Bet-a-Million" Gates wagering $10,000 on every turn of a card or spin of a wheel, or carrying away in a market basket a mound of cash won on the horses. But for the extremely rich there is still high-stakes gambling of a kind the Kefauver investigation didn't touch.

It occurs in the evenings of the second week of August in a green and white paddock two blocks east of the track. This is the sales ring of the Fasig-Tipton Company, horse auctioneers, and the name of the game is the Saratoga Annual Yearling Auction. As has always been true of Saratoga gaming, anyone can play who can afford to lose; there are no social barriers. But for the most part the horse bettors are both socially and financially supreme (a popular anecdote told at the Spa—a prominent yearling bidder, the story goes, tried to cash a check at the local bank, and the bank bounced —contains more truth than jest).

The aim of the game is simple: to purchase, at the lowest possible price, a year old, untested thoroughbred who will one day win the Kentucky Derby and go on from there to take the Triple Crown. Since some seventeen thousand thoroughbreds are foaled annually, and one fourth of the foals dropped never get to the starting gate, the odds against the horse winning the Derby alone are roughly 13,000 to 1. Lesser goals are also hedged with formidable odds. But while the great majority of young colts and fillies flounder in their efforts to reach the jackpots, the rewards are prodigious when they do. And, as in every form of gambling, it is the possible pay-off rather than the probable loss that rests pleasantly on the minds of the players who bid against one another at the Fasig-Tipton sales.

To support their optimism they can point to a fairly bulging dossier on yearlings who made good after buyers took a chance on them at the Saratoga auctions. Alsab, purchased for $700, earned over $350,000 for his owner; Globemaster, knocked down at $80,000, brought in five times the amount of his price and is presently worth half a million as a sire; Bull Lea, obtained for $14,000 in 1936 by Warren Wright (Mrs. Markey's first husband, from whom she inherited Calumet Farm), gained $95,000 in purses and displayed such a flair with the brood mares that his numerous offspring, notably Citation, Armed and Iron Liege, turned in over $13,500,000. Such major money-winners as Cavalcade and Head Play were purchased respectively for as little as $1,200 and $550. And on an August evening in 1964 a dark bay colt named Kauai King was picked up for $42,000 in the Saratoga sales ring and went on to win the 1966 Kentucky Derby and Preakness, the first horse sold at public auction ever to claim two-thirds of the elusive Triple Crown. The success stories are more than balanced, of course, by the sour vignettes of the Saratoga yearlings who were left at the post, such as Rise 'n' Shine, bought for $87,000; or who never got to it, such as Hustle On and Pericles, the first a $70,000 and the second a $75,000 investment.

The gamble in buying a yearling actually commences in the breeding stalls, long before the bidders assemble at the auctions, and is illustrated by such case histories as the mating of a mare named Geisha to a stallion named Polynesian. It produced Native Dancer, who won all but one of twenty-two races; it also produced Noble Savage, who won no races whatsoever. In 1918, a year after the sales began under the Saratoga elms, Samuel D. Riddle paid $5,000 for a colt he named Man o' War. The big red horse went on to win nearly $250,000 before he was retired to stud in 1921, and so embarrassed August Belmont, the gold-encrusted racing buff who had bred and sold him, that Belmont attempted to duplicate him by mating his sire and dam once again; the result was My Play, who rewarded the patrician sportsman with nine paltry purses in four years on the tracks. As a daddy, Man o' War also was half responsible for several flops. In 1928 his son, Broadway Limited, was sold to a bidder for $65,000 and never finished a race better than fourth. His career ended a few years later among the saddest and cheapest of platers when he dropped dead while out in front in the running for a $900 purse and lost the only chance he ever had to be a winner.

Despite the evidence that a blue-ribbon pedigree is by no means a guarantee that a yearling will be a money-maker, it is the most reliable clue to how an unraced colt or filly will do. Thus, conformation and condition (the two other guides to a yearling's worth) also being above cavil, the biggest prices are generally paid for the horses with the best bloodlines—bidders devoting as much attention to the performance and gestation records of sires, dams, grandsires and granddams as to the young thoroughbreds themselves.

Long esteemed as the Tiffany of yearling sales, the Saratoga auctions usually offer the most desirable horseflesh and inflict the most painful purchase fees. The average price per head has soared from $1,388 in 1917, the first year of the sales, to over $20,000 in 1965, and the ceiling is nowhere to be seen. The grand total rung up on the cash register during the four evenings of the 1965 auctions was $4,159,100, nearly $400,000 more than the year before, and the top price set a new high for the Saratoga sales: $125,000 paid by Raymond Guest for a bay filly by Tom Fool out of Levee.

The atmosphere in the Fasig-Tipton auction pavilion is more informal than it was in Canfield's gambling casino and the style of play is

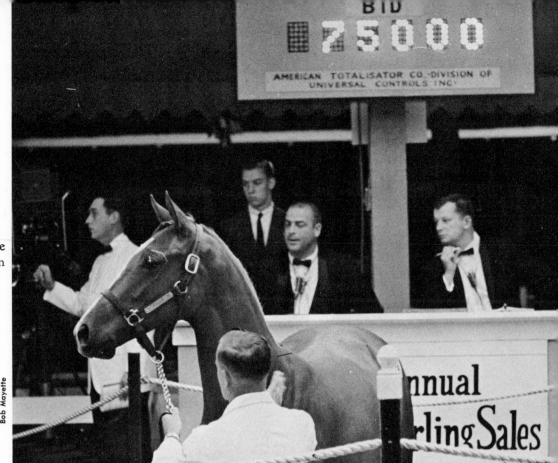

Bob Mayette

While an auctioneer encourages the bidding, the prices are registered on the bid board.

Charles H. Hutchins

The National Museum of houses both memorabilia and me of the sport. The silks of f stables are displayed along with ings of famous thoroughbreds.

Hanover, a star of the early 1880's, was one of the first ten horses admitted to the museum's Hall of Fame.

This painting of *The First Futurity* is also on view in the museum's art gallery.

polite rather than showy. But when the bidding is intense it generates the same high-voltage excitement produced in the past by five-figure betting at faro and roulette. The action begins at eight-thirty, when the first yearling is led into the roped-off sales ring with an identifying number on a patch of adhesive taped to its hip. The rustle of catalogues and whispered consultations is stilled, and Whitneys, Vanderbilts, Wideners, Sanfords and other socialite horse fanciers, together with non-social but rich stable owners and less moneyed horse proprietors hoping for an inexpensive but lucky purchase, lean forward from the tiers of white chairs encircling the tarmac for an appraising look at the young filly or colt. In the back, and outside the pavilion, Saratogans and tourists crane for a glimpse too, for the yearling auction offers both players and spectators the best diversion in town.

On the podium Humphrey S. Finney, the white-haired president of Fasig-Tipton, peers over spectacles that habitually cling to the tip of his nose, and his son, John, general manager of the company, introduces the horse. Then one of the two auctioneers, Milton (Laddie) Dance and Ralph Retler, takes over. All four are bow-tied and dinner-jacketed in splendid contrast to the majority of their guests, who, apart from a few attired in formal clothes for a late-evening party, usually arrive in whatever raiment seems comfortable.

As the amplifiers pick up the auctioneer's chant and bark the piston-like cadence at the crowd the yearling in the ring is apt to tug nervously at the bit held by its handler or, if frightened, may whinny piteously, sidle and wheel. Spotters, well educated in the language of the auction, stand in the aisles, interpret each thousand-dollar bid and counterbid signalled by a barely perceptible nod of a head or flick of a finger, a furtively raised pencil or catalogue, a briefly smoothed skirt or lapel, and with high-pitched cries relay the increases in the horse's price to the podium. Above and slightly to the rear of the platform the numbers on the bid board jump convulsively as the bids are registered and the auctioneer's liturgy is subtly invested with urgency and cajolery, an acceptable and indeed commendable ploy since Fasig-Tipton collects five per cent of the fee it turns over to the breeder of each yearling sold. And so the game continues—the secret pantomime of the bidders punctuated by the voluble commentary from the podium and the aisles—until the gavel falls for the last time and the colt or filly has a new owner. All that remains is a formality: the horse is led away and the purchaser signs the sales slip (and pays twenty-five per cent of the price before leaving); another yearling is led into the arena and a new round of bidding begins.

It will be a year—two or three years if the purchase fees were high—before the buyers will know whether they've won their gamble or lost. The horses will then be out on the tracks, bidding against one another in a high-stakes game of their own. Meanwhile, there's hope and here and there a few dreams, the imagination tantalized by the far-off drumming of a hard-bought thoroughbred's hoofs; could it be the sound of another Twenty Grand, another Whirlaway, another Kelso . . . ?

Treasure hunt The most eloquent demonstration of the determination to maintain Saratoga as the dowager queen of the American turf is on view all year round, directly opposite the race track, inside a handsome red brick, Colonial-style building, topped by a white cupola on which a symbolic horse and jockey defiantly perch. The building is named the National Museum of Racing and the intriguing collection of memorabilia it houses superbly supports this claim.

The idea of collecting and preserving "all materials and articles associated with the origin, history and development of horse racing and the breeding of the thoroughbred horse" took root in 1950 among such stout-hearted champions of the sport as F. Skiddy von Stade, George D. Widener, Jock Whitney and Cornelius Vanderbilt Whitney, but for the next four years the new museum's exhibits had to be confined to a room in the Canfield Casino. Early in 1955, however, the spacious lawn fronting the former Saratoga residence of Samuel Rosoff, the indelicate multimillionaire who had cut a swath at the Spa in the Twenties, was made available along with a sizable chunk of private funds, and the present museum * was erected and formally opened (by the then Governor of New York, W. Averell Harriman) at the peak of the 1955 racing season.

It is a turf lover's treasure trove. A thorough search of the premises will turn up such gems as a shoe worn by Kentucky, the first horse to win the Travers; a cane given to the gentleman jockey, Tod Sloan, by Britain's King Edward VII; the boots and saddle, the latter hardly larger than a postage stamp, used by Johnny Loftus when he rode the legendary Man o' War; the stopwatch employed by Mr. Fitz to time the morning workouts of his equine family and the record book in which he charted the progress of Gallant Fox; and similar items guaranteed to surprise and delight hunters of rare and historical racing curios. Other pleasures cached in the glassy, airy repository include two hundred sets of racing silks representing past and present, perennial and occasional stable owners—Whitneys, Vanderbilts, Wideners, Sanfords and the like, together with such as Bing Crosby, Fred Astaire, Sir Winston Churchill and Queen Elizabeth of England—and two hundred and fifty oil paintings of some of the horses who made their racing colors famous. There are also portraits of patrons of distinction who dedicated themselves to the sport above and beyond the struggle for profit, among them a painting by Charles Willson Peale of an early American horseman and patron of the turf, George Washington.

---

* Since the museum was dedicated, two wings have been added, a measure of the confidence and esteem it enjoys.

Alajalov's portrait of Mrs. Isobel Dodge Sloan is one of several paintings of prominent horse owners on display.

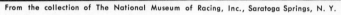
From the collection of The National Museum of Racing, Inc., Saratoga Springs, N. Y.

In 1963 Saratoga celebrated 100 years horse racing at the resort. Broadway w decorated with racing colors.

Bob Mayette

To cap the celebration, socialites turned out for a centennial ball in the restaurant of the Canfield Casino and dined and danced by candlelight. The restaurant's famous octagonal-glass ceiling can be seen.

A visit to the museum's Hall of Fame evokes misty memories of horse racing's glorious past. Golden letters spell out the names of the famous thoroughbreds who stirred America's sporting blood starting in the early 1800's: Sir Archy, Boston, Lexington, Hindoo, Hanover, Sysonby, Fair Play, Man o' War, Gallant Fox, Twenty Grand, Blue Larkspur, Sarazen, Equipoise, Seabiscuit, War Admiral, Citation, Whirlaway, Tom Fool, Count Fleet, Omaha, Nashua; of the trainers who trained them: Sam Hildreth, Sunny Jim Fitzsimmons, Ben and Jimmy Jones, Hirsch Jacobs, Max Hirsch; and of the jockeys who rode them: Tod Sloan, Snapper Garrison, Laverne Fator, Earl Sande, Sonny Workman, Ted Atkinson, Eddie Arcaro, Johnny Longden, Willie Shoemaker, Bill Hartack, Johnny Loftus and Buddy Ensor, the late father of the museum's curator, Mrs. Elaine Mann.

In August, when the horses are running at Saratoga, films of the races are shown daily in an upstairs gallery of the museum, and bettors on the winning noses are invited to enjoy their triumphs all over again. But guests intent upon recapturing the old days are more likely to wander among the trophies decked out below or stand outside on the patio, where they can reminisce over an area paved with bricks that once upon a time paved a portion of the betting ring at the race track.

Today,
yesterday
and tomorrow

Saratoga's Broadway, today, is an awkward pause between the past and the present, an uneasy union of the old and the new, with none of the grandeur and just a trace of the charm that made it one of the most famous main streets in America. The grounds on which the grand hotels stood facing one another across the wide, tree-lined thoroughfare are occupied by shops, stores, restaurants, supermarkets and such, and all but a few of the tall, arching elms have died (young maples have been planted to replace them). Here and there, however, Victorian houses still linger, their high stoops, lacy fretwork and gaudy signs advertising rooms for tourists suggesting clusters of little old ladies in faded brocade and flowered bonnets gone askew; and at the busiest section of Broadway a pair of small, venerable hotels, the Rip Van Dam and the Adelphi (the latter featuring a piazza and wicker rocking chairs) stand side by side as stubborn monuments to a departed era.

In the residential areas east and west of Broadway old and new Saratoga have become acquainted with considerably less strain; indeed, in many places they mingle with neighborly harmony. From sidewalks and lawns ancient elms, oaks and maples spread a leafy elegance over jet-slick motor cars and modern homes, and standing back from the streets the elephantine cottages with their wide, pillared porches and gingerbread frosting of porticoes, turrets, cupolas and bays, though they serve, most of them, as rooming houses now, impart to their surroundings a dignity and solidity that even Saratogans impatient for progress find attractive.* A few active springs, Red, Peerless, Lincoln and Hathorn, have also held their ground in the face of change, but the waters to which Saratoga owes its existence have retreated into the earth. High Rock, whose medicinal brew won the praise and patronage of Sir William Johnson, Washington, Hamilton, the Schuylers and other early notables, today is a sunken, cone-shaped boulder sheltered by a decaying pavilion, its mouth, from which the waters sprang, littered with discarded beer cans.

The majestic trees and mansions, the mineral springs, the race track (and the ceremonies and celebrations attending the August running), together with Congress Park, are the doughty leftovers from Saratoga's yesterdays still breathing the spark of life; the rest of the remains are museum pieces under glass or memorials in the shape of monuments and plaques. Canfield's Casino, although its downstairs rooms are occasionally used for social functions, is itself a museum, housing on one of its two upper floors a collection of community and regional memorabilia assembled by the Saratoga Historical Society and on the other an exhibition of furnishings from the Pine Grove home of Chancellor Reuben Hyde Walworth. And fourteen miles east of the city the Saratoga battlefield is now a national historical park; a memorial shaft marks the site of Burgoyne's surrender and the once elegant country house of Philip and Kitty Schuyler is a curiosity preserved for the inspection of tourists.

The vanished splendors, the lost magnificence, are of course the result rather than the cause of Saratoga's decline and fall as a great resort. The cause goes back to the turn of the century, when America crossed the threshold of an age of explosive change. Extraordinary social and technological innovations thoroughly redesigned the pattern of American life, with painful consequences to Saratoga and all other celebrated nineteenth-century summer resorts.

Prior to 1900, and for a few stubborn years while the new century was getting settled, fashionable America's way of life from late June to early September was fairly well bounded in the north by Bar Harbor, in the south by White Sulphur and Hot Springs, in the east by a sprinkling of sea-watering places of which Newport and Southampton were the most prestigious, and inland by Lenox in the Berkshires, Saratoga and Tuxedo Park. The ultra-fashionable people who established the customs, decreed the manners, supplied the taste and set the pace at these elite oases were the envied old-family aristocrats of American society, called by themselves (and thus by practically everybody else) the Four Hundred. They might better have been named the Four Hundred Musketeers, Society's Last Stand or the Charge of the Blue Book Brigade, for the status quo they strove to uphold was a tottering fortress attacked by feminists, suffragists and other

---

* Possibly the oldest of Saratoga's stately mansions is the Grecian-styled dwelling at 129 Circular Street long ago occupied by Madame Jumel and presently the residence of a physician.

social revolutionists, some of whom aimed their fire from within the ranks of society itself.

The rebels within were restless and independent-minded ladies for whom the traditional tribal rites and values had become fusty, enervating and rather ridiculous. Although turn-of-the-century society was ruled by women and its affairs were conducted by women (uppercrust gentlemen having relinquished their social responsibilities some years before in order to spend more time acquiring more wealth and power), it made no demands on either the intelligence or talents of its members, and matrons and debutantes endowed with one or both qualities had grown impatient and bored with their roles. To such as these, the struggle of women to obtain the same opportunities enjoyed by men held infinitely more challenge and satisfaction than anything society could offer, and a few daring ladies defected from the social routine and entered the fray. Soon they were joined by others, and gradually by a few dowagers so highly positioned in society that malcontents who had hesitated felt safe in following their example. When the *doyenne* of the Four Hundred, Mrs. O. H. P. Belmont*, who had wrested the scepter of social dictatorship from the formidable grasp of Mrs. John Jacob Astor, herself tired of the traditional conventions and amenities and enlisted in the battle for women's rights, society went into a spin from which it emerged shakily and hardly the same. Its eventual collapse was hastened by the behavior of Mrs. Belmont's successor, Mrs. Stuyvesant Fish, a *grande dame* who became so annoyed by the monotony and pretensions of the social world that she continually ridiculed it with a tongue that was loud, rude and frequently witty.

The things that were wrong with society went a great deal deeper, of course, than the complaints of the majority of its socialite critics. Displayed at the fashionable sea resorts, they were scaled down to a size that fairly leaped to the eye. At Newport, Southampton and other such oceanside havens favored by the first families, the aristocratic rich were snobbish to a degree that mocked the democracy that had made it possible for them to acquire their riches. Suspicious of writers and artists, scornful of politicians, spurning actors and actresses, dancers, singers and other public entertainers as slightly better than servants, they clustered together in tight little colonies designed to keep their social inferiors at a distance. They invited only each other to their luxurious private homes, dined and danced with each other at their private balls, played at games with each other at their private clubs, sunned and bathed with each other at their private beaches, went sailing with each other on their private yachts sheltered at their private docks. And to protect their wealthy-patrician-white-Protestant communities from unwanted intrusions, they imposed restrictions on the sale of property which put it out of the reach of Catholics and Jews.

With all their faults, the social elite were a force that uplifted the

* Previously the socially ambitious Mrs. William K. Vanderbilt, nee Alva Smith; in 1895 she showed her mettle by becoming the first woman in American society to get a divorce.

taste and improved the manners of the millions of Americans who avidly read about them and, so far as they were able, sought to emulate them. The great resorts became great only because the nation's best families selected them for summer residence and by their presence induced swarms of citizens of modest status to spend a week or two breathing the same air as the rich, seeing the same sights, and basking, though usually at a distance, in the radiance of their personalities and activities. To each resort the socialites brought elegance and style, and a dignity, discipline and code of decorum which gentled and refined the behavior of the mass of resort-goers.

But when society began to question itself, when ladies of breeding and luxury stepped down from their pedestals into the everyday world in search of a more satisfying life, its influence was blunted, its mystique evaporated; having decided to take themselves less seriously, the wealthy bluebloods were taken less seriously by everyone else. This too was reflected at the fashionable resorts, but not to their advantage. As society's hold loosened, the quality of their guests deteriorated (it is unlikely that Saratoga would have fallen prey to gangsters and the flashy sporting types of the Twenties and Thirties had its social leaders been cast from society's old autocratic mold). Around 1915 the confident world of traditional society started to come apart fairly rapidly, and the elegant, ceremonial summers of the great resorts dissolved with it.

In the 1920's, the Jazz Age, an innovation in popular entertainment called moving pictures seized the imagination of the public and created a new aristocracy of image-makers, the movie stars*. At the same time the automobile, and a few years later the airplane, made other modes of travel appear slow, fussy or out-of-date. The combination dealt the famous resorts a blow from which none fully recovered and only a few survived with a trace of their once proud estate. Since, for Americans at large, wealthy socialites were no longer a prime attraction, the principal reason for going to the fashionable resorts (because it was the fashionable thing to do) was no longer valid; and in autos and planes they went wherever the spirit, and the state of their finances, moved them.

Today, high-powered cars and super-jets casually erase time and space, and the places to go for a stylish summer or a brief summertime fling are distributed all over the United States (not to mention Latin America and Europe). The people who go are for the most part the products of a thriving economy: young families and young marrieds of upper-middle-class status and middle-rich means who are not much interested in the

* Today's taste-makers, trend-setters and arbiters of the thing to do consist of a hundred or so culture-oriented individuals who have achieved wealth and stature in the creative arts, and although a few of the more sophisticated film stars belong to the new elite, along with respected celebrities in operatic and symphonic music, ballet, theater, literature and other such areas, practically no Social Registerites do. There are, of course, no barriers based on money, family lineage, race or religion; membership in the new uppercrust is open to anyone with spectacular talents and the wit, charm and cultural equipment to hold his (or her) own on the frequent occasions when the group gets together. Starting with the stiffly correct posture of early American society, our native aristocracy has turned completely about-face.

activities of their social and financial superiors but want to enjoy the same splendid holiday facilities—the copper-toning sun, the wide variety of sports and the festive night life.

Three of the old renowned resorts have managed to change with the times and cater to the pleasures of the new breed of vacationists while clinging to a few of the credentials that made them famous. Bar Harbor, although many of its grand mansions were destroyed by fire in 1947 and others have since been replaced by motels, still attracts a number of socialites along with the holiday crowds who discovered that its winds and waters rank among the very best for sailing. Newport's pretentious marble palaces and imitation European chateaux, from which the pedigreed rich used to sally forth in their victorias and barouches and parade along Bellevue Avenue and out Ocean Drive to the seaside, have largely been converted into apartments for today's summer residents, but descendants of the old-family regulars continue to impart elegance to the resort in the cool, reserved, unostentatious manner of the modern rich. Southampton has lost much of its prestige to nearby East Hampton; several of its grandiloquent houses also have gone to seed; even so it keeps a stiff social upper lip, sustained "in season" by a relentless round of posh parties that send guests reeling to the sun-baked beach to dry out.

The remainder of the resorts that formed the fashionable summer circuit at the turn of the century have failed to keep up with their still stylish rivals, and in the case of Saratoga it isn't hard to understand why. Saratoga does not lie beside the ocean; although it is near one, it is not even next to a lake; its natural attractions are not composed of sunny beaches, an inviting surf, convenient marinas and the rest of the seaside accouterments today's summer colonists favor for a pleasurable and relaxing vacation. Saratoga is a spa, and a yearly visit to a spa for physical repairs is no longer deemed necessary (as it was in the days of their grandparents and great-grandparents) by twentieth-century Americans accustomed to the benefits of increasingly new and better drugs.*

Well aware of this, Saratoga has adjusted to its drop in the social ratings and is promoting the advantages of its surroundings to cultural, educational and other such institutions in need of space, a luxuriant landscape, a pleasing climate and a location just a few hours away from the populous eastern cities. But while Saratoga keeps its eye on the future, its heart belongs to the past. And so it should. For more than any of its rival resorts, the Queen of the Spas caught and reflected the spirit of its times. Its history is a diary in which we see recorded the volatile moods, manners, morals and aspirations of an ever-changing America. Its streets, piazzas, dining rooms and ballrooms were a stage on which paraded a remarkable cross section of

* Most American physicians insist that spas have no therapeutic value, but in Europe they always have been and still are a part of medical practice. Some European corporations dispatch their executives to the spas once a year to soak away the tensions accumulated from their jobs, and in the Soviet Union more than six million Russians annually spend their holidays taking the treatment prescribed at government-sponsored spas. It appears that today's Saratoga Springs is positioned in the wrong time, the wrong place and among the wrong people.

our national life. Whatever the future holds, Saratoga can look back with pride: it was the most truly American of all American resorts.

The things that made it so are brought vividly into focus when Saratoga is compared to Newport, the national social citadel of the cradle-of-liberty aristocrats. Saratoga's summer guests came from everywhere in the land and infused the resort with the characteristically American diversity of their speech, dress and other provincialisms. Newport's accents, fashion and culture were mainly those of Boston, Philadelphia, New York and similar eastern havens of early American wealth. Saratoga was host to the three social worlds that coexisted in every American city: the *haut monde,* the *beau monde* and the *demimonde.* Newport opened its doors to high and fashionable society, but turned its back on citizens who fell below its rigid social standards. Such as Diamond Jim Brady and Lillian Russell were excluded from Newport's charmed circle as celebrities of mere popular distinction; at Saratoga they were cock-of-the-walk.

The quality that marked Saratoga as wonderfully, uniquely American was not only the diversity of its guests, of course, but also the democratic manner in which they intermingled. They were greatly assisted by the physiognomy of the Spa: its accommodations were public hotels and boarding houses, its pleasures were public places available to everyone. (Newport, to employ the comparison again, was characterized by private homes and private pleasures.) From the time they got up in the morning until the time they went to bed at night Saratoga's vacationists were thrown together in a communal pursuit of the diversions of holiday life. They trooped to the springs for a glass of mineral water before breakfast, gossiped on the piazzas and shopped along Broadway, sat elbow to elbow at mealtimes and lingered collectively over the leisurely midday dinner. They strolled together in the after-dinner promenades and set out for the lake together in the coach parade (in contrast to Newport's posh excursions to the beach, anyone could join the Spa's procession just by producing a horse and carriage). They attended the band concerts and the races together, and made each other's acquaintance all over again in the salons of the Morrissey and Canfield casinos and in the ballrooms of the fashionable hotels.

The absence of social barriers at the Spa led to an open society that was in the best tradition of Americanism. A bookkeeper, a salesman, a small-town merchant could not only look at a patrician, a tycoon, a politician or statesman, but could mix with them and enjoy many of the same advantages. Their wives and daughters could not only admire the Parisian silks and satins worn by the ultra-fashionable ladies of high society but could put on a show of their own and utilize the same showcase—the daily turn-out of coaches and carriages, in which they sat flowered, beribboned, brocaded and stiffly whaleboned before an appreciative audience of onlookers. A Western Union clerk could court and win an heiress (a Twombly could marry a Vanderbilt). And one and all could, and did, share a dining table with their social and financial superiors, promenade with them, join

The Spa's newest pride is the Saratoga Performing Arts Center. One of the world's largest theaters, it is the summer home of the New York City Ballet and the Philadelphia Orchestra, held its first annual dance and music festival in July and August, 1966. Shown here is the exterior of the fan-shaped, multi-ramped pavilion, Melissa Hayden "working out" with the trotters on the Saratoga Raceway for a performance of the ballet, and the orchestra on stage during the Center's opening concert.

Bob Mayette, Saratoga Performing Arts Center

Bob Mayette, Saratoga Performing Arts Center

Bob Mayette, Saratoga Performing Arts Center

their games in the hotel parlors and dance, if not actually with them, at least in gratifying proximity to them at the hops and balls.

Quite obviously, the indiscriminate socializing at Saratoga was accepted by its aristocratic guests because the Spa's nonexistent class barriers gave them no other choice; the nature of Saratoga made it impossible for them to completely withdraw and keep to themselves. The nicest compliment they paid the resort was their devoted patronage in spite of its thoroughly democratic ways. Since they returned to it summer after summer, it can be assumed that the blueblooded old-family elite enjoyed Saratoga as an escape from the rigidly correct and socially protected lives they led at home and in their more or less private resorts (such as Newport). At Saratoga they were plunged into the mainstream of American life—a mainstream in miniature, to be sure, but one that accurately reflected the character of a young and undisciplined but vastly exciting land.

That Saratoga has vanished. Today's Saratoga reflects a different America. But in August, when the Spa is "in season," one can sense the ghostly presence of the great hotels and the magnificent *mélange* of holiday guests swarming over Broadway. One remembers a eulogy by Monty Woolley as the scenes of his Saratoga boyhood disappeared. "There was in those days," he said, "a wonderful slow tempo to life. Even the weather was warmer. God, what a lovely time it was to live!"

Bibliography

BOOKS:

Allen, Richard L., *An Analysis of the Principal Mineral Fountains of Saratoga Springs*, W. H. Arthur & Co., New York, 1858.

————, *Handbook of Saratoga and Strangers' Guide*, W. H. Arthur & Co., New York, 1859.

Amory, Cleveland, *The Last Resorts*, Harper and Brothers, New York, 1948.

————, *Who Killed Society*, Harper and Brothers, New York, 1960.

Asbury, Herbert, *Sucker's Progress: An Informal History of Gambling in America From the Colonies to Canfield*, Dodd, Mead and Company, New York, 1938.

Baker, Nina Brown, *Nellie Bly*, Henry Holt and Company, New York, 1956.

Barber, J. W., and Howe, H., *Pictorial History of the State of New York*, H. and E. Phinney, Cooperstown, N.Y., 1846.

Beer, Thomas, *The Mauve Decade*, Alfred A. Knopf, New York, 1926.

Bird, Harrison, *March To Saratoga*, Oxford University Press, New York, 1963.

Bradley, High, *Such Was Saratoga*, Doubleday, Doran and Company, New York, 1940.

Brandow, John Henry, *The Story of Saratoga and History of Schuylerville*, Brandow Printing Co., Albany, N.Y., 1900.

————, *The Story of Old Saratoga; the Burgoyne Campaign*, Brandow Printing Co., Albany, N.Y., 1919.

Bristed, C. Astor, *The Upper Ten Thousand: Sketches of American Society*, Stringer & Townsend, New York, 1852.

Brown, Henry Collins, *Brownstone Fronts and Saratoga Trunks*, E. P. Dutton & Company, New York, 1935.

Buckingham, James Silk, *America: Historical, Statistic and Descriptive*, Fisher, Son & Co., London, 1841.

Clews, Henry, *Fifty Years in Wall Street*, Irving Publishing Company, New York, 1908.

Crockett, Albert Stevens, *Peacocks on Parade*, Sears Publishing Company, New York, 1931.

Davison, G. M., *The Fashionable Tour in 1825*, Saratoga Springs, N.Y., 1825.

Dearborn, R. F., *Saratoga and How To See It*, Saratoga Springs, N.Y., 1871-2-3-4.

Depew, Chauncey M., *My Memories of Eighty Years*, Charles Scribner's Sons, New York, 1924.

Deveaux, S., *The Traveller's Own Book to Saratoga Springs*, Faxon & Read, Buffalo, N.Y., 1841.

Diamond, Sigmund, *A Casual View of America: The Home Letters of Salomon de Rothschild, 1859-1861*, Stanford University Press, Stanford, California, 1961.

Durkee, Cornelius E., *Reminiscences of Saratoga*, reprinted from *The Saratogian*, Saratoga Springs, N.Y., 1928.

Endicott, G., *Endicott's Pictures of Saratoga for 1843*, New York, 1843.

Falkner, Leonard, *Painted Lady: Eliza Jumel—Her Life and Times*, E. P. Dutton and Company, New York, 1962.

Ferber, Edna, *Saratoga Trunk*, Doubleday and Company, New York, 1941.

Flexner, James Thomas, *Mohawk Baronet: Sir William Johnson of New York*, Harper and Brothers, New York, 1959.

Gardiner, Alexander, *Canfield: The True Story of the Greatest Gambler*, Doubleday, Doran and Company, New York, 1930.

Gilpin, Henry Dilworth, *A Northern Tour*, H. C. Carey & I. Lea, Philadelphia, Pa., 1825.

Glasscock, C. B., *Lucky Baldwin: The Story of an Unconventional Success*, Bobbs-Merrill Company, Indianapolis, Ind., 1933.

Griswold, Frank Gray, *Race Horses and Racing*, the Plimpton Press, New York, 1925.

Heimer, Mel, *Fabulous Bawd: The Story of Saratoga*, Henry Holt and Company, New York, 1952.

Holley, Marietta, *Samantha at Saratoga*, Hubbard Brothers, Philadelphia, Pa., 1887.

Hone, Philip, *The Diary of Philip Hone, 1828-1851*, Dodd, Mead and Company, New York, 1927.

James, Henry, *The American Scene* (Together with Three Essays from *Portraits of Places*), Charles Scribner's Sons, New York, 1946.

Katcher, Leo, *The Big Bankroll: The Life and Times of Arnold Rothstein*, Harper and Brothers, New York, 1959.

Kofoed, Jack, *Brandy For Heroes: A Biography of the Honorable John Morrissey*, E. P. Dutton & Company, New York, 1938.

Landon, Melville, (Eli Perkins, pseud.), *Saratoga in 1901*, Sheldon & Company, New York, 1872.

Lathrop, George Parsons, *Yaddo: An Autumn Masque*, privately printed, 1897.

Marks, Edward B., and Liebling, Abbott J., *They All Sang*, Viking Press, New York, 1934.

McAllister, Ward, *Society As I Have Found It*, Cassell Publishing Company, New York, 1890.

Minnigerode, Meade, *The Fabulous Forties*, G. P. Putnam's Sons, New York, 1924.

———, *Lives and Times*, G. P. Putnam's Sons, New York, 1925.

———, *Certain Rich Men*, G. P. Putnam's Sons, New York, 1927.

Morell, Parker, *Diamond Jim*, Simon and Schuster, New York, 1934.

———, *Lillian Russell: The Era of Plush*, Random House, New York, 1940.

Morris, Lloyd, *Postscript to Yesterday: America—The Last Fifty Years*, Random House, New York, 1947.

———, *Incredible New York*, Random House, New York, 1951.

Murray, C. A., *Travels in North America*, R. Bentley, London, 1839.

Noble, Iris, *Nellie Bly*, Julian Messner, Inc., New York, 1956.

Powell, E. Alexander, *Gone Are The Days*, Little, Brown and Company, Boston, Mass,. 1938.

Powell, Lyman Pierson, *Historic Towns of the Middle States*, G. P. Putnam's Sons, New York, 1899.

Reed, John, *The Hudson River Valley*, Clarkson N. Potter, New York, 1960.

Richards, T. Addison, *Miller's Guide to Saratoga Springs and Vicinity*, J. Miller, New York, 1876.

Riedesel, F. C. L., Baroness von, *Letters and Memoirs Relating to the War of American Independence*, G. and C. Carvill, New York, 1827.

Rittenhouse, Mignon, *The Amazing Nellie Bly*, E. P. Dutton and Company, New York, 1956.

Rovere, Richard H., *Howe & Hummel: Their True and Scandalous History*, Farrar, Straus and Company, New York, 1947.

Ruggles, Eleanor, *Prince of Players: Edwin Booth*, W. W. Norton and Company, New York, 1953.

Runyon, Damon, *Short Takes*, McGraw-Hill Book Company, New York, 1931.

Saxe, John Godfrey, *Poems*, Ticknor and Fields, Boston, Mass., 1864.

Seaman, Valentine, *Dissertation on the Mineral Waters of Saratoga*, Samuel Campbell, New York, 1793.

Seymour, Flora Warren, *Lords of the Valley: Sir William Johnson and his Mohawk Brothers*, Longmans, Green and Company, London, 1930.

Shepherd, Daniel, *Saratoga: A Story of 1787*, W. P. Fetridge and Co., New York, 1856.

Smith, Joseph, *Reminiscences of Saratoga*, the Knickerbocker Press, New York, 1897.

Stone, William L., *The Life and Times of Sir William Johnson, Bart.*, J. Munsell, Albany, N. Y. 1865.

———, *Saratoga Springs*, T. Nelson & Sons, New York, 1866.

———, *Reminiscences of Saratoga and Ballston*, R. Worthington, New York, 1880.

Swanberg, W. A., *Sickles the Incredible*, Charles Scribner's Sons, New York, 1956.

————, *Jim Fisk: The Career of an Improbable Rascal*, Charles Scribner's Sons, New York, 1959.

Sylvester, Nathaniel Bartlett, *History of Saratoga County, New York*, Gresham Publishing Company, Chicago, Ill., 1893.

Talbot, Francis, *Saint Among Savages*, Harper and Brothers, New York, 1935.

Tharp, Louise Hall, *The Baroness and the General*, Little, Brown and Company, Boston, Mass., 1962.

Thayer, Bert Clark, *August in Saratoga*, the Sagamore Press, New York.

The American Heritage Book of Indians, American Heritage Publishing Company, New York, 1961.

Trask, Katrina, *The Story of Yaddo*, privately printed, 1918.

Trevathan, Charles E., *The American Thoroughbred*, the Macmillan Company, New York, 1905.

Trollope, Frances M., *Domestic Manners of the Americans*, Whittaker, Treacher & Co., London, 1832.

Van Epps, Percy M., *Stories and Legends of Our Indian Paths*, published by the Town Board, Glenville, New York, 1940.

Van Every, Edward, *Sins of New York*, Frederick A. Stokes Company, New York, 1930.

————, *Sins of America*, Frederick A. Stokes Company, New York, 1931.

Waite, Marjorie Peabody, *Yaddo: Yesterday and Today*, privately printed, Saratoga Springs, N.Y., 1933.

————, *Seeing Saratoga*, published by the Business and Professional Women's Club, Saratoga Springs, N.Y., 1935.

Wall, E. Berry, *Neither Pest Nor Puritan: The Memoirs of E. Berry Wall*, the Dial Press, New York, 1940.

Walton, G. E., *The Mineral Springs of the United States and Canada*, D. Appleton and Company, New York, 1873.

Ward, Christopher, *The War of the Revolution*, the Macmillan Company, New York, 1952.

Warshow, Robert Irving, *Bet-a-Million Gates: The Story of a Plunger*, Greenberg, New York, 1932.

Watson, W. C., *Men and Times of the Revolution; or, Memoirs of Elkanah Watson*, Dana & Co., New York, 1856.

Wecter, Dixon, *The Saga of American Society*, Charles Scribner's Sons, New York, 1937.

Weiner, Ed, *The Damon Runyon Story*, Longmans, Green and Company, London, 1948.

Wendt, Lloyd and Kogan, Herman, *Bet A Million!: The Story of John W. Gates*, Bobbs-Merrill Company, Indianapolis, Ind., 1948.

Williamson, Jefferson, *The American Hotel: An Anecdotal History*, Alfred A. Knopf, New York, 1930.

Willis, Nathaniel P., *People I Have Met; or, Pictures of Society and People of Mark*, Baker and Scribner, New York, 1850.

————, *Hurry-Graphs; or, Sketches of Scenery, Celebrities and Society*, Charles Scribner, New York, 1851.

————, *The Rag Bag*, Charles Scribner, New York, 1855.

MAGAZINES AND NEWSPAPERS:

American Artist, March 1955.

American City, September 1935; September 1950.

American Heritage, October 1955; June, October 1956; April, August, December 1957; February, April, June, August 1959; June 1960; August, October 1961; June, August 1962; February 1963.

American Mercury, March 1952.

Américas, August 1956.

Atlantic Monthly, September 1938.

Business Week, September 27, 1952; March 19, 1955.

Catholic World, May 1951.

Collier's, July 30, 1938; April 2, 16, 30, 1954.

Coronet, May 1958.

Country Life, August 1931.

Everybody's Magazine, August 1904.

Fortune, August 1935.

Godey's Lady's Book, various issues.
Harper's, Volume 53, 1876; October 1952.
Harper's Weekly, various issues.
Independent and Weekly Review, August 23, 1919.
Leslie's Weekly, various issues.
Life, July 15, 1946; June 19, July 31, 1950; September 29, 1952; July 26, 1963.
Modern Music, October 1946.
Musical America, October 1949.
New England Magazine, June 1905.
New Republic, February 19, 1951; September 29, 1952.
Newsweek, August 12, 1933; August 4, 1934; August 3, 1935; September 16, 1940; March 12, May 7, 1951; August 19, 1963.
New York American, August 17, 1930.
New York Times, July 3, 1872; July 31, August 14, 1919; August 16, 17, 24, 1930; July 30, 1950.
New York World, August 19, 1894.
Outing, December 1902.
Poetry, March 1927.
Reader's Digest, December 1958.
St. James Magazine, Volume 31.
Saratoga *County Exchange, County Press, Daily Register, Post, Republican, Saratogian, Sentinel, Sun, Whig*, various issues.
Saturday Evening Post, November 24, 1928; January 5, 1929.
Saturday Review of Literature, July 23, 1949.
Science, September 28, 1934.
Sports Illustrated, August 7, 1961; August 5, 1963.
The Commonweal, August 2, 1946.
The Delineator, June 1905.
The Forum, September 1919.
The Independent, August 28, 1926.
The Nation, March 31, 1951.
The National Police Gazette, various issues.
The New Yorker, October 14, 1944; September 18, 1954; June 25, 1955.
The Quarterly Journal (New York State Historical Association), October 1927.
The Rotarian, December 1937.
The Survey, June 5, 1920.
Time, August 5, 1935; September 5, 1938; September 16, 1940; September 4, 1944; August 9, 1963.
Tinsley's Magazine, Volume 34.
Travel, October 1941.
U.S. News & World Report, November 10, 1950.
Wilkes' Spirit of the Times, August 15, 1863.
Wilson Library Bulletin, January 1953.
World Outlook, January 1920.

OTHER:

Informative and descriptive material and maps dealing with Saratoga Springs and vicinity obtained from Saratoga Springs Authority, Saratoga Springs Chamber of Commerce, Saratoga Springs Commission, Saratoga Springs Reservation, Saratoga Performing Arts Center, Yaddo (Elizabeth Ames, Executive Director) and the New York State Historical Association at Cooperstown, New York.

Index